THE

APOCALYPSE OF BARUCH

TRANSLATED FROM THE SYRIAC

CHAPTERS I.-LXXVII. FROM THE SIXTH CENT. MS. IN THE AMBROSIAN LIBRARY OF MILAN

AND

CHAPTERS LXXVIII.-LXXXVII.—THE EPISTLE OF BARUCH FROM A NEW AND CRITICAL TEXT BASED ON TEN MSS. AND PUBLISHED HEREWITH

EDITED, WITH INTRODUCTION, NOTES, AND INDICES

BY

R. H. CHARLES, M.A.

TRINITY COLLEGE, DUBLIN, AND EXETER COLLEGE, OXFORD

LONDON

ADAM AND CHARLES BLACK

1896

TO

MY WIFE

PREFACE

THE Apocalypse of Baruch is a composite work written in the latter half of the first century of the Christian era. It is thus contemporaneous with the chief writings of the New Testament. Its authors were orthodox Jews, and it is a good representative of the Judaism against which the Pauline dialectic was directed.

In this Apocalypse we have almost the last noble utterance of Judaism before it plunged into the dark and oppressive years that followed the destruction of Jerusalem. For ages after that epoch its people seem to have been bereft of their immemorial gifts of song and eloquence, and to have had thought and energy only for the study and expansion of the traditions of the Fathers. But when our book was written, that evil and barren era had not yet set in; breathing thought and burning word had still their home in Palestine, and the hand of the Jewish artist was still master of its ancient cunning.

And yet the intrinsic beauty of this book must to a great degree fail to strike the casual reader. Indeed, it could hardly be otherwise. For the present English version is a translation of the Syriac; the Syriac was a translation of the Greek, and the Greek in turn a translation from the Hebrew original. In each translation we may feel assured the original work was shorn in large and growing measure of its ancient vigour, and this is certainly the case in the version now before the reader. For the translator, having the interests of scholars before his eyes, has made it his aim to give a literal reproduction of the Syriac. And yet, even so, much of its native eloquence has survived, so that to be prized it needs only to be known, and our appreciation of its beauty, its tragic power and worth, must grow in the measure of our acquaintance with it.

The Apocalypse of Baruch has had a strange history. Written by Pharisaic Jews as an apology for Judaism, and in part an implicit polemic against Christianity, it gained nevertheless a larger circulation amongst Christians than amongst Jews, and owed its very preservation to the scholarly cares of the Church it assailed. But in the struggle for life its secret animus against Christianity begat an instinctive opposition in Christian circles, and so proved a bar to its popularity. Thus the place it would naturally have filled was taken by the sister work, 4 Ezra. This latter work having been written in some degree under Christian influences, and forming, in fact, an unconscious confession of the failure of Judaism to redeem the world, was naturally more acceptable to Christian readers, and thus, in due course, the Apocalypse of Baruch was elbowed out of recognition by its fitter and sturdier rival.

In this edition of Baruch — which is also the *editio princeps*—no pains have been spared as regards the criticism and emendation of the text, its interpretation, and the determination of its various sources.

As regards the text, the facts are briefly as follows: The first seventy-seven chapters, as appears on the title-page, are found only in one MS., namely, *c*. For the concluding nine chapters—the Epistle of Baruch —I have made use of *c* and nine other MSS. Of these I have collated eight—several of these for the first time. Through the kindness of the publishers I have been enabled to print on pp. 125-167 a critical text of this Epistle based on those MSS. As Ceriani and Lagarde contented themselves each with reproducing a single unamended MS., scholars will, I think, be grateful for this attempt to grapple with all the Syriac MSS. available. By this comparative study of *c* and the remaining nine MSS. in the chapters common to both, I have been able to ascertain the value of *c* in the chapters in which *c* stands alone. The trustworthiness of the MS. *c*, which we have thus established, is further confirmed by a Greek work, which borrows largely from our Apocalypse, the Rest of the Words of Baruch.

There are, of course, corruptions in the text. Some of these that are native to the Syriac have been removed by Ceriani, others by the editor; others are provisionally emended, or else reproduced in the English translation. But many still remain. Of these some are manifestly peculiar to the Greek, and have been dealt with accordingly. But the rest are not so, and are, in fact, incapable of explanation save on the hypothesis of a Hebrew original. To this hypothesis, which marks a new departure in the criticism of this book, I have been irresistibly led in the course of my study. In many passages I have by its means been able to reduce chaos to order. For details the reader should consult the Introduction, pp. xliv.-liii.

The interpretation of this book has been the severest task as yet undertaken by the editor. Insuperable difficulties confronted on every side, till at last he awoke to the fact that these were due to plurality of authorship. When once this fact was recognised and the various sources determined, the task of interpretation was materially lightened, and the value of the work for New Testament and Jewish scholars became every day more manifest. As my studies in this direction began in 1891, my conclusions are, save in a few cases, the result of long study and slowly matured conviction.

A special study of the relations subsisting between this Apocalypse and 4 Ezra will be found on pp. lxvii.-lxxvi., where it is shown that whereas 4 Ezra is in many respects non-Jewish, our Apocalypse is a faithful exponent of the orthodox Judaism of the time. To this subject I may return in an edition of the former work.

Scholars are at last coming to recognise that the study of the literature to which this book belongs is indispensable for the interpretation of the New Testament. Thus Dr. Sanday and Mr. Headlam write in their recent work on the Epistle to the Romans (p. vii.): "*It is by a continuous and careful study of such works that any advance in the exegesis of the New Testament will be possible.*"

My knowledge of Talmudic literature, so far as it appears in this book, is derived from Weber's *Lehren des Talmuds,* Edersheim's *Life and Times,* etc., Wunsche's translations of the various treatises of the Babylonian Talmud, Schwab's French translation of the Jerusalem Talmud, and in passages where translations were wanting, I had the ready help of Dr. Neubauer.

My thanks are also due to Mr. Buchanan Gray, for his revision of my proofs of the Hebrew original of Baruch.

17 Bradmore Road, Oxford,
September 1896.

CONTENTS

PAGE

INTRODUCTION . . . . xv-lxxxiv

§ 1. Short Account of the Book (pp. xv.-xvi.)—§ 2. Other Books of Baruch (pp. xvi.-xxii.)—§ 3. The Syriac MSS.—only one MS. *c* for chapters i.-lxxvii., but nine other MSS. for lxxviii.-lxxxvi. A comparative study of these MSS. in relation to *c* (pp. xxii.-xxx.)—§ 4. Previous Literature on the Apocalypse of Baruch. Reprint of MS. *c*—Ceriani; of *b*—Lagarde. Edition of lxxviii.-lxxxvi.—Walton and Paris Polyglots. Translation—Ceriani, Fritzsche (pp. xxx.-xxxiii.) Critical Inquiries—Langen, Ewald, Hilgenfeld, Wieseler, Fritzsche, Stähelin, Hausrath, Renan, Drummond, Kneucker, Dillmann, Edersheim, Rosenthal, Stanton, Schürer, Thomson, Kabisch, De Faye, Ryle (pp. xxxiii.-xliii.)—§ 5. The Syriac—a Translation from the Greek (pp. xliii.-xliv.)—§ 6. The Greek—a Translation from a Hebrew Original; for (1) The Quotations from the Old Testament are from the Massoretic text. (2) Hebrew Idioms survive in the Syriac. (3) Unintelligible expressions in the Syriac can be explained and the Text restored by Re-translation into Hebrew. (4) Many Paronomasiae discover themselves by such Re-translation (pp. xliv.-liii.)—§ 7. The different Elements in the Apocalypse of Baruch with their respective Characteristics and Dates. Of these elements A^1 = xxvii.-xxx. 1, A^2 = xxxvi.-xl., A^3 = liii.-lxxiv. are Messiah Apocalypses written by different Authors before 70 A.D. (pp. liii.-lviii.) B^1, B^2, B^3 were written after 70 A.D. These are derived from different authors. They agree in expecting no Messiah, but are severally differen-

PAGE

tiated from each other by many characteristics. B^1 is the earliest—soon after 70 A.D., and B^3 is probably the latest. B^1=i.-ix. 1; xliii.-xliv. 7; xlv.-xlvi. 6; lxxvii.-lxxxii.; lxxxiv.; lxxxvi.-lxxxvii. B^2=xiii.-xxv.; xxx. 2-xxxv.; xli.-xlii.; xliv. 8-15; xlvii.-lii.; lxxv.-lxxvi.; lxxxiii. B^3=lxxxv. x. 6-xii. 4, which I have called S, is probably from a source distinct from the rest (pp. lviii.-lxv.)—§ 8. The lost Epistle to the two and a half Tribes, on many grounds is probably identical with, or is the source of the Greek Baruch iii. 9-iv. 29 (pp. lxv.-lxvii.)—§ 9. The Relations of our Apocalypse with 4 Ezra. (*a*) The composite nature of 4 Ezra. (*b*) Conflicting characteristics of 4 Ezra and Baruch, the former to some extent non-Jewish in its teaching on the Law, Works, Justification, Original Sin and Freewill. (*c*) 4 Ezra from a Hebrew Original. (*d*) Relations of the respective Constituents of our Apocalypse and 4 Ezra. A^1 is older than E of 4 Ezra, and both A^1 and A^2 than M. B^1 older than E^2, and both B^1 and B^2 than S (pp. lxvii.-lxxvi.)—§ 10. Relation of this Apocalypse to the New Testament. Bulk of parallels in these books can be explained as being drawn independently from pre-existing literature, or as being commonplaces of the time; but others may point to dependence of Baruch on the New Testament (pp. lxxvi.-lxxix.)—§ 11. Value of our Apocalypse in the Attestation of the Jewish Theology of 50-100 A.D., and in the Interpretation of Christian Theology for the same Period: The Resurrection, Original Sin and Freewill, Works and Justification, Forgiveness (pp. lxxix.-lxxxiv.)

THE APOCALYPSE OF BARUCH. TRANSLATION AND CRITICAL AND EXEGETICAL NOTES 1-167

APPENDIX 168

INDEX I.—PASSAGES FROM THE SCRIPTURES AND ANCIENT WRITERS 169

INDEX II.—NAMES AND SUBJECTS 173

INTRODUCTION

§ 1. Short Account of the Book

This beautiful Apocalypse, with the exception of nine chapters towards its close,[1] was lost sight of for quite 1200 years.

Written originally in Hebrew, it was early translated into Greek, and from Greek into Syriac. Of the Hebrew original every line has perished save a few still surviving in rabbinic writings. Of the Greek Version nothing has come down to us directly, though portions of it are preserved in the Rest of the Words of Baruch, a Greek work of the second century, and in a late Apocalypse of Baruch recently discovered in Greek and in Slavonic. Happily, the Syriac has been preserved almost in its entirety in a sixth century MS., the discovery of which we owe to the distinguished Italian scholar Ceriani. Of this MS., Ceriani published a Latin translation in 1866, the Syriac text in 1871, and the photo-lithographic facsimile in 1883. Though

[1] These chapters under the title "The Epistle of Baruch," or a similar one, were incorporated in the later Syriac Bible.

there are no adequate grounds for assuming a Latin Version, it is demonstrable that our Apocalypse was the foundation of a Latin Apocalypse of Baruch, a fragment of which is preserved in Cyprian.

The Apocalypse of Baruch belongs to the first century of our era. It is a composite work put together about the close of the century, from at least five or six independent writings. These writings belong to various dates between 50 and 90 A.D., and are thus contemporaneous with the chief New Testament writings. It is this fact that constitutes the chief value of the work. We have here contemporaneous records of the Jewish doctrines and beliefs, and of the arguments which prevailed in Judaism in the latter half of the first century, and with which its leaders sought to uphold its declining faith and confront the attacks of a growing and aggressive Christianity.

Over against many of the Pauline solutions of the religious problems of the day, Jewish answers are here propounded which are frequently antagonistic in the extreme. It was this hidden hostility to Christianity that no doubt brought it into discredit. As early as the sixth century it seems to have passed out of circulation.

§ 2. Other Books of Baruch

In addition to our Apocalypse, a considerable literature arose and circulated under Baruch's name, sometime before and after the Christian era. It will be sufficient for our present purpose to touch briefly on the different books belonging to it.

1. The Apocryphal Baruch in the LXX.—This book falls clearly into two parts—i.-iii. 8 being the first part, and iii. 9-v. constituting the second. The first part was originally written in Hebrew, the second is generally held to be of Greek origin, but this is doubtful. The first part of the book is said by Ewald and Marshall to have been composed three centuries before the Christian era, by Fritzsche and Schrader in the Maccabean period, by Kneucker and Schürer after 70 A.D. Most writers agree in assigning the second half of the book to the last-mentioned date. The second half, however, may also be composite. Thus Professor Marshall differentiates iii. 9-iv. 4 from iv. 5-v. 9, and regards the former as originally written in Aramaic, and the latter in Greek. The chief authorities on this book are Fritzsche, *Exeget. Handbuch zu den Apocryphen*, part i., pp. 165-202, 1851; Kneucker, *Das Buch Baruch*, 1879; Gifford, *Speaker's Commentary, Apocrypha*, ii. 241-286, 1888. On the probability that i. 1-3; iii. 9-iv. 29 of this book are a recast of a lost portion of our Apocalypse, *i.e.* "the Letter to the two and a half Tribes," see § 8, pp. lxv.-lxvii. There is no verbal borrowing between our Apocalypse and and the Greek Baruch, but in the following passages there is a similarity of diction or of thought or of both. This list could be enlarged.

Apoc. of Baruch.	Book of Baruch.
i. 1 (mention of Jeconiah).	i. 3.
x. 16.	iv. 10, 14.
lix. 7.	iii. 12.
lxxvii. 10.	ii. 26.
lxxviii. 7.	iv. 36, 37 (v. 5, 6).
lxxix. 2.	i. 17, 18.
lxxx. 5.	ii. 13.
lxxxiv. 2-5.	i. 19 ; ii. 2.
lxxxvi. 1, 2.	i. 14.

2. The Rest of the Words of Baruch.—This book was written in Greek in the second century of our era. It seems in parts to be a Jewish work recast. The Greek text was first printed at Venice in 1609, next by Ceriani in 1868 under the title "Paralipomena Jeremiae" in his *Monumenta Sacra*, v. 11-18, and recently it has been critically edited by Rendel Harris in 1889. This book exists also in the Ethiopic Bible. The Ethiopic Version was edited from three MSS. by Dillmann in his *Chrestomathia aethiopica* in 1866. As these MSS. are inferior, and as no attempt was made by Dillmann to revise his text by means of the Greek, the present writer hopes in due time to edit a critical text from eleven Ethiopic MSS., accompanied with translation and notes. In this edition account will be taken of all the important variations of the Greek text.

This book is deeply indebted to our Apocalypse and attests the accuracy of the Syriac text in the following passages :—

Apoc. Bar.	Rest of the Words.
ii. 1.	i. 1, 3, 7.
ii. 2.	ii. 2.
v. 1.	i. 5 ; ii. 7 ; iii. 6 ; iv. 7.
vi. 1.	iv. 1.
vi. 4, 5, 6, 8, 10.	iii. 2, 5, 8, 14.
viii. 2, 5.	iv. 1, 2, 3, 4.
x. 2, 5, 6, 7, 18.	iv. 3, 4, 6, 9.
xi. 4, 5.	iv. 9.
xxxv. 2.	ii. 4.
lxxvii. 21, 23, 26.	vii. 3, 10, 12.
lxxx. 3.	i. 5 ; iv. 7.
lxxxv. 2.	ii. 3.
lxxxv. 11.	vi. 3.
lxxxvii.	vii. 8, 30.

3. The Gnostic book of Baruch.—Of this book large fragments are found in the *Philosophumena of Hippolytus*, v. 24-27. But these fragments are wholly out of relation with the remaining literature of Baruch.

4. A Latin book of Baruch is quoted in one MS. of Cyprian's *Testimonia*, iii. 29. As this book is clearly based on our Apocalypse, I will give the passage in full. Item in Baruch: "Veniet enim tempus, et quaeretis me et vos et qui post vos venerint, audire verbum sapientiae et intellectus, et non invenietis" (cf. Apoc. Bar. xlviii. 36). "Nationes autem cupient videre sapientem praedicantem, et non obtinget eis: non quia deerit aut deficiet sapientia hujus saeculi terrae, sed neque deerit sermo legis saeculo. Erit enim sapientia in paucis vigilantibus et taciturnis et quietis" (cf. Apoc. Bar. xlviii. 33), "sibi confabulantes et in cordibus suis meditantes

quoniam quidam eos horrebunt et timebunt ut malos. Alii autem nec credunt verbo legis Altissimi: alii autem ore stupentes non credent et credentibus erunt contrarii et impedientes spiritum veritatis. Alii autem erunt sapientes ad spiritum erroris et pronuntiantes sicut Altissimi et Fortis edicta" (cf. Apoc. Bar. xlviii. 34; lxx. 5; observe also that the titles of God here are characteristic of our Apoc., see vii. 1, note; xxi. 3, note). "Alii autem personales fidei. Alii capaces et fortes in fide Altissimi et odibiles alieno."

In 5 Ezra xvi. 64, 65 (which James ascribes to the third century) we have a clear use of our text. Thus: "Certe Hic novit . . . quae cogitatis in cordibus vestris. Vae peccantibus et volentibus occultare peccata sua: propter quod Dominus scrutinando scrutinabit omnia opera eorum et traducet vos omnes," is based on lxxxiii. 3, which = "Et scrutinando scrutinabit cogitationes arcanas et quidquid in penetralibus omnium hominis membrorum positum est et in apertum coram omnibus cum increpatione educet." We should observe that not only is the thought of the two passages the same, but that the actual diction is borrowed, *i.e.* the Hebraism "scrutinando scrutinabit" and "traducet," which = "in apertum cum increpatione educet" (cf. also "quae cogitatis in cordibus" with "cogitationes arcanas").

5. The Greek Apocalypse of Baruch, or, as Mr. James names it, *Apocalypsis Baruch Tertia.*—This book belongs to the second century, for, on the one hand, it is based largely on the Slavonic Enoch, and on

the other, it is mentioned by Origen, *de Princip.* ii. 3. 6 : "Denique etiam Baruch prophetae librum in assertionis hujus testimonium vocant, quod ibi de septem mundis vel caelis evidentius indicatur." This Greek Apocalypse of Baruch was discovered some years ago by Mr. James in a British Museum MS. Through his kindness I have been permitted to examine his copy of this MS. His edition of the text will, we believe, shortly appear. The Slavonic Version of this book has been known for some time, and was published in the *Starine*, vol. xviii. pp. 205-209, 1886, by Novakovic. A German translation, preceded by a helpful introduction by Professor Bonwetsch, appeared this year in the *Nachrichten der K. Gesellschaft der Wissenschaften zu Göttingen*, 1886, Heft i. An English translation will shortly appear by Mr. Morfill in Mr. James's Cambridge edition. The Slavonic is less trustworthy and full than the Greek. This Greek is dependent in certain respects on the Rest of the Words of Baruch, and is thus of service in determining the date of the latter. With our Apocalypse it has only one or two points of contact. Thus with vi. 2, "I was grieving over Zion and lamenting over the captivity which had come upon the people," compare the opening words of the Greek Apocalypse, Ἀποκάλυψις Βαρούχ, ὃς ἔστη . . . κλαίων ὑπὲρ τῆς αἰχμαλωσίας Ἱερουσαλήμ: and with x. 5, "I, Baruch, . . . sat before the gates of the temple and I lamented with that lamentation over Zion," and xxxv. 1, "And I, Baruch, went to the holy place, and sat down upon the ruins and wept," compare the words already quoted together with *καὶ οὕτως ἐκάθητο ἐπὶ τὰς ὡραίας πόλας, ὅπου ἔκειτο τὰ τῶν ἁγίων ἅγια.* Perhaps liv. 8-9, "Even so I could not give Thee the meed of praise, or laud Thee as is befitting. . . . For what am I amongst men . . . that I should have heard all those marvellous things from the Most High?" may be the source of the following words towards the close of the Greek Apocalypse—*δόξαν ἔφερον τῷ θεῷ τῷ ἀξιώσαντί με τοιούτου ἀξιώματος.*

6. Finally, another book of Baruch, distinct from the above, and belonging to the fourth or fifth century of our era, is mentioned in the *Altercatio Simonis Judaei et Theophili Christiani*, published by Harnack (*Texte und Untersuchungen*, Bd. 1, Heft 3, 1883). In this work Theophilus makes the following quotation from the book of Baruch: "Quomodo ergo prope finem libri sui de nativitate ejus et de habitu vestis et de passione ejus et de resurrectione ejus prophetavit dicens: Hic unctus meus, electus meus, vulvae incontaminatae jaculatus, natus et passus dicitur."

Above all the foregoing works which circulated under Baruch's name, the Apocalypse of Baruch stands head and shoulders alike in respect of form or matter or real worth to the student of Judaism and Christianity.

§ 3. The Syriac MSS.

For chapters i.-lxxvii. of this book we have only one MS., the famous sixth-century Peshitto MS. which was found by Ceriani in the library in Milan. For convenience we shall call this MS. *c*. In 1871 Ceriani edited the Syriac text from this MS. in his *Monumenta Sacra et Profana*, vol. v. Fasc. 2, pp. 113-180. Of chapters lxxviii.-lxxxvi., which constitute the Epistle of Baruch, many MSS. were known to exist, and of three of them (i.e. *a*, *b*, *d*) Ceriani made collations and inserted these in their appropriate place below the printed text of *c*. He made no attempt, however, to correct the text of *c* by their means. This task was attempted in a haphazard fashion by Fritzsche (*Libri Apocryphi Vet. Test. Graece*, 1871, pp. 690-699) in an emended edition of Ceriani's Latin translation of these chapters.

It is manifest that, if we wish to ascertain the value of *c* in those chapters in which it stands alone, *i.e.* i.-lxxvii., we can do so only by an exhaustive examination of its text in those chapters which it attests in common with *a*, *b*, *d*, *e*, *f*, *g*, *h*, *i*, *k*, i.e. lxxviii.-lxxxvi., and by a determination of its critical value in respect to them. When we have discharged this task we shall know the real worth of *c* in i.-lxxvii., and familiar with its strength and its weakness shall approach with some confidence the critical problems it presents. With this end in view I have made use of all the Syriac MSS. of lxxviii.-lxxxvi. attainable. These are ten, and are as follows:—

a called A in Ceriani.

b Add. 17,105 in the Brit. Mus., Fol. 116^a-121^a. Sixth century.

c The Milan MS., Fol. 265b-267b. Sixth century.

d called *d* in Ceriani.

e No. 1 Syr. MSS., Bodley, Fol. 430-432. 1627.

f Egerton 704 Brit. Mus., Fol. 373a-374a. Seventeenth century.

g Add. 12,172 Brit. Mus., Fol. 192b-195b. Tenth or eleventh century.

h Add. 18,715 Brit. Mus., Fol. 242b-244a. Twelfth century.

i No. 2 Syr. MSS., Bodley, Fol. 492-493. 1614.

k No. 20 Syr. MSS., Bodley, Fol. 37-38.

All these MSS. with the exception of *k* contain the complete Epistle of Baruch. *k* has only lxxxiii. 7-lxxxiv. 1. Of the ten MSS. I have collated directly *b*, *e*, *f*, *g*, *h*, *i*, *k*. *b* had already been collated and published by Lagarde. I did it, however, afresh, and found only one important error in his work. For a knowledge of *a*, *d* I am indebted to Ceriani's collations. Of *c* my knowledge is derived directly from the photo-lithographic reproduction of that MS. In addition to the above MSS., I have found excerpts from the Epistle of Baruch in the three following MSS., from which I have drawn various readings.

l Add. 12,178 Brit. Mus., Fol. 111b. Ninth or tenth century.

m 14,482 Brit. Mus., Fol. 47b-48a. Eleventh or twelfth century.

n 14,684 Brit. Mus., Fol. 24. Twelfth century.

W and P stand for the Walton and Paris Polyglots.

Of the foregoing MSS. *a*, *b*, *d*, *e*, *f*, *g*, *h*, *i*, *k*, *l*, *m*, *n* represent one type of text as *c* represents another. But although the former belong to one family they are of very different values. To the more ancient and trustworthy belong *a, b, g, h, k* to the latter and less trustworthy *d, e, f, i*. For convenience' sake we shall denote the parent of *a, b, g, h, k* by the symbol β, that of *d, e, f, i* by γ, and the ancestor of both by α. First of all we shall study the general relations of *c* to α and to the sub-groups β and γ.

c stands frequently alone alike when it is right and when it is wrong. In lxxviii. 1; lxxxi. 4; lxxxii. 7; lxxxv. 1, 7; lxxxvi. 3; lxxxvii., it is right against α, i.e. *a, b, d, e, f, g, h, i*; and most probably also in lxxix. 2, 3; lxxxiii. 3, 7, 8; lxxxiv. 1, 9; lxxxv. 15. On the other hand, it is frequently wrong. Thus it attests a corrupt text against α in lxxviii. 1, 2, 3, 4, 7 (?); lxxx. 1, 2, 3; lxxxi. 3; lxxxii. 2 (twice), 3, 4, 5; lxxxiii. 2, 3, 4, 5, 8, 13, 15, 16, 18, 19, 21; lxxxiv. 1, 2, 8, 10; lxxxv. 7, 8, 12, 13; lxxxvi. 1. Thus we see that whereas *c* independently preserves the true text in many passages, α preserves it in thrice as many.

Again, as we have already remarked, the MSS. *a, b, d, e, f, g, h, i, k* are of very different values. Thus *a, b, g, h* agree with *c* in attesting the true text against *d, e, f, i* in lxxviii. 3, 5; lxxix. 1; lxxx. 3; lxxxi. 4; lxxxiv. 4, 6, 7, 10; lxxxv. 6, 11. In lxxxii. 1 *a, b, g, h* agree alike against *c* and *d, e, f, i*. Only in lxxxiii. 17 do *d, e, f, i* agree with *c* against *a, b, g, h*. In the above passages *k* is wanting, but where it exists it belongs as a rule to β, and agrees with *a* more than with any other member of this group. Thus if we represent *a, b, d, e, f, g, h, i, k* by α, and *a, b, g, h, k* by *β*, and *d*, *e*, *f*, *i* by *γ*, as we have already arranged, we arrive at the following genealogy :—

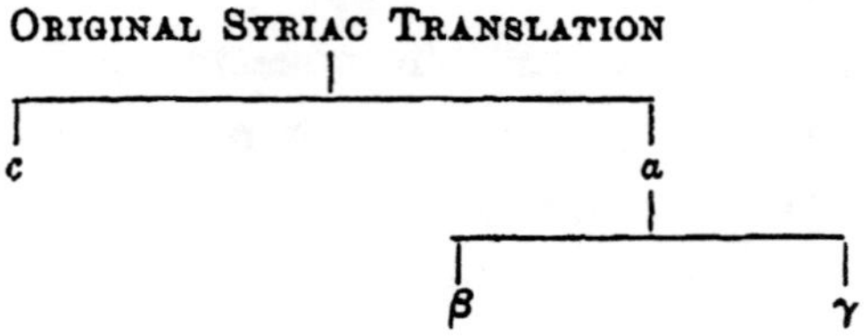

We have also seen from what precedes that *c* often agrees with *β* in giving the true text against *γ*, but *c* and *γ* never agree in attesting the true text against *β*, except perhaps in lxxxiii. 17.

l, *m*, *n*, so far as they exist, support *a* as against *c*, and where the attestation of *a* is divided they generally agree with *γ* against *β*, *i.e.* with *d*, *e*, *f*, *i* against *a*, *b*, *g*, *h*, *k*.

Having now learnt in some measure the relations of the various groups of MSS. to each other, we have still to study those of the individual MSS., so far as our materials admit. The special study of *c* we reserve till later.

Amongst *a*, *b*, *g*, *h*, *b* and *g* are closely related. They agree against all else in lxxx. 4 ; lxxxi. 3 ; lxxxii. 2, 3 ; lxxxiii. 2, 9, 11 ; lxxxv. 12 ; but this combination is generally wrong. *b* is never right when it stands alone. *a* and *h* are excellent authorities when supported by *c*. Thus *a*, *c* are right in lxxxiii. 4 ; lxxxiv. 6 ; lxxxv. 9. They agree in the wrong in lxxix. 2 ; lxxx. 7 ; lxxxv. 9. *a* agrees also with *b*, *c*, *g* against all else in lxxxv. 14, and with *c*, *h* against all in lxxxiv. 3. *h* stands alone with *c* in lxxxi. 4; lxxxiv. 4; lxxxv. 13; but the combination is untrustworthy. From these facts we infer that amongst *a, b, g, h, b* and *g* are very closely related, but that no such close relations exist between *a* and *h* or between either of these with *b, g*. Thus the relations of the sub-group to each other might be represented as follows:—

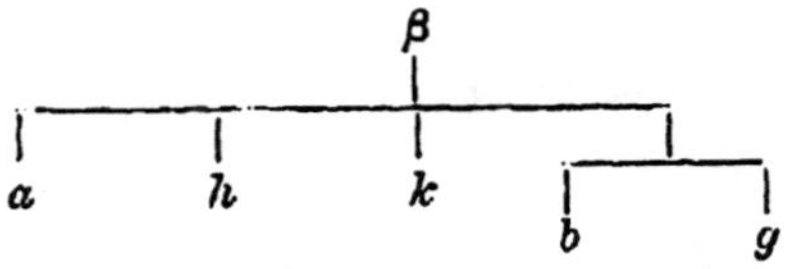

As regards the γ group, we have learnt above that it is quite untrustworthy when it stands alone against *c*. Yet it is upon two of the members of this group that the text of the Walton and Paris Polyglots is based.

The text of these Polyglots may be shortly described as follows. In all cases where it stands in opposition to *c*, WP follow *a* except in lxxxii. 8, lxxxv. 10, where their text is most probably due to conjecture as they here stand alone. Secondly, in cases where γ is opposed to *c*β, WP agree with γ. Thirdly, within the group γ, WP are most closely associated with, and in all probability are based upon, *e, f*. For they agree with *e* against all other MSS. in lxxx. i., lxxxii. 9 in omitting "and," in lxxx. 2 in giving an impossible form, and in lxxxiii. 14 in omitting half the verse. But WP are not based on *e* alone; for though *e* omits a word in lxxxv. 5, it is given in WP. This defect of *e* was made good from *f;* for we find that *f*WP stand alone in lxxx. 7. It is of no little interest to have traced the sources of the text in the Polyglots; for, as their editors have given no information on the subject, scholars have hitherto been quite in the dark in this respect. We are now in a position to give the genealogy of the MSS. dealt with above. This is as follows:—

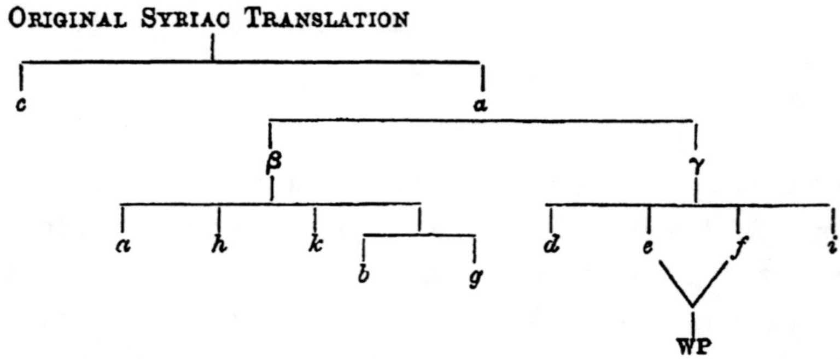

Special Study of c.—It is now time to study the special characteristics of *c*. We have already seen that *c* has independently preserved the true text in many passages against corruptions in *a*. (A list of these passages will be found above, where also it is shown that *a* has preserved the true text much more frequently than *c*.) I have found *c* trustworthy when supported by *a* in lxxxiii. 4; lxxxiv. 6; lxxxv. 9; but not so in lxxix. 2; lxxx. 7; lxxxv. 9; or by *a, b, g* in lxxxv. 14; or by *a, h* in lxxxiv. 3; or by *b, g* in lxxxv. 1. But the character of *c* appears more clearly in its errors. Thus it is wrong (1) *through omission* in lxxx. 1, 2 (omission due here to an attempted emendation); lxxxii. 2, 3; lxxxiii. 4, 5, 16, 18; lxxxiv. 1, 10; lxxxv. 4 (through homoioteleuton), 12. Cf. li. 16 and lvi. 14 for omissions of the negative. (2) *Through additions to the text* in lxxviii. 2; lxxxiii. 5; lxxxv. 8, 9, 15. (3) *Through transposition of words or letters whereby the sense is generally destroyed. Transposition of letters* in lxxxii. 4 whereby "drop" becomes "pollution"; lxxxiii. 21 where "by truth" becomes "in silence." For similar transpositions in the earlier chapters see xiv. 6; lxx. 8. *Transposition of words* in lxxxi. 3; lxxxii. 2, 3; lxxxiii. 5; lxxxiv. 8. For similar transpositions see xiv. 11; xxi. 16. (4) *Through clerical errors* in lxxviii. 3 (for a similar error see xxiv. 4), 4; lxxx. 3; lxxxii. 5; lxxxiii. 2, 3, 13, 15, 16, 19; lxxxiv. 1 (observe that there is the same erroneous pointing in lxx. 5), 3, 8; lxxxv. 12, 13. In lxxxiv. 2 we have an intentional variation. Cf. in earlier chapters li. 1.

We have now completed our study of the MSS. The knowledge which we have thus gained from our comparative criticism of *c* and the other MSS. helps to secure us against the characteristic errors of the former in the chapters where the friendly aid of the latter cannot be invoked. We can thus address ourselves with a certain degree of confidence and skill to the obscurities and corruptions that arise in these chapters. As a further result of this examination, we have come to feel that so long as we follow its guidance, we can nowhere greatly err from the sense of the Hebrew original.

Date of the Common Ancestor of c and a.—Since *c* and *b* are both of the sixth century, we find that already at that date there existed two distinctly developed types of text, both of which must have been for no brief period in existence, owing to the variety of readings already evolved. Further, though *b* belongs to the sixth century, many of its readings are decidedly later than *c* and even than *a* and *h*. In fact, *a, h* represent the text at an earlier period than *b*. The common parent, therefore, of *a, h,* and *b* was probably not later than the fifth century. Such a variety of related yet different MSS. as *a, b, g, h, k* could not well have arisen from an MS. of a later date. This being so, the common progenitor of *c* and *a* can hardly be sought later than the fourth century.

§ 4. Previous Literature on the Apocalypse of Baruch

The Syriac Text.—As we have seen in the foregoing section, we have only one MS., i.e. *c*, for chapters i.-lxxvii. For Ceriani's edition of this MS. see pp. xxii.-xxiii. Of the text of the remaining chapters, which form the Epistle of Baruch, many editions have appeared:—(1) That which is published in the Walton and Paris Polyglots. This text is, as we have shown above (pp. xxvii.-xxviii.), founded on two indifferent MSS., *e* and *f*. (2) Lagarde's edition of *b*, pp. 88-93 of his *Libri Vet. Test. Apocryphi Syriace*, 1861. This is merely *b* in a printed form, and not an edition of the Syriac text based on the Nitrian MSS. in the British Museum, as is everywhere wrongly stated both by German and English writers. Though *b* is a very old and valuable MS., we have now several MSS. at our disposal containing a more ancient text (see pp. xxvi.-xxvii.) (3) Ceriani's published text of *c*, to which he has appended collations of *a*, *b*, *d* in his *Monumenta Sacra et Profana*, vol. v. Fasc. 2, pp. 167-180. As we have already remarked, Ceriani has contented himself with printing the text of *c*, and has not sought to correct it by means of *a*, *b*, *d*.

Translations.—Only one translation of our Apocalypse has hitherto appeared, *i.e.* the Latin translation of Ceriani in the *Monumenta Sacra et Profana*, vol. i. Fasc. 2, pp. 73-98, 1866. This is certainly a model translation in point of style, and considering the fact that Ceriani was not a specialist in Apocalyptic literature, it is also very accurate. Not quite accurate, indeed, as Ceriani himself was aware in 1871 when he wrote—"Omisi tamen plenam revisionem meae versionis Latinae . . . quia omnino in meis occupationibus tempus me deficit, et quidquid corrigere opus erit, alii ex textu per se poterunt." Some of the errors are as follows:—In xiii. 8 we must expunge "enim est." In verses 4-5 of the same chapter we find the peculiar construction "ut . . . dic." In xv. 6 read "transgressus est" for "fecit." In xix. 1 for "te" read "vos." In xxv. 4 for "terrae" read "terram." In xxxii. 4 for "coronabitur" read "perficietur." In xl. 1 for "qui tunc" read "illius temporis." In xlix. 3 for "vestient" read "induent." In lv. 1 expunge "ejus." In lx. 1 add "eorum" after "magiarum." In lxii. 2 add "et" before "idololatria." In lxxii. 2 for "vivificabit" read "parcet." In lxxxv. 9 for "veritatem cujuspiam" read "veritas quodpiam." In lxxxvi. 12 for "viae" read "recreationis" (= ἀνέσεως); "viae" is a rendering of *d* but not of *c*, Ceriani's text. Although Ceriani made no critical study of the text of *c*, he has nevertheless made some most felicitous emendations in x. 14; xiv. 6; li. 1; lvi. 4, 14; lx. 2; lxix. 1, 4; lxx. 8. A critical study of the text and matter would have helped him to deal with the corruptions of the Syriac in xxiv. 4; xlviii. 32; li. 16; lxvii. 2; lxx. 5; lxxii. 1, etc.

As Ceriani did not believe in a Semitic original of our Apocalypse, he was naturally unable to deal with corruptions that were not native to the Syriac Version, but had already appeared in the Hebrew text or had arisen through the misconceptions of the Greek translator.

Ceriani's Latin translation was republished by Fritzsche in his *Libri Apocryphi Vet. Test. Graece,* 1871, pp. 654-679. Though Fritzsche introduces several changes into Ceriani's translation, hardly any of these can be justified. Sometimes he makes the change because he has failed to understand the text; thus in xx. 4; xxi. 9, 10, he has emended Ceriani's "investigabiles" into "ininvestigabiles"; but "investigabilis" in the Vulgate frequently means "unsearchable." The change of "omne" into "vanum" in xix. 8 is quite wanton. The Latin text also is carelessly edited;

thus for "ego" there is "ergo" in lxxxiv. 1; for "ibi" there is "tibi" in lxxxv. 13; and "opulus" for "populus" in xlviii. 24. In the critical notes on pp. 690-699 there are many confusions and mis-statements of authorities. It is needless to add that none of Ceriani's actual errors were corrected by Fritzsche, for the Syriac text had not yet been published.

Notwithstanding all these defects, every scholar who has used Fritzsche's book is rightly grateful to him for making Ceriani's translation so generally accessible.

Critical Inquiries.—Langen, *De Apocalypsi Baruch anno superiori primum edita commentatio*, Friburgi in Brisgovia, 1867. This treatise, which consists of twenty-four quarto pages, maintains that our Apocalypse was written in Greek in the reign of Trajan. Although no grounds worthy of consideration are advanced in support of a Greek original, Langen's view has been universally accepted. Only two scholars have expressed a doubt on the subject, Mr. Thomson and Professor Ryle of Cambridge. This fact in itself serves to show how inadequately hitherto this Apocalypse has been studied. In other respects, Langen's work is admirable.

Ewald, *Göttinger Gel. Anzeigen*, 1867, pp. 1706-1717, 1720; *Gesch. des Volkes Israel*, vii. 83-87 (English trans. vol. viii. 57-61). In a short but interesting article Ewald assigns the date of our author to the reign of Domitian. He regards 4 Ezra and this Apocalypse as the work of one and the same author.

Hilgenfeld, *Zeitschrift für wissensch. Theologie*, 1869, pp. 437-440; *Messias Judaeorum*, pp. 63-64. Hilgenfeld ascribes our Apocalypse to the earlier years of Vespasian, possibly to 72 A.D. Vespasian is the leader mentioned in xl. The Baruch Apocalypse is subsequent to 4 Ezra.

Wieseler, "Das Vierte Buch Ezra," *Theol. Stud. und Kritiken*, 1870, p. 288. This writer criticises Hilgenfeld's date. The seven weeks (xxviii. 2) are to be reckoned from the fall of Jerusalem to 119 A.D. The two weeks in that verse point to the years 105-119, *i.e.* to the time of Trajan.

Fritzsche, *Libri Apocryphi Vet. Test.* 1871, pp. xxx.-xxxii. On Fritzsche's reprint of Ceriani's Latin translation see pp. xxxii.-xxxiii.

Stähelin, "Zur paulinischen Eschatologie," *Jahrbücher für Deutsche Theologie*, 1874, pp. 211-214.

Hausrath, *Neutestamentl. Zeitgesch.* 2nd ed. iv. 88-90, 1877.

Renan, "L'Apocalypse de Baruch," *Journal des Savants*, 1877, pp. 223-231; *Les Évangiles*, 1877, pp. 517-530. Renan regards this Apocalypse as an imitation of 4 Ezra and in part designed as a correction of it, as, for instance, on the question of original sin (cf. also Langen). The latter was written in Nerva's reign, the former in the last year of Trajan's. The sombre clouds which obscured the last months of Trajan roused the hopes of the Jews and gave birth to the furious revolt of 117, of which this book is a monument. The fact that this book was accepted amongst the Christians excludes a later date. No

Jewish product later than Hadrian gained currency in Christian circles.

Drummond, *The Jewish Messiah*, 1877, pp. 117-132. Dr. Drummond is of opinion that, "notwithstanding the Hebraic colouring of its thoughts and language, this book may very well have been written in Greek." Its author was a Jew: there is "not a single expression which betrays a Christian hand." It is probably subsequent in date to 4 Ezra, and is divided into the following groups of chapters—i.-ix.; x.-xii.; xiii.-xx.; xxi.-xxx.; xxxi.-xliii.; xliv.-xlvii.; xlviii.-lxxvi.; lxxvii.-lxxxvii.

Kneucker, *Das Buch Baruch*, 1879, pp. 190-196. Kneucker believes that the Apocryphal Book of Baruch is the letter which Baruch undertakes in ch. lxxvii. to send by "three men" to the brethren in Babylon. This view needs to be greatly modified; as it stands, he has found none to follow it. The present book, he holds, is defective.

Dillmann, art. "Pseudepigraphen" in Herzog's *Real-Enc.* 2nd ed. xii. 356-358. Baruch, according to Dillmann, was undoubtedly later than 4 Ezra, and was written under Trajan. The writer was an orthodox Jew and wrote in Greek. Dillmann rightly thinks that parts of the book are lost, but he is wrong in supposing it to be not more truly Jewish than 4 Ezra. He falls also into the same mistake as so many other scholars in supposing Lagarde's edition of MS. *b* to be an edition of the Syriac text, based on the Nitrian MSS.

Edersheim, *The Life and Times of Jesus the Messiah*, 2nd ed. 1884, ii. p. 658.

Rosenthal, *Vier Apocryphische Bücher*, 1885, pp. 72-103. This writer has made a painstaking study of Ceriani's Latin translation. He has likewise given no little thought to the subject matter, and discovered many connections between our book and Talmudic literature. It cannot, however, be said that he has thrown much light on the difficult problems of this book. In most respects Rosenthal follows the traditional lines of interpretation. The work is from the hand of one author. It was written in Greek in the reign of Trajan. Like previous writers Rosenthal regards our Apocalypse as subsequent to 4 Ezra, and as designed in some respects to correct its statements. He accepts Wieseler's interpretation of xxviii., and reckons the seven weeks there mentioned as dating from 70 A.D. Hence $70 + 49 = 119$ and the two last weeks point to the years 105-119, the period of the last woes. 119 is the year of the Messiah's advent. But Rosenthal thinks he can determine the exact year of the book's publication. Thus the letter to the Jews in Babylon shows that it was written before the rebellion of the Jews in Cyrene, Egypt, Cyprus, Babylon, and their extermination by Quietus in 116. On the other hand, he believes that the great earthquake in Syria, which did not affect Palestine in December 115, is referred to in lxx. 8-lxxi. 1. Thus the book was written in the beginning of 116. With many of Dr. Rosenthal's statements, in which he departs from the traditional interpretation of this book, the present writer dissents strongly. Some of these statements are as follows:—The Messiah, he says, has a less active *rôle* in 4 Ezra than in Baruch. The real facts are that a passive *rôle* is assigned to the Messiah in xxix. 3 of this Apocalypse and in vii. 28-29 of 4 Ezra, and a highly active *rôle* in xxxix.-xl. and lxx.-lxxii. of this Apocalypse and xii. 32-34 and xiii. 32-50 of 4 Ezra. Rosenthal charges our author with being an ignorant man and unacquainted with Scripture. This is strange, seeing that in every instance save one the quotations from the Old Testament are made from the Hebrew and not from the LXX., and that a large and accurate knowledge of Jewish history is shown throughout the work. Again, he says our author makes the resurrection from the dead depend on faith therein, and then quotes as a proof xxx. 1, which says nothing of the kind, and further adduces lxv. 1, where he alleges Manasseh is reproved for not believing in the future, "dass er an keinen Zukunft glaubte!" This last assertion rests on a strange misconception of the Latin translation—"cogitabat tempore suo quasi ac futurum non esset ut Fortis inquireret ista." This is, of course, "he thought that in his time the Mighty One would not inquire into these things!" "Futurum" cannot mean "the future."

Stanton, *The Jewish and Christian Messiah*, 1886, pp. 72-75. This writer ascribes our Apocalypse to the years immediately subsequent to 70 A.D. He divides the book as follows—i.-ix; x.-xii.; xiii.-xx.; xxi.-xxx.; xxxi.-xliii.; xliv.-lxxvi.; lxxvii.-lxxxvii.

Schürer, *A History of the Jewish People in the Time of Jesus Christ* (translated from the second and revised edition of the German), 1886, vol. iii. Div. ii. pp. 83-93. We have here an admirable account of our Apocalypse. Schürer regards it as written shortly after 70 A.D., and argues strongly for its priority to 4 Ezra. After citing passages on the question of original sin from both books, he proceeds: "Here, then, we have not even an actual difference of view, far less a correction of the one writer on the part of the other. Further, such other reasons as have been advanced in favour of the priority of Ezra and the dependent character of Baruch are merely considerations of an extremely general kind which may be met with considerations equally well calculated to prove quite the reverse." "My own opinion is that . . . it is precisely in the case of Baruch that this problem is uppermost, *i.e.* How is the calamity of Israel and the impunity of its oppressors possible and conceivable? while in the case of Ezra, though this problem concerns him too, still there is a question that lies almost yet nearer his heart, *i.e.* Why is it that so many perish and so few are saved? The subordination of the former of these questions to the other, which is a purely theological one, appears to me rather to indicate that Ezra is of a later date than Baruch." It must be admitted that these arguments are as conclusive as are the counter-arguments of Ewald, Langen, Hilgenfeld, Hausrath, Stähelin, Renan, Drummond, and Dillmann for the priority of 4 Ezra. And beyond this *impasse* it is impossible for criticism to advance until it recognises the composite nature of both books. Schürer appends a valuable bibliography.

Baldensperger, *Das Selbstbewüsstsein Jesu*, 1888, pp. 23-24, 32-35. The composition of Baruch is here assigned to a Jew living in Palestine in the reign of Trajan.

Thomson, *Books which Influenced our Lord and His Apostles*, 1891, 253-267, 414-422. This writer believes with Schürer in the priority of Baruch, but his hardihood goes still farther: he assigns the date of its composition to 59 B.C. Such a date of necessity argued a Semitic original, and this Mr. Thomson contends for, and we hold rightly, though his reason may be wrong. This his sole reason is that in v. 5 we find the proper name Jabish ܝܒܝܫ. "This," he says, "almost certainly represents 'Ιγαβής of the Septuagint, 1 Chron. iv. 9, 10 (Heb. יעבץ, Syriac ܝܥܒܨ)." There is no ground for this identification; in fact, everything is against it; and even if the identification were right, it would not necessarily prove a Hebrew original. Jabish or Jabesh, for the Syriac is unpunctuated, implies a Greek form Ιαβις or Ιαβης, and this in turn יבש. Here, as elsewhere, I have had occasion to regret that Mr. Thomson acquainted himself inadequately with the facts before he gave loose rein to his vigorous imagination.

Kabisch, "Die Quellen der Apocalypse Baruchs," *Jahrbücher f. Protest. Theol.* 1891, pp. 66-107. With this writer the criticism of Baruch enters on a new stage. So long, indeed, as it pursued the old lines, finality on the question of the chronological relations of our Apocalypse and 4 Ezra was impossible, and the champions of the one book with excellent reasons demolished their rivals, and with reasons just as excellent were demolished in turn. The explanation is obvious: both books are composite, and if some parts of 4 Ezra are older than certain parts of Baruch, no less certainly are some parts of Baruch older than some of 4 Ezra.

Kabisch emphasises at the outset certain facts which point to a plurality of authorship. Thus he shows that we find in Baruch side by side, on the one hand, a measureless pessimism and world-despair which look for neither peace nor happiness in this world; and, on the other hand, in the same work, a vigorous optimism and world-joy which look to a future of sensuous happiness and delight, of perfect satisfaction and peace.

Kabisch further points out that the same subjects are treated several times, and often without any fresh contribution to the subject at issue. Thus the Messianic Kingdom is twice delineated, the advent of the Messiah twice foretold, and the Messianic woes just as often depicted. Yet the latter are neither so identical as to point to the same author, nor are the novelties so great as to justify the repetition of the whole complex statement already once given.

On these grounds he shows that the book is derived from at least three or four authors. Thus he distinguishes i.-xxiii.; xxxi.-xxxiv.; lxxv.-lxxxvii. as the groundwork written subsequently to 70 A.D., since the destruction of the temple is implied throughout these chapters. Further, these sections are marked by a boundless despair of this world of corruption, which fixes its regards on the afterworld of incorruption. In the remaining sections of the book, however, there is a faith in Israel's ultimate triumph here, and an optimism which looks to an earthly Messianic Kingdom of sensuous delights. In these sections, moreover, the integrity of Jerusalem is throughout assumed. Kabisch, therefore, rightly takes these constituents of the book to be prior to 70 A.D. These sections, however, are not the work of one writer, but of three, two of them being unmutilated productions, *i.e.* the Vine and the Cedar Vision, xxxvi.-xl., and the Cloud Vision, liii.-lxxiv., but the third a fragmentary Apocalypse, xxiv. 3-xxix. Finally, these different writings were incorporated in one book by a Christian contemporary of Papias, and to this editor are probably due xxviii. 5; xxx. 1; xxxii. 2-4; xxxv.; lxxvi. 1. With the bulk of this criticism I have no reason for variance, as by independent study, and frequently on different grounds, I have arrived at several of these conclusions. But taken as it stands, Kabisch's criticism is only an additional stage on the way. It is far from being final, as a more prolonged study would have convinced this writer. Thus, as we shall presently learn (see pp. liii.-lxiv.), the so-called groundwork of Kabisch is as undoubtedly composite as the whole work is composite, and edited from at least two or three distinct writings. In this and in other respects the criticism of our book is indefinitely more difficult than Kabisch conceives it. But we must not anticipate our conclusions here. Kabisch's work is based on the Latin translation of Ceriani. He follows the traditional views of a Greek original. The possibility of a Semitic original does not seem to have occurred to him.

De Faye, *Les Apocalypses juives*, 1892, pp. 25-28, 76-103, 192-204. It is interesting to find that some of Kabisch's conclusions were reached by this French scholar independently. Thus De Faye, like Kabisch, distinguishes xxxvi.-xl. and liii.-lxxv. as distinct works written before 70 A.D. The rest of his analysis is not likely to gain acceptance. His main conclusions are as follows:—i.-xxxii. 7 constitute an Apocalypse of Baruch written after 70 A.D.; i.-v. and vi.-xxxii. 7, however, were originally derived from two hands (pp. 193-196). Another quite distinct work was the Assumption of Baruch, which consists of xlviii.-lii.; xli.-xliii. 2; lxxvi. 1-4 (p. 97 note). The date of this work is also after 70 A.D. xliii. 3-xlvii. is for the most part the work of the final editor. They are much later in date than the Apocalypse or the Assumption. Thus the following chapters and verses are derived from the final editor: xxxii. 7-xxxv.; xliii. 3-xlvii.; lxxvi. 5-lxxxvii. (pp. 201-202). Much praise is due to M. de Faye for the abundant scholarship and pains he has expended on this book; but his work is unconvincing: a profounder study would have led him to abandon many of the positions which are maintained by him.

Ryle, "The Book of Baruch," *Dictionary of the Bible*, ed. Smith, 1893, vol. i. pp. 361-362. Professor Ryle regards our Apocalypse as written shortly after the destruction of Jerusalem, and possibly in Hebrew. He reverts to Ewald's idea of the common authorship of this book and 4 Ezra as a means of explaining their manifold points of identity and similarity. He divides it into the following sections: i.-xii.; xiii.-xx.; xxi.-xxxiv.; xxxv.-xlvi.; xlvii.-lii.; liii.-lxxvi.; lxxvii.-lxxxv.

§ 5. The Syriac—A Translation from the Greek

That the Syriac text is a translation from the Greek is to be concluded on several grounds. 1. It is so stated in the sixth-century MS. *c*. 2. There are certain corruptions in the text which are explicable only on the hypothesis that the translator misinterpreted the Greek, or else found the corruption already existing there. Thus in iii. 7 (see note) the Syrian translator renders "ornament" where the text requires "world." It is obvious here that he followed the wrong sense of κόσμος. The corrupt readings in xxi. 9, 11, 12; xxiv. 1, 2; lxii. 7 are to be explained on this principle (see notes *in loc.*). 3. Imitations of Greek constructions are found. In lxv. 1 we have *hau* = the Greek article in connection with a proper name. 4. We have frequent transliterations of Greek words, as in vi. 4, 7; x. 17; xvii. 4; xxi. 7, etc. It is possible, of course, that these borrowed Greek words may have been part of the current language when the translation was made. In lxxvii. 14, however, we have a Greek word transliterated which gives no sense in its context. Hence this word was not written first-hand by a Syriac writer, but was taken by the Syriac translator from the Greek text before him. 5. The Rest of the Words of Baruch is largely based on our Apocalypse, and frequently reproduces it word for word. This book was written in Greek by a Christian Palestinian Jew in the second century. It implies, therefore, the existence of our Apocalypse in a Greek form, and preserves important fragments of the Greek Version.

§ 6. The Greek—A Translation from a Hebrew Original

It is hard to understand how such an unbroken unanimity has prevailed amongst scholars on the question of a Greek original. Indeed, it is impossible to explain it, save on the hypothesis that they gave the subject the most cursory notice, or more probably none at all. In fact, since the discovery of the book not a single serious attempt has been made to grapple with this problem, and yet, in nearly every instance, scholars have spoken with an assurance on this subject that only a personal and thorough study of the subject could justify. To this strong and unanimous tradition of the learned world I bowed without hesitation at the outset of my studies, but with an awakening distrust and an ever-growing reluctance during the subsequent years in which the present Translation and Notes were completed. In fact, the feeling grew steadily stronger that only a Hebrew original could account for many of the phenomena of the text. And yet my gathering certainty on this head did not lead to action till the MSS. of the Translation and Notes were partially in type. I then felt that I could no longer stay my hand, and with the kind permission of my publishers I have been enabled to introduce the necessary changes into the Translation and Notes. The facts which have obliged me to maintain a Hebrew original may be summarised as follows:—1. The quotations from the Old Testament agree in all cases but one with the Massoretic text against the LXX. 2. Hebrew idioms survive in the Syriac text. 3. Unintelligible expressions in the Syriac can be explained and the text restored by retranslation into Hebrew. 4. There are many paronomasiae which discover themselves on retranslation into Hebrew. 5. One or two passages of the book have been preserved in Rabbinic writings.

1. *The quotations from the Old Testament agree in all cases but one with the Mass. text against the LXX.*—See vi. 8; xxxviii. 2; xli. 4; li. 4; lviii. 1, with notes *in loc.* In two other passages our text departs alike from the Mass. and LXX.: thus in iv. 2 it agrees with the Syriac Version of Is. xlix. 16 against the Mass., LXX., and Vulg.; and in xxxv. 2 it reproduces Jer. ix. 1, freely and independently. Finally, in lxxxii. 5 only does it agree with the LXX. of Is. xl. 15. It is to be observed, however, that neither does the Vulgate

in that passage agree with the Mass. The Mass. = כדק יטול; the LXX. = ὡς σίελος λογισθήσονται = כרֹק נחשבו; Vulg. = "quasi pulvis exiguus." Here the Vulg. omits יטול and the LXX. replaces it by repeating a previous verb. Hence this passage is inconclusive, as the text of Isa. xl. 15 seems to have been uncertain.

2. *Hebrew idioms survive in the Syriac text.*—We shall treat this section under four heads.

(*a*) *Survival of the familar Hebrew idiom of the infinitive absolute combined with the finite verb.*—The Syriac equivalent of this Hebraism is frequently found in this Apocalypse: cf. xiii. 3 (note); xxii. 7; xli. 6; xlviii. 30; l. 2; lvi. 2; lxxv. 6; lxxvi. 2; lxxxii. 2; lxxxiii. 1, 2, 3, 6; lxxxiv. 2. In this circumstance alone we have sufficient evidence to establish a Hebrew original. This idiom is, it is true, also found in original Syriac, but is comparatively rare. It is not, however, with original Syriac that we have here to do, but with a Syriac translation. We shall now proceed to show that *in a Syriac translation of a Hebrew or a Greek text this idiom does not appear except as a rendering of the corresponding idiom in the Hebrew or Greek before it.*

In order to prove this statement we shall examine the Peshitto Version of Genesis and Exodus. In these two books I have found fifty-seven instances of the occurrence of the infinitive absolute with the finite verb in the Massoretic text.

As we shall require presently to know the usage of the LXX. in this matter, we shall now give a table furnishing the facts we are in search of from both versions.

Syriac-Peshitto.	Genesis-Massoretic Text.	LXX.
Noun and verb.	ii. 17.	Noun and verb.
Infinitive and verb.	iii. 4.	,,
,,	iii. 16.	Participle and verb.
,,	xvii. 12.	Noun and verb.
,,	xviii. 18.	Participle and verb.
Finite verb only.	xix. 9.	Noun and verb.
Infinitive and verb.	xxii. 17 (twice).	Participle and verb.
,,	xxvi. 11.	Finite verb only.
,,	xxvi. 13.	Different text followed.
,,	xxvi. 28.	Participle and verb.
Finite verb only.	xxvii. 30.	Finite verb only.
Infinitive and verb.	xxviii. 22.	Noun and verb.
,,	xxx. 16.	Finite verb only.
Finite verb only.	xxxi. 15.	Noun and verb.
Infinite and verb.	xxxi. 30.	,,
,,	,,	Finite verb only.
,,	xxxii. 12.	Adverb and verb.
,,	xxxvii. 8 (twice).	Participle and verb.
,,	xxxvii. 10.	,,
Different text followed.	xxxvii. 33.	Different text followed.
Infinitive and verb.	xl. 15.	Noun and verb.
,,	xliii. 2.	,,
,,	xliii. 6.	Participle and verb.
,,	,,	Finite verb only.
Finite verb only.	xlvi. 4.	Different text followed.
Infinitive and verb.	l. 24 (twice).	Noun and verb.

Thus in Genesis there are twenty-nine instances of this idiom. These are rendered by the Peshitto as follows: twenty-three by the infinitive and verb; one by cognate noun and verb; four by finite verb only; and in one case a different text is followed. In the case of the LXX., eleven by cognate noun and verb; nine by participle and verb; five by finite verb only; while in four a different text is followed.

An examination of Exodus supplies the following evidence :—

Syriac-Peshitto.	Exodus-Massoretic Text.	LXX.
Infinitive and verb.	iii. 7.	Participle and verb.
,,	iii. 16.	Noun and verb.
Different text followed.	xi. 1.	,,
Infinitive and verb.	xiii. 19.	,,
,,	xviii. 18.	,,
Finite verb only.	xix. 12.	,,
Infinitive and verb.	xxi. 12, 15, 16, 17.	,,
Different text followed.	xxi. 19.	Finite verb only.
Infinitive and verb.	xxi. 20, 22, 28.	Noun and verb.
Finite verb only.	xxi. 36.	Finite verb only.
Infinitive and verb.	xxii. 6, 14.	,,
,,	xxii. 16, 19.	Noun and verb.
Finite verb only (twice) Infinitive and verb	xxii. 28 (thrice).	Noun and verb (twice). Participle and verb.
Infinitive and verb.	xxiii. 4.	Participle and verb.
,,	xxiii. 5.	Finite verb only.
,,	xxiii. 22, 24.	Noun and verb.
,,	xxxi. 14.	,,
,,	xxxi. 15.	Finite verb only.

Thus in Exodus there are twenty-eight instances of this idiom. These are rendered in the Peshitto : twenty-two by the infinitive and verb ; four by finite verb only ; in two cases a different text is followed. In the LXX., nineteen by cognate noun and verb; three by participle and verb; and six by the finite verb only. By combining the facts on both books, we arrive at the following results. The Hebrew idiom occurs fifty-seven times. In the Peshitto forty-five are rendered by infinitive and verb; one by cognate noun and verb; eight by finite verb only; in three cases a different text is followed. In the LXX., thirty are rendered by cognate noun and verb; twelve by participle and verb;

eleven by finite verb only; in four cases a different text is followed. Finally, we should mention here that in no case have we found this idiom in the Syriac Version where the same idiom was not also present in the Hebrew from which it was derived, and the same holds true of the LXX. save in one case, *i.e.* Exod. xxiii. 26.

From the above results obtained from the Peshitto Version of Genesis and Exodus we learn that *whereas the Syriac translator on the one hand never inserts this idiom unless as an equivalent of the corresponding Hebrew idiom before him, on the other he has failed to render it in eight cases out of fifty-seven.* In these he gives the finite verb only. Thus the irresistible conclusion is: *if we find this idiom occurring at all in a Syriac translation, it is a presumption that it existed in the language from which the translation was made; whereas if we find it frequently* (as in our Apocalypse) *the presumption changes to a certainty.*

The above conclusions drawn from a study of the Peshitto Version of the Hebrew text of Genesis and Exodus may be further confirmed and extended in their application by a short consideration of the corresponding phenomena in the New Testament. So far as I can discover, the Peshitto Version of the New Testament in no case inserts this idiom where it does not already exist in the Greek. This idiom occurs, as we know, at least six times: see Matt. xiii. 14; xv. 4; Luke vii. 34; xxii. 15; Acts vii. 34; Hebrews vi. 14. Five of these passages are quotations from the LXX., and thus the idiom goes back to the Hebrew. In the remaining one, Luke xxii. 15, it implies undoubtedly an Aramaic or Hebrew original. The Peshitto renders these instances by the infinitive and verb except in Matt. xiii. 14, where it misses the point, and in Luke xxii. 15, where it gives the noun and verb. In both these verses the Sinaitic MS. gives the infinitive and verb.

The Syriac translator therefore is so far from inserting this idiom, unless it exists already in the Hebrew or Greek text before him, that, as we found above, *he occasionally fails to do so when he ought.* The bearing of this conclusion on our present investigation is obvious. This idiom is found fifteen times in our Apocalypse; we can therefore conclude with confidence that it occurred at least fifteen times in the Greek, and in all likelihood oftener.

Having now found that this idiom occurred frequently in the Greek, we have now to ask, could it have appeared there for the first time, *i.e.* in an original Greek writing?

The answer does not require a long investigation. The idiom is thoroughly Semitic, and is only once found in all Greek literature, and that in Lucian. In the New Testament there is no instance of it unless in a quotation from the Old Testament; in the Old Testament only once, Exod. xxiii. 26, without a Semitic background.

Hence we conclude that its frequent occurrence in our Apocalypse is in itself demonstrable evidence of a Hebrew original. Further, it is probable that it occurred in the Hebrew original more frequently than in the Greek translation; for we found above that out of fifty-seven instances of this idiom in Genesis and Exodus, the LXX. failed to render eleven.

(*b*) *The survival of various Hebraisms.*—In xx. 2 (see note); xxiv. 2, where Syriac for "throughout all generations" = ἐν πάσῃ γενεᾷ καὶ γενεᾷ = בכל־דור ודור; cf. Ps. cxlv. 13; the same idiom is found in xxix. 7, where I render "every morning"; xxxviii. 4, where "from my (earliest) days" is the Hebrew idiom found in 1 Kings i. 6.

(*c*) *Probable survival of Hebrew order against Syriac idiom.*—In xiii. 12 (see notes); lxiii. 8. In connection with the notes on xiii. 12 it is worth observing that, in Western Aramaic, unlike Syriac, the order of the participle and the substantive verb in the compound past imperfect indicative is indifferent. Thus in Dan. v. 19; vi. 4, 5, 11, 15, etc., the substantive verb precedes, whereas in Dan. ii. 31; iv. 7, 10, 26; vii. 2, 6, 8, etc., the participle.

(*d*) *Probable survival of syntactical idioms against Syriac idiom.*—For omission of relative see xx. 3, note; imperative used as jussive, xi. 6, note; Hebrew perfect with strong vav in xxi. 21, and the voluntative with weak vav in xlviii. 6, reproduced literally but not idiomatically.

3. *Unintelligible expressions in the Syriac can be explained and the text restored by retranslation into Hebrew.*—In xxi. 9, 11, 12; xxiv. 2; lxii. 7, I have been able to explain and restore an unintelligible

text by retranslation first into Greek and thence into Hebrew. The Syriac in these verses is the stock rendering of δικαιοῦσθαι, and this in turn of צדק. But צדק also = δίκαιος εἶναι, and this is the meaning required in the above passages (see notes *in loc.*), but the Greek translator erroneously adopted the more usual rendering.

Again in xliv. 12 we have another interesting restoration through the same means. There we find in the Syriac "on its beginning" set over antithetically against "to torment." Here the context requires "to its blessedness." Now the corrupt text = בראשו, which by the transposition of the single letter ר gives us the text באשרו = "to its blessedness." Again in lxxxv. 12 we have another instance of the Greek translator following the wrong of two alternative meanings.

Again in xi. 6; xx. 3; xxi. 21; xxix. 5; xlviii. 6, we are obliged by the context to translate not the Syriac text but the Hebrew text presupposed by the Syriac, but mistranslated by the Greek translator, and, therefore, of necessity by the Syriac. See notes *in loc.*; also 2 (*d*) above, p. xlvii. For other restorations the reader should consult the notes on x. 13; lxx. 6; lxxx. 2. Finally in lxxvii. 14 we have a transliteration of the Greek word ὕλη. ὕλη is either a corruption or a mistranslation of some Hebrew word. It could not have been written for the first time in Greek. I have hazarded a conjecture in the note on the passage.

4. *Many paronomasiae discover themselves on retranslation into Hebrew.*—We have in xv. 8 (see note) one that is already familiar to us in Isaiah and Ezekiel. As many as three spring into notice in xlviii. 35 (see note), and probably two in lxxxiv. 2. The most interesting perhaps are those on the proper names, Hezekiah and Sennacherib, in lxiii. 3, 4 (see notes). In the case of the former, I had the good fortune to conjecture the existence of the same paronomasia in Ecclus. xlviii. 22, and to restore the Hebrew there as it actually stood before Dr. Neubauer's discovery of the Hebrew MS. of Ecclus. xl.-l.

5. *One or two passages of this book have been preserved in rabbinic writings* (see notes on x. 18; xxxii. 2-4; lxiv. 3).

§ 7. The Different Elements in the Apocalypse of Baruch with their Respective Characteristics and Dates.

As we have seen above, the composite nature of this book has already been recognised independently by Kabisch and De Faye. And the more thoroughly we study it, the more conscious we become of the impassable gulf which sunders the world-views which underlie the different parts. In one class of the passages there is everywhere manifest a vigorous optimism as to Israel's ultimate well-being on earth; there is sketched in glowing and sensuous colours the blessedness which awaits the chosen people in the kingdom of the Messiah which is at hand (xxix.; xxxix.-xl.; lxxiii.-lxxiv.), when healing will descend in dew, and disease and anguish and lamentation will flee away; when strife and revenge and hatred will go into condemnation; when gladness will march throughout the earth, the reapers not grow weary, nor they that build toil-worn; when child-birth will entail no pangs, and none shall die untimely (lxxiii.-lxxiv. 1); when Israel's enemies shall be destroyed (xxxix.-xl.; lxx. 7-lxxii.), and to God's chosen people will be given a world-wide empire with its centre at Jerusalem (xl. 2; lxxiii.-lxxiv.). Over against these passages which ring with such assurance of coming victory and untold blessedness stand others wherein, alike to Israel's present and its future destiny on earth, there is written nothing save "lamentation and mourning and woe." These veritable cries from the depths give utterance to a hopeless pessimism — a bottomless despair touching all the things of earth. This world is a scene of corruption, its evils are irremediable; it is a never-ceasing toil and strife, but its end is at hand; its youth is past; its strength exhausted; the pitcher is near to the cistern, the ship to the port, the course of the journey to the city, and life to its consummation (lxxxv.). The advent of the times is nigh, the corruptible will pass away, the mortal depart, that that which abides for ever may come, and the new world which does not turn to corruption those who depart to its blessedness (cf. xxi. 19; xliv. 9-15; lxxxv.).

Thus we discover that whereas (1) optimism as to Israel's future on earth is a characteristic of some sections of the book, pessimism in this respect characterises others. The former are the Messiah Apocalypses, xxvii.-xxx. 1; xxxvi.-xl.; liii.-lxxiv. (which for convenience I designate respectively as A^1, A^2, A^3), and a short original Apocalypse of Baruch, B^1. The remaining sections are B^2, B^3. The contents of these we shall determine presently. Again (2), A^1, A^2, A^3, B^1, agree in teaching the advent of the Messianic kingdom, but this doctrine is absolutely relinquished in B^2, B^3.

Thus, A^1, A^2, A^3, B^1, agree in presenting an optimistic view of Israel's future on earth, and in inculcating the hope of a Messianic kingdom; whereas in B^2, B^3, such expectations are absolutely abandoned, and the hopes of the righteous are directed to the immediate advent of the final judgment and to the spiritual world alone. But at this point a difference between A^1, A^2, A^3, and B^1, emerges. The former look for a Messiah and a Messianic kingdom, the latter for a Messianic kingdom without a Messiah.

As we pursue our study, other features, one by one, disclose themselves which belong to A^1, A^2, A^3, but not to B^1, B^2, B^3, and thus differentiate them from the latter. Some of these are: (1) In A^1, A^2, A^3, Jerusalem is still standing—hence they were written before 70 A.D.; whereas in B^1, B^2, B^3, it is already destroyed (for details see pp. 49, 61, 87, 101, 111). In B^1, Jerusalem is to be restored; (2)

in A^1, A^2, A^3, the advent of the Messiah is looked for, but not in B^1, B^2, B^3; (3) in A^1, A^2, A^3, it is only to the actual inhabitants of Palestine that the promise of protection is given in the time of the Messianic woes (see xxix. 2; xl. 2; lxxi. 1)—thus the Jews are still in Palestine; but in B^1, B^2, B^3, the Jews are already carried into exile. In B^1 they are to be ultimately restored.

These conclusions as to the different authorship of A^1, A^2, A^3, and B^1, B^2, B^3, are confirmed by the following facts:—

(1) According to the scheme of the final editor of this book (see v. 7; ix. 2; pp. 36, 61), events proceed in each section in a certain order: first a fast, then a divine disclosure, then an announcement or address to the people based on this disclosure. This being so, it is significant that in the various addresses in v. 5; x. 4; xxxi. 2-xxxiv.; xliv.-xlvi.; lxxvii. 1-17, there is not a single reference to these Messianic Apocalypses, A^1, A^2, A^3. (2) From (1) it follows that A^1, A^2, A^3, have no real organic connection with the rest of the book, B^1, B^2, B^3. And a detailed examination of their immediate contents shows that the removal of A^1 (= xxvii.-xxx. 1), A^2 (= xxxvi.-xl.), A^3 (= liii.-lxxiv.) serves to restore some cohesion to the text (see xxx. 2, note; xli. 1, note; lxxv.-lxxvi., note).

Having thus seen that A^1, A^2, A^3, were written prior to 70 A.D., and are of different authorship to B^1, B^2, B^3, which were written subsequent to that date, we have next to deal with the relations in which A^1, A^2, A^3 stand to each other.

A^1, A^2, A^3; *their relations to each other and dates.*—On pp. 61, 87, we have shown that A^1 is of distinct authorship to A^2 and A^3, on the ground that in A^1 the Messiah pursues an entirely passive *rôle*, and does not appear till the enemies of Israel are destroyed and the kingdom established; whereas, in A^2 and A^3, it is the Messiah that destroys the enemies of Israel and establishes the Messianic kingdom. As regards the date of A^1, all that can be said with safety is that it was composed before 70 A.D.

It is hard to determine with certainty the relation of A^2 and A^3. In many points they are at one: their differences are few. Some of these are: A^2 has more affinities in matter and character with the older Jewish Apocalyptic, *i.e.* that of Daniel; A^3 is more nearly related in form and spirit to later Judaism, to the rabbinic type of thought. Further, whereas in xl. 2, it is the Messiah that defends the inhabitants of the Holy Land, in lxxi. 1, it is the Holy Land itself; and whereas in A^2 (= xxxvi.-xl.) the law is only passingly alluded to, in A^3 (= liii.-lxxiv.) its importance is frequently dwelt upon. The latter difference may partly be due to their diversity in subject and method as well as to the brevity of A^2. On the whole, we are inclined to regard A^2 and A^3 as springing from different authors; but the evidence is not decisive.

As to the date of A^2 we are unable to say anything more definite than that it was composed before 70 A.D. The case of A^3 is different. Like A^1 and A^2, it was written before 70 A.D., as we have seen above (see also p. 87 and lxviii. 6, note). The earlier limit of composition is fixed by lix. 5-11. In the notes on that passage we have shown that in our Apocalypse there is a transference of Enoch's functions to Moses, and an attribution to Moses of revelations hitherto ascribed to Enoch (see also xiii. 3, note). This glorification of Moses at Enoch's expense is a clear sign of Jewish hostility to Christianity, and a tribute to Enoch's influence in the Christian Church of the first century. This acceptance of Enoch as a prophet in Christian circles became the ground of his rejection by the Jews, and of a hostility which was unswervingly pursued for several centuries. This aggressive attitude of Judaism could not have originated before the open breach of Christianity with the Synagogue, which was brought about by the Pauline controversy. Hence A^3 cannot be earlier than 50 A.D. Thus the limits of its composition are 50-70 A.D.

B^1, B^2, B^3, *the later constituents of Baruch, their characteristics and dates.*—We have seen above the grounds on which we are obliged to ascribe B^1, B^2, B^3, to a different authorship and later date than A^1, A^2, A^3. We have now to study the relations which subsist between B^1, B^2, B^3. We shall consider B^3 first, as it consists of a single chapter.

B^3 = lxxxv. This chapter agrees with B^1, B^2, in being written after 70 A.D.; but differs from B^1 and agrees with B^2 in despairing of a national restoration, and in looking only for spiritual blessedness in the world of incorruption. But, again, it differs from B^2 also, in that B^2 was written in Jerusalem or Judæa, whereas B^3 was written in Babylon or some other land of the Dispersion—in the former most probably; for it was written in Hebrew (cf. lxxxv. 2, 3, 12, notes). Again, whereas, according to B^2, Jeremiah was with the captivity in Babylon, it is here definitely stated that the righteous and the prophets are dead, and that the exiles have none to intercede for them (see notes on pp. 154, 156). B^3 was thus written after 70 A.D. in Hebrew, and most probably in Babylon.

B^1, B^2.—After the removal of A^1, A^2, A^3, and B^3, the remaining chapters, when submitted to a searching scrutiny, betray underlying suppositions, statements, and facts which are mutually irreconcilable.

Thus certain sections, i.-ix. 1; xliii.-xliv. 7; xlv.-xlvi. 6; lxxvii.-lxxxii.; lxxxiv.; lxxxvi.-lxxxvii., are optimistic and hopeful as to this world, whereas certain others, ix.-xii. (?); xiii.-xxv.; xxx. 2-xxxv.; xli.-xlii.; xliv. 8-15; xlvii.-lii.; lxxv.-lxxvi.; lxxxiii., are decidedly of an opposite character. The former sections we have named B^1, and the latter B^2. That B^1 and B^2 are derived from different authors will be clear from the following considerations:—

(1) In B^1 the earthly Jerusalem is to be rebuilt (i. 4, note; vi. 9, note; lxxviii. 7, note), but not so in B^2, where it is said that Jerusalem is removed with a view to usher in the judgment (see xx. 1, 2).

(2) In B^1 the exiles are to be restored, but not in B^2; see notes cited in (1).

(3) In B^1 an earthly felicity or a Messianic kingdom is expected (i. 5; xlvi. 6; lxxvii. 12), whereas in B^2 no earthly consolation of any kind is looked for (xliv. 8-15), and the judgment is close at hand (xlviii. 39; lxxxiii.).

(4) In B^2 there is a strongly ascetic tone (see xv. 8, note); but this is wholly absent from B^1.

(5) In B^1, Baruch is to die an ordinary death, whereas in B^2 he is to be taken up or translated and preserved till the last day, to testify against the Gentile oppressors of Israel (see xiii. 3, note).

(6) In B^1, Jeremiah is not sent to Babylon, but in B^2 he is (see x. 2, note; xxxiii. 2, note; lxxvii. 12, note).

(7) In B^1, Jerusalem is destroyed by angels lest the enemy should boast; this idea seems foreign to B^2 (see lxvii. 6, note).

(8) In B^1 the main interest of the writer is engaged in dealing with the recent destruction of Jerusalem; in tracing this calamity to the nation's sins; in exhorting to renewed faithfulness; and in inculcating the sure and certain hope of Israel's restoration. In B^2 the writer has relinquished all hopes of national restoration, and is mainly concerned with theological problems and questions of the schools.

In x. 6-xii. 4 it is not improbable, as we have shown in the notes on the passage, that we have a fragment of a Sadducean writing, which I have marked by the symbol S. It may possibly belong to B^2; it cannot to B^1. Having now recognised that the groundwork is in the main derived from the two sources B^1 and B^2, and having already acquainted ourselves with the leading characteristics of each, it is next incumbent on us to consider the use made of these sources.

B^1, *its extent in this book.*—It is not difficult to ascertain the extent to which B^1 has been put in requisition by the final editor. Thus i.-ix. 1, with the exception of the interpolation iv. 2-7, clearly belongs to it, as it discovers most of the characteristics which belong to B^1 as over against their contraries in B^2. B^2 begins clearly with x. 1.-5, for these verses give the account of Jeremiah's departure to Babylon, which is peculiar to B^2; ix. 2 and other references to fasts of seven days are probably due *in their present positions* to the final editor. The next fragments of B^1 are xliii.-xliv. 7; xlv.-xlvi. 6 (see pp. 68, 69, for detailed criticism), and the rest that are drawn from this source are lxxvii.-lxxxvii., with the exception of lxxxiii. = B^2 and lxxxv. = B^3 (see pp. 119, 140, 154, 156).

B^2, *its extent in this book.*—Criticism encounters its chief difficulty in dealing with the source B^2, and with the use to which it has been put by the final editor. From B^1 the editor borrowed materials and used them in a straightforward fashion, but those from B^2 he mutilated and transposed in every imaginable way. This will be manifest to every serious student of xiii.-xxv. It was my sheer inability to write any connected or reasonable commentary on these chapters in their present order, that led me at last to recognise the true nature of the case. Then I came to see that these chapters could not have been written originally as they stand at present, and further study made it clear that we had here a most complete but instructive example of the perverse ingenuity of a redactor, by which the original text was dislocated and transposed, the original development of thought arrested and inverted, questions frequently recorded after their specific answers had already been given in full, and passages torn from their original setting in Baruch's address to the people and inserted in Baruch's prayers to God, where they are bereft of all conceivable meaning.

The reader will find a list of these logical *anacoloutha* and inversions on pp. 20, 21, and likewise an attempt to restore these chapters to their original order in B^3. With the paucity of materials at our disposal, this can only be partially satisfactory. The original order was probably xiii. 1-3*a*; xx.; xxiv. 2-4; xiii. 3*b*-12; xxv.; xiv.-xix.; xxi.-xxiv. 1.

The next fragment from B^2 is xxx. 2-5, which forms a good sequel to xxiv. 1. Of the intervening chapters xxvii.-xxx. 1 is an independent Apocalypse, as we have already found, *i.e.* A^1 and xxvi. is an addition of the editor; xxxi.-xxxv.; xli.-lii., with the exception of xliii.-xliv. 7; xlv.-xlvi. 6, which belong to B^1 and xxxii. 2-4; xlvi. 7, which are due to the editor, are also fragments of B^2 (see pp. 57, 58, 66, 68, 69, 74). These chapters from B^2 have met with no better treatment at the hands of the editor than those already mentioned. Thus we find that xxxi.-xxxii. 6, which contains an address of Baruch to the people, presupposes xlii.; xlviii.; lii. to be already in the background; for the subject of each address is founded on a previous revelation (see p. 57). Thus xxxi.-xxxv. was read originally after xlviii.-lii., but not immediately, for lxxv. intervened (see p. 117), forming the natural sequel to lii. when A^3, *i.e.* liii.-lxxiv. is removed; xli.-xlii. appear to have followed close on xxx. (see p. 66). Thus so far the order roughly was: xxx. 2-5; xli.-xlii.; xlviii.-lii.; lxxv.; xxxi.-xxxv. But there are grounds for regarding xliv. 8-15; lxxxiii. as intervening after xxxii. 6. Finally, the last fragment of B^2 is found in lxxvi., but this cannot have formed the end of B^2. It was probably closed with an account of the Assumption of Baruch.

For further disarrangements of the text by which words used originally by Baruch in addressing the people, are used in their present context in an address to God, though quite impossible in that connection, and the probable restoration of these fragments, see xlviii. 48-50; lii. .5-7; liv. 16-18, notes. The surviving fragments of B^2, which we have just dealt with, may be restored as follows to what seems to have been their original order in their source: xiii. 1-3*a*; xx.; xxiv. 2-4; xiii. 3*b*-12; xxv.; xiv.-xix.; xxi.-xxiv. 1; xxx. 2-5; xli.-xlii.; xlviii. 1-47; xlix.-lii. 3; lxxv.; xxxi.-xxxii. 6; liv. 17, 18; xlviii. 48-50; lii. 5-7; liv. 16; xliv. 8-15; lxxxiii.; xxxii. 7-xxxv.; lxxvi.

S, *its relation to B^1 and B^2*.—We have adjourned

to the present the treatment of x. 6-xii. 4, which in the notes on this passage we have assigned to a Sadducean author, S. However this may be, I cannot but regard it as of different authorship to B^1 and B^2. Several grounds for this conclusion will be found in pp. 14-19. We might further observe that although, in vividness of grief and the still overwhelming consciousness of national calamity, S has features in common with B^1, it is sundered from it as resigning all hope of the restoration of the temple and its sacrifices, and as presenting the most hopeless pessimism in the book. And again, whereas S is related to B^2 in its world despair, it is no less certainly sundered from it in its complete absorption in the present wreck of the nation's material interests. Of this subject as now far distant B^2 recks little, and gives its chief energies and affections to religious problems and the conservation of Israel's spiritual interests.

Dates of S, B^1, B^2, B^3.—In respect of date, S seems to have been written immediately after the fall of Jerusalem, in 70 A.D.; B^1 soon after this date, when the destruction of Israel and its hoped-for restoration were still the supreme subject of interest and speculation. B^2 is much later; its interests have passed from the material to the spiritual world; patriotic aims have ceased to affect it. B^3 is probably still later than B^2.

Date of editing entire book.—Since the author of the Rest of the Words of Baruch has used portions of ii., v., vi., viii., x., xi., xxxv. 2 (?), lxxvii., lxxx., lxxxv., lxxxvii. of our Apocalypse, it is clear that he had the present form of our book before him in Greek. Thus, as this Christian Apocalypse was written between 130 and 140 A.D., the date of the Greek translation of our Apocalypse may be taken as not later than 130. The editing of the Hebrew may have been one or more decades earlier.

§ 8. The Lost Epistle to the Two and a Half Tribes

A portion of this letter is probably to be found in the Apocryphal Book of Baruch, *i.e.* in i. 1-3 ; iii. 9-iv. 29. This section corresponds in many respects with the writings we are in search of. Thus (1) the lost Epistle was addressed to Judah and Benjamin in exile (lxxvii. 12, 17). Now it is clear that iii. 9-iv. 29 was also addressed *to Judah and Benjamin in exile.* It is *Judah and Benjamin* that are addressed ; for throughout iv. 5-29 it is Jerusalem that is represented as being deprived of her children. Further, it is Judah and Benjamin *in exile,* for they are said to be "sold to the nations and delivered to their enemies" (iv. 6), and Jerusalem describes herself as robbed of her sons and daughters (iv. 16), and the writer asks in iii. 10 : "Why is it, Israel, that thou art in thine enemies' land, and that thou art waxen feeble (so Kneucker) in a strange country ?"

(2) The lost Epistle was "an epistle of doctrine and a scroll of good tidings" (lxxvii. 12). This forms an admirable description of iii. 9-iv. 29,

which is essentially a writing of consolation and encouragement.

(3) The lost Epistle was to hold out the promise of return (lxxvii. 6); this is done in iv. 22-24.

(4) The lost Epistle was written by Baruch *to Babylon* (lxxvii. 12, 17).

Now i. 1-3; iii. 9-iv. 29, which purport to have been written by Baruch in Babylon and addressed to the exiles there, appear rather to have been written by Baruch in Jerusalem and addressed to the exiles in Babylon; for (*a*) the speaker does not identify himself with those who are in exile. Cf. iii. 10: "Why is it, Israel, that thou art in thine enemies' land"; and iv. 5, 6, where he calls them the remnant dispersed among the nations; (*b*) the speaker rather identifies himself with Jerusalem; at all events, in iv. 9-29 he personifies Jerusalem, and represents her as addressing the neighbouring peoples, and then her own children as they are being led into captivity, and promising them a safe return to her.

(5) Finally, in B^1, to which the lost Epistle belongs, the blamelessness of Jerusalem over against her children is insisted on (cf. lxxvii. 8). The same thought would naturally recur in some form in the lost Epistle. And so, in fact, we find it underlying iv. 8-29. And as in B^1 it is taught that Israel is punished only as a chastisement (cf. i. 5; lxxix. 2), the same idea would most probably appear in the lost Epistle as an encouragement to the exiles. Now this is emphatically declared to be so in iv. 6.

On the above grounds to which others could be added, I am inclined to regard iii. 9-iv. 29 as a recast of, or, at all events, as based upon the lost Epistle. This Epistle was probably introduced by some form of i. 1-3. These verses are, as Kneucker has shown, corrupt in their present form.

iv. 39-v. 9, which consists of a direct address to Jerusalem, is derived by the final editor from a different source, mainly from the eleventh of the Psalms of Solomon.

§ 9. The Relations of this Apocalypse with 4 Ezra

In this section we shall deal with the following questions:—

(*a*) The composite nature of 4 Ezra.
(*b*) Conflicting characteristics of 4 Ezra and Baruch, the former to some extent non-Jewish.
(*c*) 4 Ezra from a Hebrew original.
(*d*) Relations of the respective constituents of our Apocalypse and 4 Ezra.

(*a*) *The composite nature of Ezra.*—Into this question this is not the place to enter. I shall content myself with expressing my acceptance in the main of Kabisch's masterly criticism[1] of this work. Though many of his positions cannot be maintained, the greater number of them will, I believe, be ultimately accepted as final. The work is very unequal.

[1] Kabisch, *Das vierte Buch Esra*, 1889, Göttingen.

In it there stand side by side numerous instances of extremely fine insight and not a few gross misapprehensions and bizarre conclusions. His analysis is as follows:—

S = an Apocalypse of Salathiel written *circ.* 100 A.D. at Rome, preserved in a fragmentary condition: iii. 1-31; iv. 1-51; v. 13*b*-vi. 10; vi. 30-vii. 25; vii. 45-viii. 62; ix. 13-x. 57; xii. 40-48; xiv. 28-35.

E = an Ezra Apocalypse, *circ.* 31 B.C., written in the neighbourhood of Jerusalem: iv. 52-v. 13*a*; vi. 13-25, 28; vii. 26-44; viii. 63-ix. 12.

A = Adlergesicht—an Eagle Vision, written 90 A.D. by a Zealot: x. 60-xii. 40.

M = Menschensohn—a Son-of-Man Vision, written in Jerusalem about the time of Pompey: xiii., but much interpolated by R.

E^2 = an Ezra fragment, *circ.* 100: xiv. 1-17*a*, 18-27, 36-47.

R = the Editor—a Zealot, *circ.* 120: iii. 1 (*qui et Ezras*), 32-36; vi. 11, 12, 26, 27, 29; x. 58, 59; xii. 9, 34, 37-39, 49-51; xiii. 13*b*-15, 16-24, 26*b*, 29-32, 54-58; xiv. 8, 17*b*, 48-50, as well as parts of iv. 52; vi. 20, etc.

The above analysis may be taken as a good working hypothesis. Among other grounds which Kabisch might have pressed to show that the book as it stands has been edited from various independent sources and edited most ignorantly, I will adduce only one. The title, *Dominator Domine*, which in the Apocalypse of Baruch is used only of God, and rightly so, in 4 Ezra is a designation of God in five instances—iii. 4; v. 23; vi. 38 (in Syr., Eth., and Arm. Versions); xii. 7; xiii. 51; but of an angel in six—iv. 38; v. 38; vi. 11;

vii. 17, 58, 75. The attribution of this divine title to an angel can only be due to gross confusions or interpolations in the text (see note on iii. 1 of our text). It is to be observed that this phenomenon is found only in the late source S and R.

(*b*) *Conflicting characteristics of* 4 *Ezra and Baruch, the former to some extent non-Jewish.*—On the following doctrines the teaching of our Apocalypse represents faithfully the ordinary Judaism of the first century, whereas that of 4 Ezra holds an isolated position or is closely related to Christianity.

1. *The Law.*—From an exhaustive comparison of the passages dealing with this subject in the two books (see xv. 5, note) it is clear that the possession of the law by Israel is less a subject of self-gratulation in 4 Ezra than in Baruch. In the latter, especially in B^2, it protects the righteous (xxxii. 1), justifies them (li. 3), is their hope (li. 7) and never-failing stay (xlviii. 22, 24). This is decidedly orthodox Judaism. In 4 Ezra, on the other hand, man trembles before the law; he needs mercy, not the award of the law, for all have sinned (viii. 35); it has served rather unto condemnation; for only a very few are saved through good works (vii. 77) or the divine compassion (vii. 139). It is hardly necessary to point out that this conception of the law approximates to the Pauline view.

2. *Works.*—In my note on xiv. 7 I have contrasted the teaching of the two books on this subject, and arrived at the conclusion that in 4 Ezra the

doctrine of works as it is found in Baruch can hardly be said to exist. Here again Baruch represents traditional Jewish orthodoxy, but 4 Ezra not. We should observe also that the latter guards carefully against the doctrine of salvation by works by making salvation depend on works and faith combined (cf. ix. 7; xiii. 23; cf. St. James ii. 14-26).

3. *Justification, i.e.* by the law or by works.—This subject might have more logically been treated under the preceding head. For my own convenience I have given it separately. On p. 39 I have shown that justification by the law, though taught in Baruch, is absent from 4 Ezra. In this respect again the latter is non-Jewish.

4. *Original Sin and Freewill.*—On pp. 92-93, from a study of the passages in 4 Ezra bearing on these subjects, we have found that there was in man to begin with a wicked element ("granum seminis mali," iv. 30); and that through Adam's yielding to this evil impulse a hereditary tendency to sin was created, and the *cor malignum* developed (iii. 21-22). The evil element having thus gained the mastery over man, only a very few are saved through mercy (vii. 139; viii. 3); hence the writer of vii. 118 naturally charges Adam with being the cause of the final perdition of man.

In the face of such a hopeless view of man's condition, human freewill cannot be maintained: *practically* man has none, for only a handful out of the whole human race are saved (vii. 51-61; ix. 16);

theoretically he is said to have it, but this is to justify his final condemnation (see p. 93).

This teaching is practically unique in Judaism between 1-300 A.D.—in fact it is not Jewish but Christian doctrine. In Baruch, on the other hand, conformably to early Rabbinic teaching, it is declared that Adam is not the cause of man's perdition, but that each man is the Adam of his own soul (liv. 19). There is not, moreover, a trace of Ezra's elaborate theory, and the doctrine of original sin is stoutly denied in liv. 15, 19—not a trace save only in xlviii. 42, where spiritual death is traced to Adam. Elsewhere—xvii. 3; xxiii. 4; liv. 15—it is only physical death that is ascribed to Adam's transgression. But in Ezra, as we might expect from what precedes, both spiritual and physical death are always traced to Adam—iii. 21, 22; iv. 30; vii. 118-121.

Thus on various grounds we see that *whereas Baruch is a pure product of the Judaism of the time, 4 Ezra is the result of two influences at work, first and mainly a Jewish, and secondly a Christian. It was no doubt owing to this Christian element in the latter that it won and preserved a high position in the Christian Church. It constitutes, in fact, a confession of the failure of Judaism.*

The above peculiarities of doctrine in 4 Ezra discover themselves almost universally in S. The author of S was undoubtedly a Jew, but a Jew who had been impressed and imbued to some extent by Christian teaching, probably by Pauline.

(*c*) 4 *Ezra from a Hebrew Original.*—Though this question could only be settled by an exhaustive study of the text presupposed by the Versions, I am convinced that a Hebrew groundwork underlies at all events the greater part of this book. I might call attention here to the frequent occurrence of the Hebraism—the finite verb combined with the cognate infinitive—as evidence in this direction. Thus in iii. 33 we have "pertransiens pertransivi"; iv. 13, "festinans festinavit"; iv. 26, "proficiscens profectus sum"; v. 30, "odiens odisti"; v. 45, "viventes vivent"; vi. 32, "auditu audita est"; vii. 5 "volens voluerit," and so on in vii. 14, 21, 67, 70, 75; viii. 8, 15, 58; ix. 1; x. 32; xi. 45; xiv. 3, 29. All these appear in the Syriac Version, save five—iv. 26; vii. 5, 14; x. 32; xiv. 29. Still more are omitted in the Ethiopic Version. On the weight to be assigned to this feature of the text as evidence of a Hebrew background, see pp. xliv.-li. I may add that in the late work 5 Ezra xv. 9; xvi. 65, this idiom is found; but in the latter passage it is a quotation from our Apocalypse (see p. xx.), and in the former it is apparently a quotation also.

(*d*) *Relations of the respective constituents of our Apocalypse and* 4 *Ezra.*—My present purpose does not call for an exhaustive list of the passages common to the two books. This will be given elsewhere. It will be sufficient to indicate the direction such an inquiry should pursue, and to mention some of the chief grounds for determining the relations in which the various constituents of

Baruch stand to those of 4 Ezra. These determinations must, however, pending further investigation, be regarded as provisional.

Of the multitude of thoughts, phrases, and commonplaces that are common to both books, a large number already occur in previously existing literature; and as these may possibly be drawn independently from such sources by both books, they are not helpful at the outset in determining the priority of either book or of their respective constituents. Again, of many other common passages, the sources, it is true, are no longer found; yet that such did exist in certain cases we have ample grounds for believing; see the note on xxix. 4 for the common original of 4 Ezra vi. 49-52 and of our Baruch xxix. 4. Thus we must be on our guard against tracing relations of dependence where both books have been borrowing independently from the same lost source.

We shall now point out the relations in which A^1, A^2, A^3, B^1, B^2 stand to Ezra. I shall refer to the following constituents of the latter, S, E, E^2, M (according to Kabisch's analysis on p. lxviii.).

A^1.—A^1 and S are apparently related in only one passage: Bar. xxix. 4 and 4 Ezra vi. 49-52. But this relation is not of dependence on either side, but of common derivation from the same lost source; see xxix. 4, note. As regards A^1 and the E constituent of Ezra, xxix. 3*b*-6 of the former, "*The Messiah will* then *begin to be revealed* . . . and those who hungered will *rejoice;* moreover also they will *behold marvels,*" and vii. 27*b*-28 of the latter, "Videbit *mirabilia mea; revelabitur* enim *filius meus* . . . et *jocundabit* qui relicti sunt," are certainly connected. If we add to these connections in thought and diction the fact that only in A^1 and E in the Baruch and Ezra literature is the passive *rôle* assigned to the Messiah, we may reasonably conclude that there is a direct relation of dependence between them. A^1, I think, is earlier than E; both are prior to 70 A.D. Finally, A^1 and M may be connected in xxix. 3 and xiii. 16-20. The thought seems earlier and more vigorous in A^1. In M it is threshed out; but such considerations are indecisive. If there is a relation of dependence between them, A^1 is probably earlier than M, for in A^1 the Messiah has a passive *rôle*, in M an active one. The idea of a passive Messiah conceived as early as 160 B.C. was not likely to hold its ground in later times when the needs of the people called for an active leader and combatant in the Messiah.

A^2.—A^2 and M, *i.e.* xiii. of 4 Ezra, are related. Cf. xl. 2, "My Messiah will convict him of all his impieties . . . and set before him all the works of his hosts," with 4 Ezra xiii. 37, "Ipse autem filius meus arguet quae advenerunt gentes impietates eorum . . . et improperabit" ("improperabit" is a mistaken rendering; read "ordinabit" with Syr. and Eth.) "coram eis mala cogitamenta eorum." The connection is manifest.

The first halves of these sentences agree verbally, so likewise do the second; for "set before him" = παραστήσει κατὰ πρόσωπον αὐτοῦ = יערך לעיניו; and "improperabit" (or "ordinabit," Syr. and Eth.) "coram eis" = ἐπιστοιβάσει κατὰ πρόσωπον αὐτῶν = יערך לעיניהם; for παριστάναι and ἐπιστοιβάζειν are both LXX. renderings of ערך. The phrase is derived from Psalm xlix. 22 (cf. also Leviticus i. 1, 7, 8, 12; vi. 12).

A number of features into which I cannot enter here show that it is M that is dependent on A^2, and not *vice versa*.

The verse just dealt with reappears in xii. 32, in the Eagle Vision designated A by Kabisch, in a form which shows it dependent on M. A^2 is thus earlier than M and A in 4 Ezra.

A^3.—Although there are many points of contact between A^3 and 4 Ezra, there are none that necessitate the theory of dependence on either side save in liv. 15, 19. These verses which represent the teaching of orthodox Judaism *circ.* 50-70, were before the writer of the S element in 4 Ezra (cf. iii. 21-22; iv. 30; vii. 48), where a non-Jewish turn is given to the borrowed thoughts and phrases.

B^1.—Although there are many similar and identical thoughts and phrases in B^1 and 4 Ezra, these are not sufficiently characteristic or definite to furnish grounds for determining the dependence of either. This question must be settled on other grounds, *i.e.* chronological. From the use of like thought or diction, one might argue, on the one hand, that B^1 is dependent on the E element of 4 Ezra; compare iii. 7 with vii. 30; on the other, that B^1 is a source of E^2 of 4 Ezra; compare lxxvii. 3-6 with xiv. 30-33, and lxxvii. 14 with xiv.

20; that it is likewise a source of S; compare lxxxiv. 10 with x. 24. In these latter passages a different turn is given to the phrases found first in Baruch.

B^2.—Between B^2 and 4 Ezra there are almost innumerable points of contact, but the bulk of them are indecisive for our purposes. With the older elements of 4 Ezra its points of similarity are few and unimportant; but the relations between B^2 and S are very close. The fact of man's sinning consciously is frequently emphasised in B^2 and S (cf. Bar. xv. 6; xix. 3; xlviii. 40; and 4 Ezra viii. 56, 58-60; vii. 72). The doctrine that the world was made for man is confined to B^2 and S; see notes on xiv. 18; xv. 7. Their teaching on the law and on works and justification is allied—*in some particulars identical but as a whole at variance*, owing to Christian influences at work in S; see pp. lxix.-lxx. In B^2 we have an exposition of the views of orthodox Judaism 70-100 A.D.; in S we find much of the actual teaching in B^2 recast under Christian influences. S seems to us in every respect to be later than B^2.

§ 10. Relation of this Apocalypse with the New Testament

The points of contact between this Apocalypse and the New Testament are many in number. The most of these, however, are insufficient to establish a relation of dependence on either side; for the thoughts and expressions in question could be explained from pre-existing literature, or were commonplaces of the time.

Of these a list will be given immediately, followed by another list of passages which seem to show that our text may in a few instances be derived from the New Testament:

New Testament.	Parallels in our Apocalypse.	Probable source of both.
Mt. iii. 16.—Lo, the heavens were opened.	xxii. 1.—Lo, the heavens were opened.	Ezek. i. 1.
Mt. iii. 17 (xvii. 5; John xii. 28).—A voice from heaven.	xiii. 1; xxii. 1.—A voice from the height.	Dan. iv. 31.
Mt. iv. 8.	lxxvi. 3.	Deut. xxxiv. 1-4.
Mt. xxiv. 7 (Mk. xiii. 8; Luke xxi. 11).—Famines . . . and earthquakes.	xxvii. 6, 7.	Commonplaces of Jewish Apocalyptic.
Mt. xxiv. 11, 24.—Many false prophets.	xlviii. 34 (see note).	...
Mt. xxiv. 19 (Luke xxiii. 29).	x. 13, 14 (resemblance slight).	Isa. liv. 1.
Mt. xxvi. 24.—It had been good for that man, etc.	x. 6.—Blessed is he who was not born, etc.	A Jewish Commonplace.
Mt. xxiv. 27.—For as the lightning . . . so shall be the coming of the Son of Man.	liii. 9.—Now that lightning shone exceedingly so as to illuminate the whole earth. (The lightning here symbolises the Messiah.)	A coincidence (?).
Luke xx. 36.—Equal unto the angels.	li. 10.	Eth. En. civ. 4, 6.
Luke xxi. 28 (1 Pet. iv. 7).—Your redemption draweth nigh.	xxiii. 7.—My redemption has drawn nigh.	Eth. En. li. 2.—The day of their redemption has drawn nigh.

New Testament.	Parallels in our Apocalypse.	Probable source of both.
Acts xv. 10 (where the law is spoken of as a "yoke"; cf. Gal. v. 1).	xli. 3.—The yoke of Thy law.	A current expression.
Rom. ii. 14, 15.	xlviii. 40 (see note).	A Jewish Commonplace.
Rom. viii. 18 (2 Cor. iv. 17).—The sufferings of this present time are not worthy to be compared with the glory, etc.	xv. 8.—This world is to them a trouble and a weariness . . . and that which is to come, a crown with great glory.	A Jewish Commonplace (?).
1 Cor. iv. 5 (Heb. iv. 13).	lxxxiii. 3.	(Cf. Eth. En. ix. 5).
2 Cor. iv. 17 (Rom. viii. 18).	xv. 8.	A Jewish Commonplace.
1 Tim. i. 2.—Mercy and peace.	lxxviii. 2.—Mercy and peace.	A coincidence.
2 Peter iii. 9.	xxi. 20.	A coincidence.
2 Peter iii. 13 (Mt. xix. 28; Rev. xxi. 1).—New heavens and a new earth.	xxxii. 6.—Renewed His creation.	Isa. lxv. 17, etc.
Rev. xx. 12.—The books were opened.	xxiv. 1.—The books will be opened.	Dan. vii. 10.

In the following passages our text is dependent on the New Testament, or on some lost common source:—

Mt. xvi. 26.—For what shall a man be profited, if he shall gain the whole world, and forfeit his soul? or what shall a man give in exchange for his soul?	li. 15.—For what then have men lost their life or for what have those who were on the earth exchanged their soul?
Luke i. 42.—Blessed art thou among women, etc.	liv. 10.—Blessed be my mother among those that bear, etc. (probably interpolated).

1 Cor. xv. 19.—If in this life only we have hoped in Christ, we are of all men most miserable.	xxi. 13.—For if there were this life only . . . nothing could be more bitter than this.
1 Cor. xv. 35.—How are the dead raised? and with what manner of body do they come?	xlix. 2.—In what shape will those live who live in that day?
James i. 2.—Count it all joy when ye fall into manifold temptations.	lii. 6.—Rejoice ye in the suffering which ye now suffer.
Rev. iv. 6.—In the midst of the throne, and round about the throne, four living creatures.	li. 11.—The living creatures which are beneath the throne.

§ 11. Value of our Apocalypse in the Attestation of the Jewish Theology of 50-100 A.D., and in the Interpretation of Christian Theology for the same Period.

This book presents us with a vivid picture of the hopes and beliefs of Judaism during the years 50-100 A.D. As it was written at different dates during this period and by different authors, its composition was thus contemporaneous with that of the New Testament. It is, therefore, of very great value to the New Testament student, as it furnishes him with the historical setting and background of many of the New Testament problems. We are thereby enabled to estimate the contributions made in these respects by Christian thought, as well as to appreciate the world's need of the Pauline dialectic. For the purpose of illustrating our meaning we shall first of all draw attention to the doctrine of the Resurrection in our Apocalypse. Of the Jewish doctrine here set forth, St. Paul's teaching on this subject will be seen to be in some respects a development. Secondly, we shall briefly advert to the doctrines of Original Sin and Freewill, Works and Justification, Forgiveness, in which the Jewish teaching and the Christian stand in strong antagonism.

(*a*) *The Resurrection.*—In xlix. 2-li. a view of the resurrection is expounded, which sets forth first the raising of the dead with their bodies in exactly the same form in which they had been committed to the earth with a view to their recognition by those who knew them, and next their subsequent transformation with a view to a spiritual existence of unending duration. In my notes on pp. 83, 84, I have shown that the Pauline teaching in 1 Cor. xv. 35-50 is in many respects not an innovation, but a developed and more spiritual exposition of ideas already current in Judaism.

(*b*) *Original Sin and Freewill.*—According to our Apocalypse,[1] the penalties which man has incurred through Adam's sin affect only his *physical* existence. He still preserves his freewill; whether he is saved or lost, it is his own doing. Adam's sin is limited in

[1] Only in B^2, xlviii. 42, is spiritual death traced to Adam. This passage may be interpolated; for (1) in all other passages in B^2 it is only physical death that is so traced. (2) It conflicts with the presupposition underlying B^2 that man can work righteousness and acquire merit as against God (see xiv. 7, note). (3) In A^3 (see liv. 15, 19) original sin is denied and freewill asserted in the clearest terms. (4) The doctrine of original sin is unknown to the Talmud (see Weber, 217, 240; Edersheim, *Life and Times*, etc., i. 165). We have shown elsewhere (pp. lxix.-lxxi.) that the teaching of 4 Ezra on this subject is largely non-Jewish.

spiritual consequences to himself; every man is the Adam of his own soul (see pp. 44-45, 93).

St. Paul's doctrine is strongly antagonistic. Both *physical* and *spiritual* death are due to Adam's sin. Owing to that sin man is henceforth dominated by a power (= original sin) which makes his fulfilment of law and therefore his realisation of righteousness impossible. He is not, however, robbed wholly thereby of freewill, but retains it in a degree only sufficient to justify his condemnation.

Works and Justification.—In our Apocalypse the righteous are saved by their works (li. 7), and their righteousness is of the law (lxvii. 6). In the consciousness of their justification by the law (li. 3) they can with confidence approach God and look to Him for the fulfilment of their prayers because of their works wherein they trust (lxiii. 3, 5; lxxxv. 2), and owing to the same ground of confidence they depart from this world full of hope (xiv. 12). But their works are not limited to themselves in their saving influences. So long as the righteous live, their righteousness is a tower of strength to their people (ii. 2), and after their death it remains to their country a lasting ground of merit (xiv. 7; lxxxiv. 10); see notes on xiv. 7; xxi. 9.

With every position here maintained Christianity is at variance, and rabbinic teaching in full accord.

Forgiveness.—How far did this doctrine exist in Pharisaic Judaism, and in what relation does it stand to the Christian doctrine of forgiveness? In Pharisaic Judaism forgiveness was a wholly subordinate conception, and can only be considered in conjunction with its views on merit and demerit. If we wish to discover the Pharisaic doctrine of forgiveness we must have recourse to the Talmud; for that the Pharisaic views of the first century on this subject were those which later prevailed in the Talmud, is to be inferred on these grounds:—(1) In Matt. iii. 9 the words "Think not to say within yourselves, we have Abraham to our father," show that the doctrine of the vicarious righteousness of Abraham was a popular belief. Now this latter doctrine at once presupposes and forms an organic part of the Talmudic doctrine. (2) The teaching on works in our Apocalypse and partially also in 4 Ezra, as well as that of St. Paul's Jewish antagonists, belong also organically to the Talmudic doctrine of works and forgiveness.

The Talmudic doctrine of works may (see Weber, pp. 267-300) be shortly summarised as follows:—Every good work—whether the fulfilment of a command or an act of mercy—established a certain degree of merit with God, while every evil work entailed a corresponding demerit. A man's position with God depended on the relation existing between his merits and demerits, and his salvation on the preponderance of the former over the latter. The relation between his merits and demerits was determined daily by the weighing of his deeds (see Eth. En. xli. 1; lxi. 8; Weber, 272). But as the results of such judgments were necessarily unknown, there could not fail to be much uneasiness, and to allay this the doctrine of the vicarious righteousness of the patriarchs and saints of Israel was developed, not later than the beginning of the Christian era (cf. Matt. iii. 9). A man could thereby summon to his aid the merits of the fathers, and so counterbalance his demerits.

It is obvious that such a system does not admit of forgiveness in any spiritual sense of the term. It can only mean in such a connection a remission of penalty to the offender, on the ground that compensation is furnished, either through his own merit or through that of the righteous fathers. Thus, as Weber vigorously puts it: "Vergebung ohne Bezahlung gibt es nicht."[1] Thus, according to popular Pharisaism, *God never remitted a debt until He was paid in full, and so long as it was paid it mattered not by whom.*

It will be observed that with the Pharisees forgiveness was *an external thing;* it was concerned not with the man himself but with his works—with these indeed as affecting him, but yet as existing independently without him. This was not the view taken by the best thought in the Old Testament. There forgiveness dealt first and chiefly with the direct relation between man's spirit and God; it was essentially a restoration of man to communion with God. When, therefore, Christianity had to deal with these problems, it could not accept the Pharisaic solutions, but had in some measure to return to the Old Testament to

[1] In certain extraordinary cases, the divine forgiveness was conceived possible where no merit was at hand, see 4 Ezra viii. 36; Weber, 292, 300.

authenticate and develop the highest therein taught, and in the person and life of Christ to give it a world-wide power and comprehensiveness.

We thus see that forgiveness was conceived as (1) *the restoration of man to communion with God*; (2) *the remission of penalty on the receipt of certain equivalents.* Of these two the former alone is taught in the Gospels. In the Pauline Epistles, however, the writer maintains indeed the former as the essential element in forgiveness, but he also incorporates in some degree the latter conception, and not unnaturally as having been originally a Pharisee of the Pharisees. Thus in his doctrine of the Atonement, he introduces the Pharisaic conception by representing the penalty due to man's sin as endured by Christ. This is undoubtedly a more spiritual form of the Pharisaic doctrine, and rightly interpreted it preserves the element of truth which underlies the Pharisaic teaching. It needs, however, to be kept in complete subordination to the former. But that it has not been so kept is obvious from every page of the history of this doctrine since the Christian era. In every age this Pharisaic error has won an evil eminence in the Church—before the eleventh century in representing Christ's death as a debt paid to the devil in lieu of the latter's claim on man, and in the subsequent centuries as a sacrifice to the alleged unforgivingness of God. Wherever or whenever this evil leaven has appeared, it has been followed by shallowness, unreality, and every vice of the unspiritual life.

THE APOCALYPSE OF BARUCH

[Translated from the Greek into Syriac]

I. And it came to pass in the twenty-fifth year of I.-IV. 1=B[1].

The First Section

I.-V. 6. These chapters constitute the first of the seven sections into which, according to the scheme of the final editor, the book was originally divided by fasts. These sections were divided by fasts which generally lasted seven days (see v. 7, note; ix., note). In each section there is a definite movement or order of events observed. This order briefly is: first a fast, then a divine command or revelation, and finally the publication of the command or matter so revealed. In some cases a prayer follows the fast, and a lamentation the publication of the divine disclosure (see notes already referred to).

It will be observed that iv. 2-7 is interpolated probably from B[3].

In this section the word of the Lord comes to Baruch announcing the coming, though temporary, destruction of Jerusalem on account of the wickedness of the two tribes (i.); with a view to this destruction Baruch is to bid Jeremiah and the remaining righteous to withdraw (ii.); Baruch then in his alarm asks, will this destruction be final? will chaos return and the number of souls be completed (iii.)? God replies that the punishment is only temporary (iv. 1). Yet, rejoins Baruch, even so, the enemy will, by the pollution and fall of Zion, glory before their idols over the nation loved of God (v. 1). Not so, answers God; judgment must be executed on Judah, yet the heathen will have no cause to glory, for it is not they that will destroy Zion (v. 2, 3). Baruch thereupon assembled the people in the Cedron valley, and delivered the divine message; and the people wept (v. 5, 6).

I. [*Translated from Greek into Syriac.*] These words are found in their above position in the Syriac MS. As they were placed there either by the Syriac translator or a subsequent scribe, I have bracketed them. The statement they convey, however, is borne out by all other evidence. Thus we find (1) transliterations of Greek words; (2) renderings explicable only on the hypothesis that the translator followed the wrong meaning of the Greek word before him.

I. 1. *In the twenty-fifth year of Jeconiah.* Jeconiah was eighteen years when he began to reign in 599 (2 Kings xxiv. 8). After reigning three months he was carried into

Jeconiah king of Judah, that the word of the Lord came to Baruch the son of Neriah, and said to him: 2. "Hast thou seen all that this people are doing to Me, that the evils which these two tribes which remained have done are greater than (those of) the ten tribes which were carried away captive? 3. For the former tribes were forced by their kings to commit sin, but these two of themselves have been forcing and compelling their kings to commit sin. 4. For this reason, behold I bring evil upon this city, and upon its inhabitants, and it will be removed from before Me for a time, and

captivity. Yet during his captivity he is still called king (2 Kings xxv. 27; Jer. xxix. 2; Ezek. i. 2). Thus his twenty-fifth year would be 592, or two years before the approach of Nebuchadrezzar. It is no objection to this that, according to vi. 1, only one day and not two years should elapse between the prediction and its fulfilment; for in like manner the siege of Jerusalem, which lasted two years, is represented as lasting one day. The unities of time are sacrificed to suit the dramatic purposes of the writer. Why the writer spoke of Jeconiah and not of Zedekiah here, I cannot say. It was not from ignorance of the latter (cf. viii. 5).

The Lord. This title of God is found in iii. 1, 4; iv. 1; v. 2; x. 4, 18; xi. 3; xv. 1; xvii. 1; xxiv. 3; xxviii. 6; xlviii. 2; liv. 1, 20; lxxv. 1; lxxvii. 3. It is, therefore, not peculiar to any of the different elements of the book. This, however, may be due in part to the final editor. See note on iii. 1.

Baruch the son of Neriah. Cf. Jer. xxxii. 12; xxxvi. 4; Bar. i. 1.

2. *The ten tribes.* Elsewhere in this Apocalypse called "the nine and a half tribes." See lxxviii. 1, note.

3. *Forced by their kings.* *I.e.* by Jeroboam and others of the kings of Israel.

These two . . . compelling their kings to commit sin. It was in some instances the princes of Judah, and not Zedekiah, that resisted the teaching and prophecy of Jeremiah: cf. Jer. xxxviii.; and Josephus, *Ant.* x. 7. 2, ὁ δὲ Σεδεκίας ἐφ' ὅσον μὲν ἤκουε τοῦ προφήτου ταῦτα λέγοντος, ἐπείθετο αὐτῷ, καὶ συνῄδει πᾶσιν ὡς ἀληθεύουσι . . . διέφθειραν δὲ πάλιν αὐτὸν οἱ φίλοι, καὶ διῆγον ἀπὸ τῶν τοῦ προφήτου πρὸς ἅπερ ἤθελον.

4. *I bring evil upon this city, and upon its inhabitants* (2 Kings xxii. 16; 2 Chron. xxxiv. 28; Jer. vi. 19; xix. 3, etc.)

Will be removed from before Me (2 Kings xxiii. 27; xxiv. 3; Jer. xxxii. 31).

For a time. This phrase recurs in iv. 1; vi. 9; xxxii. 3. Since we must on other grounds regard xxxii. 2-4 in its present context as an interpolation, this phrase is peculiar to i.-viii., *i.e.* to B^1. Although Jerusalem has fallen under the Romans, the writer of these chapters believes that its desolation will be but "for a time." The future restoration of

I will scatter this people among the Gentiles that they may do good to the Gentiles. 5. And My people will be chastened, and the time will come when they will seek for the prosperity of their times.

II. "For I have said these things to thee that thou mayst say (them) to Jeremiah, and to all those who are like you, in order that ye may retire from this city. 2. Because your works are to this city as a firm pillar, and your prayers as a strong wall."

Jerusalem is implied also in lxxvii. 6; lxxviii. 7, where the return of the ten tribes is foretold. In B^2, *i.e.* ix.-xxvi.; xxxi.-xxxv.; xli.-xliii.; xliv. 9-15; xlvii.-lii.; lxxxiii.; B^3, *i.e.* lxxxv., no such restoration is looked for; Jerusalem is removed, xx. 2 (see note *in loc.*), in order to usher in the judgment more speedily; in x. 10 the writer abandons all hope of a restored Jerusalem.

Scatter this people, etc. Jer. xxx. 11; Ezek. xxxvi. 19.

Do good to the Gentiles. This seems to mean to make proselytes of the Gentiles. Cf. xli. 4; xlii. 5; see also xiii. 12.

5. *My people will be chastened.* Cf. xiii. 10; xiv.; lxxix. 2; Pss. Sol. vii. 3; x. 1-3; xiii. 6-8; xviii. 4.

Seek for the prosperity of their times. The writer looks forward to a Messianic kingdom or period of blessedness for Israel on earth.

II. 1. According to Jer. xxxviii. 13, 28, Jeremiah was a prisoner in the court of the guard till the capture of Jerusalem.

Jeremiah is mentioned again in v. 5; ix.; x. 2, 4.

Those who are like you. This phrase is found in three of the sections of this book (cf. xxi. 24; lvii. 1; lix. 1; lxvi. 7). Cf. 4 Ezra iv. 36; viii. 51, 62; xiv. 9, 49.

Withdraw from the city. This reappears in the Rest of the Words of Baruch i. 1: "Jeremiah . . . go forth from this city." Cf. also i. 3, 7. The reason for this command appears in the Talmud. Thus, as in *Taanith*, 19, we are told that a house cannot fall so long as a good man is in it; so in *Pesikta*, 115b (Buber's edition, 1868), it is said: "So long as Jeremiah was in Jerusalem, it was not destroyed, but when he went forth from it, it was destroyed."

2. *Your works are to this city as a firm pillar*, etc. We have here quite an illegitimate application of Jer. vi. 27: "I have made thee a tower and a fortress among my people." It is, however, a natural inference from Gen. xviii. 23-33. This verse is reproduced in the Rest of the Words of Baruch i. 2: *αἱ γὰρ προσευχαὶ ὑμῶν ὡς στῦλος ἑδραῖος ἐν μέσῳ αὐτῆς, καὶ ὡς τεῖχος ἀδαμάντινον περικυκλοῦν αὐτήν.* It will be remarked that the reference to "works" is omitted by this latter book, as we should naturally expect in a work of Christian authorship.

Your works. On the doctrine of works taught in this book see note on xiv. 7.

III. And I said: "O LORD, my Lord, have I come into the world for this purpose that I might see the evils of my mother? not (so) my Lord. 2. If I have found grace in Thy sight, first take my spirit that I may go to my fathers and not behold the destruction of my mother. 3. For two things vehemently constrain me: for I cannot resist Thee, and my soul,

III. 1. *O LORD, my Lord.* This title of God is found also in xiv. 8, 16; xvi. 1; xxiii. 1; xxxviii. 1; xlviii. 4, 5, and is thus, except in one instance, confined to B and B[1]. It is remarkable that, whereas it is used only of God in the Apocalypse of Baruch, in 4 Ezra it is a designation of God in five instances (iii. 4; v. 23; vi. 38 (in Syriac, Eth., and Arm. versions); xii. 7; xiii. 51), and of an angel in six (iv. 38; v. 38; vi. 11; vii. 17, 58, 75). This fact makes it probable that the introduction of the angel in 4 Ezra is the work of the final editor. The usual titles used in addressing an angel in that book are *dominus meus* (iv. 3, 5; v. 33; vii. 3; x. 34). This is applied also to Ezra in ix. 41; *domine* (iv. 22, 41; v. 34, 35, 41, 56; vii. 10, 53, 132; viii. 6, 20, 36, 63). These last two titles are probably equivalents of אֲדֹנִי which is employed in Dan. x. 17, 19, in addressing an angel. The words ܡܪܝܐ ܡܪܝ are to be rendered *O* LORD, *my Lord* as above and not *Dominator Domine*, as we find in Ceriani and Fritzsche. Linguistically indeed either rendering is right, but the frequent occurrence of this phrase in the Syriac Version of 4 Ezra enables us to see that the suffix is not moribund but living; for it appears in the Ethiopic Version and occasionally in the Armenian. The Syriac is a translation either of δέσποτα κύριέ μου or κύριε κύριέ μου; these in turn would point either to אֲדֹנָי יְהוִֹה, as in Gen. xv. 2, 8, or יְהוִֹה אֲדֹנָי. Since such titles could only be used of God, we can with certainty conclude that their attribution to an angel in 4 Ezra is due to gross confusions or interpolations in the text.

My mother. Cf. iii. 2, 3; x. 16; Baruch iv. 9-16. This was a very natural term for a Jew to apply to Jerusalem. We find the correlative expression in Isa. xlix. 21; Matt. xxiii. 37; Gal. iv. 25. It is the earthly Jerusalem that is referred to here, for the writer of B[1] looks for a restored earthly Zion (see note on i. 4). Again the same title is applied to the fallen Jerusalem in 4 Ezra x. 7: "Sion mater nostra omnium," though there the writer looks for the restoration of Zion. In Gal. iv. 26 St. Paul uses it of the heavenly Jerusalem; for he has no further interest in the earthly. The earthly was the mother of Jews, but the heavenly of Christians. The earthly Jerusalem, as we should expect, in Matt. v. 35 is still "the city of the great King."

O Lord. See i. 1, note.

2. *If I have found grace.* xxviii. 6; 4 Ezra v. 56; vii. 102; viii. 42; xii. 7.

Take my spirit. An O. T. expression (cf. Ps. xxxi. 13; Jer. xv. 15).

Go to my fathers. xliv. 2; cf. also xi. 4; lxxxv. 9; Gen. xv. 15.

moreover, cannot behold the evils of my mother. 4. But one thing I will say in Thy presence, O Lord. 5. What, therefore, will there be after these things? for if Thou destroyest Thy city, and deliverest up Thy land to those that hate us, how shall the name of Israel be again remembered? 6. Or how shall one speak of Thy praises? or to whom shall that which is in Thy law be explained? 7. Or shall the world return to its nature (of aforetime), and the age revert to primeval silence? 8. And shall the multitude of souls be taken away, and the nature of man not again be named? 9. And where is all that which Thou didst say to Moses regarding us?"

IV. And the Lord said unto me: "This city will be delivered up for a time, and the people will be

4-IV. 1. Baruch asks God if the end of all things will follow on the delivery of Jerusalem into the hands of its enemies; will Israel be blotted out? will there be no longer any students of the law? will all men die and chaos return? In iv. 1 God answers that Jerusalem will again be restored; the chastisement of its people soon be accomplished and chaos will not return. The writer thus looks forward to the returning felicity of Jerusalem.

III. 6. *To whom shall that which is in Thy law be explained?* The real answer to this question is given in Baruch's own words in xlvi. 4.

7. We should observe that the Syriac word ܨܒܬܐ, here translated "world," really means "ornament." Thus the translator followed a wrong sense of κόσμος here.

Revert to primeval silence. Cf. 4 Ezra vii. 30. In. iv. 1 this is answered in the negative, but in xliv. 9 (*i.e.* B^2) in the affirmative.

IV. 2-7. In these verses we have an undoubted interpolation. The earthly Jerusalem, the restoration of which has just been promised, is here derided. This of itself is suspicious. When, however, we turn to vi. 9 and see there that *the very Jerusalem* that is now delivered up to its foes will hereafter be restored, and that for ever, the incongruity of these verses with their present context emerges still more clearly. This incongruity is still further emphasised when we observe that the actual vessels of the earthly temple are committed to the earth by an angel, that they may be preserved for future use in the restored Jerusalem (vi. 7-9). The vessels of the heavenly Jerusalem would naturally be of a heavenly kind, and are in fact already there (iv. 5).

chastened during a time, and the world will not be
IV. 2-7 = B^2(?). given over to oblivion. 2. [Dost thou think that this is that city of which I said: 'On the palms of My hands have I graven thee'? 3. It is not this building which is now built in your midst; (it is) that which will be revealed with Me, that which was pre-

2. It is noteworthy that the words "On the palms of My hands," etc., which are taken from Isa. xlix. 16, agree letter for letter with the Syriac Version, which here stands alone against the Mass., LXX., and Vulg., in presupposing על כפות ידי instead of Mass. על כפים. This fuller phrase which the Syriac presupposes is the usual one (cf. 1 Sam. v. 4; 2 Kings ix. 35; Dan. x. 10).

3. *It is not this building . . . (it is) that which will be revealed.* These words represent one of the final stages of a movement which had already its beginnings in the O. T. Throughout the O. T. Jerusalem had always been singled out as the one place on earth in which it had pleased God to dwell, and with which He had inseparably connected His name. But from the growing transcendence and enlargement of the idea of God, combined with the deepened consciousness of sin, and the consequent sense of the unfitness of Jerusalem as God's habitation, the doctrine of a heavenly Jerusalem complete in all its parts came to be evolved.

Of the existence indeed of heavenly antitypes of the Tabernacle and its furniture we are told already in the Priest's Code (Exod. xxv. 9, 40, cf. Heb. viii. 5). It needed only a step further to postulate the existence of the heavenly temple and city. That the earthly copies needed to be purified or even wholly renewed, we are taught in Isa. lx.; Ezek. xl.-xlviii.; but that nothing else could suffice save the actual descent of the heavenly Jerusalem to the earth was not concluded till the revival of religion under the early Maccabees. In Isa. liv. 11 and Tob. xiii. 16, 17, there are highly figurative accounts of the rebuilding of Jerusalem, but it is the earthly. The first actual emergence of the idea of the heavenly seems to be in the Eth. En. xc. 28, 29, where the old Jerusalem is removed and the new is brought and set up by God Himself, though even there a prior existence is not assigned to the latter. This would be about 164 B.C. But the older ideas still held their ground. Thus in the Psalms of Solomon xvii. 25, 33 (*circ.* 70-40 B.C.), as in the oldest part of the Eth. En. x. 16-19; xxv. 1 (*circ.* 180 B.C.), the purification of Jerusalem is all that appears needful to the writers as a preparation for the Messianic kingdom. Even when we come down to the first century of the Christian era, such purification is deemed sufficient for the *temporary* Messianic kingdoms depicted in Apoc. Bar. xxix.; xxxix.-xl.; lxxii.-lxxiv.; Ezra vii. 27-30 (for vii. 26 is an interpolation, as Kabisch points out); xii. 32-34; and possibly in xiii. 32-50, where xiii. 36 seems also an intrusion. In all these passages a Messiah is expected. In B^1 of the Apoc. Bar. *i.e.* vi. 9, Jerusalem is to be restored

pared beforehand here from the time when I took counsel to make Paradise, and showed it to Adam before he sinned, but when he transgressed the commandment, it was removed from him, as also Paradise. 4. And after these things I showed it to My

and to be established for ever, but this is not the new Jerusalem coming down from heaven. The latter is mentioned in xxxii. 2-4. It was indeed a very current conception in the latter half of the first century A.D. Thus we find it in Gal. iv. 26; Heb. xii. 22; Rev. iii. 12; xxi. 2, 10. In Gal. iv. 26 the heavenly Jerusalem is a symbol of the spiritual commonwealth of which the Christian is even now a member. But in Rev. iii. 12; xxi. 2, 10, it is an actual city, the counterpart of the earthly Jerusalem, with its own buildings and vessels. Here we should probably class the passage in Test. Dan. v. This city was to descend from heaven, but this expectation does not apparently lie at the base of Heb. xii. 22. Similar conceptions to that found in Rev. iii. 12; xxi. 2, 10, appear in 4 Ezra viii. 52, 53; x. 44-59; and also in vii. 26 and xiii. 36, though we must regard one or both of the last two as interpolated. With these last we might reckon also the heavenly Jerusalem mentioned in the text. The heavenly Jerusalem is variously described as the *νέα* (Test. Dan. v.), *ἡ ἄνω* (Gal. iv. 26), *καινή* (Rev. iii. 12; xxi. 2), *ἐπουράνιος* (Heb. xii. 22). It was created in the beginning of creation, and preserved in heaven. It was shown to Adam before he sinned. To Adam indeed the heavens had been open originally (Slav. En. xxxi. 2; Philo, *Quaest.* xxxii. in *Gen.*; Book of Adam and Eve, i. 8); but when he transgressed the commandment the vision of the heavenly Jerusalem was taken from him and likewise the possession of Paradise. Among the Rabbins the heavenly Jerusalem was called ירושלים של מעלה (= *ἡ ἄνω Ἰερουσαλήμ*). For the various Rabbinic conceptions regarding it, see Schöttgen, *de Hieros. Coelest.* in his *Horae Hebr.* 1205 *sqq.*; Meuschen, *N.T. ex Talm. ill.* p. 199 *sqq.*; Bertholdt, *Christologia*, 217-220; Eisenmenger, *Entdecktes Judenthum*, ii. 839-845; Weber, *Lehren d. Talmud*, 356-359, 386.

Took counsel to make Paradise. Which Paradise is this? The context might support either. For we might regard it as the Paradise which is kept in heaven like the heavenly Jerusalem. Adam could see both before his fall, but after it he lost the vision of both. It may, however, be the earthly Paradise in which he was placed at the first. The period to which the creation of the earthly Paradise is assigned varies. In Gen. ii. 8-17 it is apparently one of the last works of the creation. When, however, we come down to the Christian era, its creation was attributed to the third day (Jub. ii. 7; Slav. En. xxx. 1). The heavenly Paradise, on the other hand, is described as already existing before the creation of the world either actually or in the mind of God (see *Pesach.* 54*a*; *Beresh.* 20 in Weber *L. d. T.* 191).

4. *I showed it to My servant Abraham.* There is naturally no mention of this in Gen. xv. 9-21; but in the *Beresh. rabba* on Gen. xxviii. 17 we are told that this

servant Abraham by night among the portions of the victims. 5. And again also I showed it to Moses on Mount Sinai when I showed to him the likeness of the tabernacle and all its vessels. 6. And now, behold, it is preserved with Me, as also Paradise. 7. Go, therefore, and do as I command thee."]

V.-IX. 1 = B[1]. V. And I answered and said: "I shall, therefore, be in great straits in Zion, because Thine enemies will come to that place and pollute Thy sanctuary, and lead Thine inheritance into captivity, and will lord it over those whom Thou hast loved, and they will depart again to the place of their idols, and will boast before them. And what wilt Thou do for Thy great name?" 2. And the Lord said unto me: "My name and My glory have an eternal duration; My judgment, moreover, will preserve its rights in its own time. 3. And thou wilt see with thine eyes that the enemy will not overthrow Zion, nor burn Jerusalem, but be subservient to the judge for a time. 4. But do thou go and do whatsoever I have said unto thee." 5. And I went and took Jeremiah, and Adu, and Seriah, and Jabish,

vision was accorded to Jacob when sleeping at Bethel.

5. Cf. Exod. xxv. 9, 40.

6. See note on verse 3.

7. *As I command thee.* A frequently recurring phrase (cf. v. 4; x. 4; xxi. 1; 4 Ezra v. 20; xii. 51).

V. 1. *Thine inheritance.* Deut. iv. 20; ix. 26, etc.; Rest of Words of Baruch, ii. 7; iii. 6.

Whom Thou hast loved. Ephes. xxi. 20; 4 Ezra iv. 23.

Boast before them. Cf. vii. 1; lxvii. 2, 7; lxxx. 3; Rest of Words of Baruch, i. 5; iv. 7.

What wilt Thou do, etc. Joshua vii. 9; cf. 4 Ezra iv. 25; x. 22.

2. *My name and My glory*, etc. Ps. cxxxv. 13.

My judgment, moreover, will preserve its rights. This phrase in a slightly different form recurs in xlviii. 27, and lxxxv. 9.

3. This is carried out in vi. 5; vii.

4. This refers to the command given in ii. 1.

5. *Adu.* There is a priest of this name who went up with Zerubbabel (Neh. xii. 4). According to Mass. he is called Iddo, but both the

and Gedaliah, and all the honourable men of the
people, and I led them to the valley of Cedron, and
I narrated to them all that had been said to me. 6.
And they lifted up their voice, and they all wept. 7.
And we sat there and fasted until the evening.

VI. And it came to pass on the morrow that, lo!

Syriac and Vulgate give Addo. In Ezra viii. 17 another Iddo is mentioned who returned with Ezra from Babylon.

Seriah. This Seriah was brother of Baruch and chief chamberlain of Zedekiah. He went with the latter to Babylon (see Jer. li. 59, 61).

Jabish. This name has been identified with Ἰγαβής = יַעְבֵּץ (1 Chron. iv. 9), but both the form of the name and the time of Jabez are against this identification.

Gedaliah. This is Gedaliah the son of Ahikam (see Jer. xl. 14). But Gedaliah might also be from Γοθολίας = עֲתַלְיָה (cf. 1 Chron. viii. 26) a companion of Ezra (see Ezra viii. 7). Gedaliah is again mentioned in xliv. 1 in a fragment of B[1].

Cedron, i.e. קִדְרוֹן (2 Sam. xv. 23). The valley of the Cedron is again the scene of Baruch's fast in xxi. 1, and of an assembly of the people in xxxi. 2.

Narrated to them, etc. After most of the revelations which Baruch receives, he makes known their disclosures to his friends and the elders of the people (see x. 4; xxxi. 3-xxxii. 7; xliv.-xlvi.; lxxvii. 1-17). There is no need of such a disclosure in the second section, *i.e.* v. 7-viii., and such disclosure is forbidden in the fourth, *i.e.* xii. 5-xx.

The Second Section

V. 7-VIII. This is a short section. First there is the fast of one day (v. 1). Thereupon to Baruch in his grief (vi. 2) is disclosed a vision. In this he sees the sacred vessels committed to the earth for a season and the city destroyed by angels, lest the enemy should triumph (vi. 3-vii.) The realisation of this vision which follows thereupon dispenses with the need of its publication by Baruch (viii.)

7. *Fasted until the evening.* The other fasts mentioned are of seven days. Of these there are four (see ix. 2; xii. 5; xxi. 1; xlvii. 2). The symmetry of the book would require another such fast after xxxv. For the scheme of the final editor is first a fast, then generally a prayer, then a divine message or revelation, then an announcement of this either to an individual, as in v. 5; x. 4, or to the people (xxxi. 2-xxxiv.; xliv.-xlvi.; lxxvii. 1-17), followed occasionally by a lamentation. In xx. 5, at the close of the fourth section, Baruch is bidden to make no announcement.

It will be observed that this scheme is broken through in the fifth section only, *i.e.* in xxi.-xlvi., where there is a fast, a prayer, an address to the people followed by a lament over Zion, a revelation and an address to the people (see ix. 2, note). In 4 Ezra there are four fasts of seven days (see v. 20; vi. 35; ix. 26, 27; xii. 51).

VI. 1. *On the following morning,* etc. These words are reproduced in Rest of Words (iv. 1).

the army of the Chaldees surrounded the city, and at the time of the evening I, Baruch, left the people, and I went forth and stood by the oak. 2. And I was grieving over Zion, and lamenting over the captivity which had come upon the people. 3. And, lo! suddenly a strong spirit raised me, and bore me aloft over the wall of Jerusalem. 4. And I beheld, and lo! four angels standing at the four angles of the city, each of them holding a lamp of fire in his hands. 5. And another angel began to descend from heaven, and said unto them: "Hold your lamps, and do not light them till I tell you. 6. For I am first sent to speak a word to the earth, and to place in it what the Lord the Most High has commanded me." 7. And I saw him descend into the Holy of Holies, and take from thence the veil,

By the oak. This oak is outside the city; for in ii. 1 Jeremiah and all that were like him were bidden to leave the city. This they and Baruch did in v. 5, and they fasted in the valley of the Cedron. On the following day the Chaldees surround the city. On that day Baruch left Jeremiah and the rest and went forth (probably from the cavern in the Cedron valley mentioned in xxi. 1) and stood by the oak. The oak thus appears to be near or in the Cedron valley, and thus in the neighbourhood of Jerusalem. This oak is mentioned again in lxxvii. 18. We are not, therefore, to compare this oak with the well-known one at Hebron, as Fritzsche, who compares LXX.; Gen. xiii. 18; xiv. 13; xviii. 1.

It is noteworthy that no mention of this oak appears in B^2. In B^1 it is found twice (vi. 1 and lxxvii. 18). A tree is referred to in A^3 in lv. 1.

3. As the Chaldeans encompassed Jerusalem, Baruch was unable to draw dear to the wall. But a strong angel lifts him on high above the wall.

4. Cf. Rev. vii. 1, "I saw four angels standing on the four corners of the earth"; Rest of Words of Bar. iii. 2.

5. Cf. Rev. vii. 2; Rest of Words, iii. 4.

6. The office of the angel here is executed by Jeremiah in Rest of Words, iii. 8.

The Lord the Most High. Occurs here only in this book. It is not found in 4 Ezra.

7. *Take from thence*, etc. According to Josephus, *Bell*, V. 5, 5, the Holy of Holies in Herod's temple was empty.

See Appendix for a similar account

and the holy ephod, and the mercy-seat, and the two tables, and the holy raiment of the priests, and the altar of incense, and the forty-eight precious stones, wherewith the priest was adorned, and all the holy vessels of the tabernacle. 8. And he spake to the earth with a loud voice: "Earth, earth, earth, hear the word of the mighty God, and receive what I commit to thee, and guard them until the last times, so that, when thou art ordered, thou mayst restore them, so that strangers may not get possession of them. 9. For the time comes when Jerusalem also will be delivered up for a time, until it is said, that it is again restored for ever. 10. And the earth opened its mouth and swallowed them up."

VII. And after these things I heard that angel say-

in Macc. *The veil, i.e.* פָּרֹכֶת (Exod. xxvi. 31). *The ephod, i.e.* אֵפֹד (Exod. xxix. 5).

Mercy-seat, כַּפֹּרֶת (Exod. xxv. 17).

Forty-eight precious stones. How this number is made up I cannot discover. There were twelve stones on the breastplate (Exod. xxviii. 15-21), and two on the ephod (Exod. xxviii. 9).

The altar of incense. The Syriac implies *θυμιατήριον*, which in Josephus and Philo = מזבח הקטרה. See Appendix.

According to *Bammidbar rabba*, 15, five things were taken away and preserved on the destruction of Solomon's temple: the candlestick, the ark, the fire, the Holy Spirit, and the cherubim.

8. In the Rest of Words, iii. 8, these words in a greatly altered shape are attributed to Jeremiah.

Earth . . . of the mighty God; drawn from Jer. xxii. 29. Text agrees with Mass., Syr., Vulg., against LXX., which gives "earth" only twice.

Mighty God. This title recurs in vii. 1, and xiii. 2, 4. It is not found in 4 Ezra.

Guard them until the last times. Cf. Rest of Words, iii. 8, "Preserve the vessels of worship until the coming of the Beloved."

That . . . thou mayst restore them, i.e. for use in the temple of the rebuilt Jerusalem.

That strangers may not get possession of them (cf. x. 19). For a slightly different reason see lxxx. 2.

9. *For a time.* See i. 4, note.

Restored for ever. It is not necessary to take the phrase "for ever" literally. In any case a Messianic kingdom of indefinite duration is looked forward to with Jerusalem as its centre, and likewise the temple in which the sacred vessels of the former temple will again be used. During this kingdom the dispersion will again return to Palestine (lxxvii. 6; lxxviii. 7, notes).

ing unto those angels who held the lamps: "Destroy, therefore, and overthrow its walls to its foundations, lest the enemy should boast and say: 'We have overthrown the wall of Zion, and we have burnt the place of the mighty God.'" 2. And the Spirit restored me to the place where I had been standing before.

VIII. Now the angels did as he had commanded them, and when they had broken up the angles of the walls, a voice was heard from the interior of the temple, after the wall had fallen, saying: 2. "Enter ye enemies, and come ye adversaries; for He who kept the house has forsaken (it)." 3. And I, Baruch, departed. 4. And it came to pass after these things that the army of the Chaldees entered and seized the house, and all that was around it. 5. And they led the people away captive, and slew some of them, and bound Zedekiah the king, and sent him to the king of Babylon.

VII. 1. *Destroy, therefore, and overthrow*, etc. Cf. v. 3; lxxx. 1.

Boast. Cf. v. 1; lxvii. 2, 7; lxxx. 3; Rest of Words, i. 5; Ps. xxxv. 19; xxxviii. 16; Ecclus. xxiii. 3; Pss. Sol. xiii. 7, ἐν περιστολῇ παιδεύεται δίκαιος, ἵνα μὴ ἐπιχαρῇ ὁ ἁμαρτωλὸς τῷ δικαίῳ.

Mighty God. See vi. 8, note.

2. *And the Spirit restored me.* I have here made a necessary emendation of the text. Thus I have emended ܘܐܚܕܬܘܢܝܗ̇ = "and you have seized it," into ܘܪܘܚܐ ܐܬܦܢܬܢܝ, "And the spirit restored me." The unamended text gives no sense, whereas the change just made restores the harmony of the context. Thus in vi. 31, "a strong spirit" carried Baruch aloft in order to see the vision. After the vision this spirit restores him to where he had been before. From this place Baruch departs in viii. 3.

VIII. 1. Cf. vii. 1; lxxx. 1.

2. Cf. Rest of Words, iv. 1. *He who kept the house has forsaken (it)*. Cf. Josephus, *De Bello Jud.* vi. 5. 3: μετὰ δὲ ταῦτα (ἀντιλαβέσθαι) καὶ φωνῆς ἀθρόας μεταβαίνωμεν ἐντεῦθεν.

Tacitus, *Hist.* v. 13, "Et apertae repente delubri fores et audita major humana vox, excedere deos."

5. *Led . . . away captive.* lxxx. 4; Rest of Words, iv. 2.

Bound Zedekiah the king, and sent, etc. Whatever explanation we give of i. 1, it is clear from these words that the writer was acquainted with the history of the kings of Judah and the captivity of Judah under Zedekiah.

IX. And I, Baruch, came, and Jeremiah, whose heart was found pure from sins, who had not been captured in the seizure of the city. 2. And we rent our garments, and wept, and mourned, and fasted seven days. IX. 2-X. 5 = E and B^2.

X. And it came to pass after seven days, that the word of the Lord was upon me, and said unto me: "Tell Jeremiah to go and confirm the captivity of the

Bound and sent to the king of Babylon. Cf. lxxx. 4.

IX. 1. *Heart . . . pure from sin.* Contrast the "wicked heart" in 4 Ezra iii. 20, 21, 26; iv. 4, etc. In Pss. Sol. xvii. 41, the Messiah is said to be καθαρὸς ἀπὸ ἁμαρτίας.

THE THIRD SECTION

IX. 2-XII. 4. We have first the fast of seven days amid the ruins of Zion (ix., cf. x. 3). Then the word of the Lord comes to Baruch and bids him to tell Jeremiah to go to Babylon (x. 2), and promises a revelation of what should be in the end (x. 3). Then follows Baruch's announcement of the divine message to Jeremiah (x. 4). The section closes with Baruch's lament before the gates of the temple over Zion (x. 5-xii. 4).

We have shown below that x. 6-xii. 4 comes probably from the hand of a Sadducean priest.

IX. 2. ***Fasted seven days.*** See v. 7, note. This is the first fast of seven days. It is observed amid the ruins of Zion (cf. x. 3). There are three others to follow, though, as we have shown in the note just referred to, there should be four. The insertion of the fasts ***in their present positions*** is the work of the final editor. There seem to have been fasts in his sources (B^1 and B^2). Fasting was the usual preparation for the reception of supernatural communications (cf. Dan. ix. 3, 20-21, and all the instances in this book and 4 Ezra cited in note on v. 7). In Test. Jos. iii. there is likewise a fast of seven days (Armenian Version), and in 2 Macc. xiii. 12, and Ass. Mosis ix. 6, of three days.

The scene of the first and fourth fasts is Cedron; of the second and sixth, Mount Zion; of the third, the gates of the temple; the account of the fourth is lost.

X. 1. *God.* This word is found only twice again, *i.e.* liv. 12; lxxxii. 9. Its use is more frequent in 4 Ezra (see vii. 19, 20, 21, 79; viii. 58; ix. 45; x. 16).

2. The divine communication that follows on the fast consists of a command to be given through Baruch to Jeremiah. Jeremiah is bidden to go to Babylon. We have here a violation of historical truth. According to Jer. xliii. 4-7, both Jeremiah and Baruch were carried down into Egypt. In the Apocryphal Baruch i. 1, Baruch is represented as being in Babylon five years after the capture of Jerusalem. In the Rest of Words, iv. 5, Jeremiah was dragged an unwilling captive to Babylon, whereas in our text he goes there at the bidding of God. The words "go and confirm the captivity" recur in xxxiii. 2.

people unto Babylon. 3. But do thou remain here amid the desolation of Zion, and I will show to thee after these days what will befall at the end of days." 4. And I said to Jeremiah as the Lord commanded me. 5. And he, indeed, departed with the people, but I, Baruch, returned and sat before the gates of the temple, and I lamented with that lamentation over Zion and

X. 6.-XII. 4 = B[2] or S. said: 6. "Blessed is he who was not born, or being

It is probable that the references to Jeremiah in connection with Babylon belong to B[2]; for it is noteworthy that in lxxvii. 17, 19; lxxx. 4; lxxxv. 6, Baruch always speaks of writing to the brethren in Babylon, but never to Jeremiah. This would be strange if the writer believed Jeremiah to be there. The people also urge Baruch in lxxvii. 12 to write to their brethren in Babylon to confirm them. Now if Jeremiah were in charge of the people there, as x. 2, 5; xxxiii. 2, clearly imply, any letter of Baruch to Babylon would have been addressed to him. As a matter of fact, in the Rest of Words of Baruch, when Baruch writes to Babylon, he directs the letter to Jeremiah.

It is probable, therefore, that the account of B[1] does not conflict with Jer. xliii., where Johanan takes Jeremiah with him down into Egypt.

3. Baruch is commanded to remain among the ruins of Zion, and is promised a revelation of what will befall in the last days. The words "after these days" show that this revelation will be accorded on a future occasion, after a fast, no doubt.

At the end of days. Cf. xxv. 1.

5. *Before the gates of the temple.* This is the scene of the following lamentation of Baruch, and probably of the fast in xii. 5. It is again the scene of his lamentation in xxxv. 1. A passage in the beginning of the Apoc. Bar. Tert. seems to be derived from our text: *οὕτως ἐκάθητο ἐπὶ τὰς ὡραίας πύλας ὅπου ἔκειτο τὰ τῶν ἁγίων ἅγια.* Mount Zion, on the other hand, is the scene where revelations are accorded to him (cf. xiii. 1; xxi. 2; xlvii. 2).

X. 6-XII. 4. This fragment appears to be the work of a Sadducee—probably a Sadducean priest writing just after the fall of the temple. For (1) in x. 6 and xi. 7 we have a thoroughly Sadducean sentiment, *i.e.* it were best not to be born at all, or, being born, to die; for the dead enjoy a sorrowless rest and a tranquil sleep (xi. 4); they know not the anguish of the living (xi. 5). No resurrection of the individual or of the nation is looked for, but only that retribution in due course may come upon the enemies of Israel (xii. 4). (2) The conception of Sheol in xi. 6 is Sadducean. (3) In x. 6-xii. 4 we have the saddest dirge in the Jewish literature of the time. This might well be; for for the priesthood there was no future. As false stewards they relinquish their charge and restore the keys of the temple to God (x. 18). Never again should sacrifices be offered in Zion (x. 10).

X. 6. *Blessed is he who was not born,* etc. Similar expressions of pessimism and despair return time and again in the later literature of Judaism. But in this passage and in xi. 7 the

born has died. 7. But as for us who live, woe unto us, because we see the afflictions of Zion, and what has befallen Jerusalem. 8. I will call the Sirens

phrase is used with a significance that severs it from all other instances of its occurrence. For whereas repeatedly elsewhere, as we shall see presently, it is said that it were better man had never been born because of sin and future condemnation, here non-existence or death is said to be preferable to witnessing the present woes of Jerusalem. Lest we should suppose this to be an accidental exaggeration, we should observe that it recurs in an intensified form in xi. 7, where the state of the dead in Sheol is said to be better than that of the living. Such a sentiment was impossible for the Pharisaic author of B², or indeed for any of the authors of this Apocalypse. It is a genuinely Sadducean sentiment, and the conception of Sheol in xi. 6, 7 is likewise Sadducean —practically that of the O. T. or of Hades in the Greek world. To a Pharisee no condition of earthly life could in any way approach the horrors of the existence of the wicked in the after-world.

In 4 Ezra and elsewhere, as we have remarked, quite a different turn is given to the expression in our text. There it is said that it were better man had not been at all than be born and have to face *future torment and judgment*. Thus in vii. 66 the writer declares: "It is much better for them (*i.e.* the beasts of the field) than for us; for they expect not a judgment and know not of torments." Again in vii. 116, 117, it is urged that "it would have been best not to have given a body to Adam, or, that being done, to have restrained him from sin; for what profit is there that man should in the present life live in heaviness and after death look for punishment?" Finally, in iv. 12 the nexus of life, sin and suffering, just referred to is put still more strongly: "It were better we had not been born at all than that we should be born and live in sin and suffer." A perfect parallel to the last passage is found in the Slav. En. xli. 2: "Blessed is the man who was not born, or, having been born, has never sinned . . . so that he should not come into this place (*i.e.* hell);" and to 4 Ezra vii. 116, 117, in the Eth. En. xxxviii. 2, where it is said, in reference to the future destiny of the wicked: "It had been good for them if they had not been born." For a N. T. parallel see Matt. xxvi. 24. It is worth observing that there is a perfect parallelism of thought between the passage in our text and in Sophocles, *Oed. Col.*, 1220—

μὴ φῦναι τὸν ἅπαντα νι-
κᾷ λόγον· τὸ δ', ἐπεὶ φανῇ,
βῆναι κεῖθεν ὅθεν περ ἥ-
κει, πολὺ δεύτερον ὡς τάχιστα,

and in Theognis, 425—

πάντων μὲν μὴ φῦναι ἐπιχθονίοισιν ἄριστον,
μὴ ἐσιδεῖν αὐγὰς ὀξέος ἠελίου·
φῦντα δ' ὅπως ὤκιστα πύλας Ἀΐδαο περῆσαι,
καὶ κεῖσθαι πολλὴν γῆν ἐπαμησάμενον.

8. *Sirens.* These are said in the Eth, En. xix. 2 (Greek Version) to have been the wives of the angels who went astray. It is strange that we have here the Greek conception of the Sirens, *Σειρῆνες*, *i.e.* that of sea-nymphs. But with the Greek translators of the O. T. it had quite a different meaning. Thus it is a

from the sea, and ye Lilin, come ye from the desert, and ye Shedim and dragons from the forests: awake and bind your loins unto mourning, and take up with me lamentation, and mourn with me. 9. Ye husbandmen, sow not again; and thou, earth, wherefore givest thou the fruits of thy produce? keep within thee the sweets of thy sustenance. 10. And thou, vine, why further dost thou give thy wine? for an offering will

rendering of בנות יענה = ostriches in Isa. xiii. 21; Jer. l. 39; Mic. i. 8; of תנים or תנין = jackals in Isa. xxxiv. 13; xliii. 20. It is similarly used by Symmachus, Theodotion, and Aquila in rendering the above words.

Lelioto. These are the Lilin (לִילִין) from the singular Lilith (לִילִית). Male and female demons named Lil and Lilit belong to Assyrian and Babylonian demonology. They were thought, as were also the Lilin (Shabbath, 151*b*), to attack men and women in their sleep (Lenormant, *La Magie*, p. 36). The Lilith, or night demon, is mentioned in Isa. xxxiv. 14, along with the satyr שָׂעִיר. The Lilin, according to the Talmud, were female demons corresponding to the Shedim or male demons. They were partly the offspring (*Erub*, 18*b*; *Beresh*. 42) of Adam and Lilith, Adam's first wife, a demon, and partly were derived from the generation that God dispersed (Gen. xi.), for God (*Jalkut Shim.*, *Beresh*. 62) transformed that generation into Shedim, Ruchin, and Lilin. These Lilin inhabited desert places. They were said to kill children. They have been compared with the Lamiae and Striges; ὀνοκένταυροι is the LXX. rendering of the word in Isa. xxxiv. 14. For further details on the subject see Weber, *Lehren d. Talm.*, pp. 245, 246, 248; Bochart, *Hierozoicon*; iii. 829-831; Eisenmenger, *Entd. Judenthum*, ii. 413-426, 452.

Shedim. These were male demons to which various origins were assigned. Their souls were created by God, but as the Sabbath intervened before they received bodies they had to remain without them (*Beresh. rabba*, c. 7); or they were sprung from Adam and a demon wife, or from Eve and a demon husband (*Beresch. rabba*, c. 24); or were originally the generation that God transformed into Shedim, Ruchin, and Lilin. Their place of resort is the wilderness. For an account of their activities, see Weber, 245, 246.

Dragons. The word ܝܪܘܢܐ is found in the Peshitto of Isa. xiii. 22 as a translation of תנים. Levy (*Neuhebräisches Wörterbuch*, ii. 265) defines it as "Drache oder sonst ein Thier mit klagendem, heulendem Tone." The word frequently occurs in the Targums and later Hebrew as ירוד (ירוד).

10. The writer of x. 6 - xii. 4 resigns absolutely all hope of the restoration of Jerusalem. This is throughout the attitude of B[2] (see i. 4, note).

With the thought of this verse, cf. *Kethuboth* 112*a*: "O land, land, let thy fruit shrivel: for whom art thou producing thy fruit? is it not

not again be made therefrom in Zion, nor will first-fruits again be offered. 11. And do ye, O heavens, withhold your dew, and open not the treasuries of rain. 12. And do thou, O sun, withhold the light of thy rays; and do thou, O moon, extinguish the multitude of thy light; for why should light rise again where the light of Zion is darkened? 13. And you, ye bridegrooms, enter not in, and let not the brides adorn themselves with garlands; and, ye women, pray not that ye may bear. 14. For the barren shall rejoice more, and those who have no sons shall be glad, and those who have sons shall have anguish. 15. For why should they bear in pain and bury in grief? 16. Or wherefore, again, should mankind have sons; or wherefore should the seed of their nature again be named, where that mother is desolate, and her sons are led into captivity? 17. From this time forward speak not of beauty and discourse not of gracefulness. 18. Moreover, ye priests, take ye the keys of the sanctuary and cast them into the height of heaven, and give them to the

for the Gentiles who rose up against us because of our sins?

13. Cf. Jer. vii. 34; xvi. 9; xxv. 10; Baruch ii. 23.

Brides. Syriac gives "virgins," but this idea is out of place in verses 13-16, where everything refers to marriage. The first right mention of virgins is in verse 19. The wrong text may be explained by a corruption of כלות into בתולות or עלמות. In the original Hebrew we should then have a paronomasia, כלילים אל תעדינה כלות. In *Git.* 7*a*, and in *Shabbath*, 59*b*, bridegrooms are forbidden to use garlands.

14. Cf. Matt. xxiv. 19; Luke xxiii. 29: "Blessed are the barren, and the wombs that never bare, and the breasts that never gave suck" (cf. Isa. liv. 1).

16. *That mother.* See iii. 1, note

18. The priesthood have proved faithless to their duty, and the charge of the temple is no longer theirs. Cf. Rest of Words, iv. 3, 4, where another turn is given to the text: "And thereupon Jeremiah took the keys of the temple . . . and cast these keys before the sun, saying: 'I say unto thee, O sun, take the keys of the house of God and keep

Lord, and say: 'Guard Thy house Thyself, for lo! we are found false stewards.' 19. And you, ye virgins, who spin fine linen and silk with gold of Ophir, hasten and take all things and cast (them) into the fire, that it may bear them to Him who made them, and the flame send them to Him who created them, lest the enemy get possession of them."

XI. Moreover, I, Baruch, say this against thee, Babylon: "If thou hadst prospered, and Zion had dwelt in her glory, it would have been a great grief to us that thou shouldst be equal to Zion. 2. But now, lo! the grief is infinite, and the lamentation measureless, for lo! thou art prospered and Zion desolate. 3. Who will be judge regarding these things? or to whom shall we complain regarding that which has befallen us? O Lord, how hast Thou borne (it)? 4. Our fathers went to rest without grief, and lo! the righteous sleep in the earth in tranquillity. 5. For

them till the days when the Lord shall ask thee concerning them. For we are not worthy to keep them; for we have been found false stewards.'"

This verse reappears in the *Jalkut Shim.* on Isa. xxi. as follows: "The flower of the priests . . . gathered together . . . the keys of the court and the sanctuary and said before God: 'Lord of the universe, we are not fit to be stewards before Thee (לא זכינו להיות גוברים לפניך). Behold Thy keys are returned to Thee.' And they cast them aloft" (quoted by Rosenthal).

19. *Fine linen and silk.* Cf. Ezek. xvi. 10.

Lest the enemy get possession. Cf. vi. 8.

XI. 1. *Babylon* stands here for Rome, as in Rev. xiv. 8; xvi. 19; xvii. 5; xviii. 2.

Prospered. Cf. xii. 1-3.

3. *How hast Thou borne (it)?* Cf. 4 Ezra iii. 30: "I have seen how Thou dost bear with them that sin." In Pss. Sol. ii. 1 and 4 Ezra iii. 8 the writers complain that God did not prevent such wrong-doing. With the latter cf. Isa. xiv. 6.

4. *Our fathers went to rest.* Cf. lxxxv. 9.

Sleep in the earth. Cf. xxi. 24; while the diction corresponds to Dan. xii. 2, "sleep in the dust of the earth," the thought is Sadducean and belongs to the earlier sphere of O.T. thought, presupposed in such a phrase as "slept with his fathers" (1 Kings ii. 10; xi. 21,

they knew not this anguish, nor yet had they heard of that which had befallen us. 6. Would that thou hadst ears, O earth, and that thou hadst a heart, O dust, that ye might go and announce in Sheol, and say to the dead: 7. 'Blessed are ye more than we who are living.'"

XII. But I will say this as I think, and I will speak against thee, O land, which art prospering. 2. The noonday does not always burn, nor do the constant rays of the sun (always) give light. 3. Do not conclude or expect that thou wilt always be prosperous and rejoicing, and be not greatly uplifted and boastful. 4. For assuredly in its own season wrath will awake against thee, which now in long-suffering is held in as it

etc.) There is no ground for supposing with Kabisch (*Das vierte Buch Ezra*, 68, 69) that this phrase in the mouth of a Pharisee of this period implied a capacity of life as still existing in the body even when interred. That "to sleep in the earth" and "to be in Sheol" are equivalent expressions for a Pharisee, is clear from Eth. En. li. 1 and 4 Ezra vii. 32. The former phrase, "to sleep in the earth," is merely a figure of speech, and must not be pressed. Yet see l. 2, note. These phrases are equivalents in verses 6, 7. Sadducean thought admitted of no resurrection; hence "life in Sheol" or "sleep in the earth" were interchangeable expressions for the same fact.

5. To a Pharisee this would be a trifling pain compared with the torments of the damned. But the Sadducee looked for no retribution in the world to come, but, like most of the writers in the O.T. and in Ecclesiasticus, only for a shadowy existence in Sheol.

6. *That ye might go*, etc. The Syriac = "and go ye." Here we have a Hebrew idiom, *i.e.* an imperative is used instead of a jussive in order to express the intention signified by the preceding verb (see Driver, *Hebrew Moods and Tenses*, p. 82).

Sheol. We have here the O.T. conception of Sheol—the eternal abode of the shades. This view of Sheol was maintained in N.T. times by the Sadducees. In xxiii. 5; xlviii. 16; lii. 2; lvi. 6, Sheol seems to be the abode of all departed souls prior to the final judgment. This also may be its meaning in xxi. 23 and in 4 Ezra iv. 41. In 4 Ezra viii. 53 it seems to bear the meaning of "hell." For a history of the various meanings borne by this word see Eth. En. lxiii. 10, note.

7. The condition of the shades was for the writer undoubtedly more blessed than that of the living (cf. x. 6, note).

XII. 3. *Boastful.* I have here emended ܠܬܫܥܒܕܘܢ = "do (not) oppress" into ܠܬܫܬܒܗܪܘܢ = "be (not) boastful."

XII. 5=E. were by reins. 5. And when I had said these things, I fasted seven days.

XIII.-XXV.=B[2]. XIII. And it came to pass after these things, that

THE FOURTH SECTION

XII. 5-XX. This section begins with a fast of seven days (xii. 5). Then follows a long revelation to Baruch (xiii. 2-xx. 2). (Owing to the complete disarrangement and confusion of the text, this revelation cannot be summarised here. For a discussion of these chapters see pp. 20-34.) Contrary to the usual procedure, Baruch is bidden not to publish this revelation (xx. 3).

XII. 5. On the fasts of Baruch see v. 9, note; ix. 2, note.

XIII.-XXV. The text of these chapters is inexplicable as it stands. The difficulties are due not to corruption, though that undoubtedly exists, but to a recasting of the original text by the final editor. In this process many passages were torn from their original contexts and placed in settings which are quite unsuitable. Some of the incongruities thus produced are as follows: (1) The words "those prosperous cities" are represented as speaking in xiii. 4 without a single note of introduction. (2) In the next verse the words, "thou and those like thee who have seen," are similarly unexplained, and are in fact inexplicable in their present context; for though Baruch was to be preserved till the consummation of the times, his *contemporaries* were not, and hence they could not see the future retribution of the Gentiles. If, however, xxiv. 2 originally preceded xiii. 3*b*-5, the words, "thou and those like thee who have seen," would be perfectly intelligible. (3) Again the retribution of the Gentiles referred to in xiii. 4, 5 has not been mentioned before, though the text presupposes some such mention. It is intelligible if xxv. or xxiv. 4 precedes where Baruch asks what will befal the enemies of Israel. (4) In xiv. 1 Baruch replies that God has shown him "the method of the times," whereas in xx. 6 this appears not to have been yet done, and it seems that a revelation of "the method of the times" is still to come. (5) In xxiv. 4 Baruch asks what retribution awaits the enemies of Israel, and when will the judgment be? In xxv. we find the answer to the latter question, whereas the answer to the former is already given in xiii. 4-12. (6) I can discover no adequate explanation of the "therefore" with which xx. 1 begins in its present context. If xx. were read immediately after xiii. the text would at once become clear. On these and other grounds we must attempt to restore the original order of the chapters before they were broken up and rearranged, mutilated, and interpolated by the final editor. Owing to the paucity of materials the attempt to restore the original order can only be partially successful. This order was probably xiii. 1-3*a*; xx.; xxiv. 2-4; xiii. 3*b*-12; xxv., xiv.-xix.; xxi.-xxiv. 1; xxx. 2. To reassure Baruch, who is plunged in grief over Jerusalem (xiii. 3*a*), God declares (xx. 1, 2) that the days and years will speed more quickly by in order to usher in the judgment which will right all wrongs, and that even Jerusalem was removed with this end in view. On the "method of the times" Baruch is then promised disclosures (xx. 6), and "he and many with him" will see the mercy of God on those that sinned and were righteous

I, Baruch, was standing upon Mount Zion, and lo! a voice came from the height and said unto me: 2. 'Stand upon thy feet, Baruch, and hear the word of the mighty God. 3. Because thou hast been astonied at what has befallen Zion, thou shalt therefore be assuredly preserved to the consummation of the times,

(xxiv. 2). Baruch, thereupon, asks two questions (xxiv. 4): (*a*) what will befal Israel's enemies? (*b*) when will God judge the world (of which event He had already spoken, xx. 2)?

The answer to (*a*) is given in xiii. 3*b*-12. But the first words of this answer are lost. In these words there was a statement of this nature: "retribution will come upon the prosperous cities of your enemies" (cf. xiii. 4). Baruch, moreover (xiii. 3*b*-12), will be preserved until those days for the express purpose of testifying the reason of the retribution that has befallen these cities, and the date of its consummation. "He and those like him who have seen" (cf. xxiv. 2) should answer the remonstrances of the tormented Gentiles. And in answer to Baruch's second question, he is informed (xxv. 1, 2) that he shall likewise be preserved till the sign of the last days has come. This sign will be a stupor that shall seize the inhabitants of the earth (xxv. 3, 4). Baruch, thereupon, acknowledges: "Behold Thou hast shown me the method of the times" (xiv. 1). After this the thought advances connectedly through xiv. - xix.; xxi. - xxiv. 1; xxx. 2. For like rearrangements of already existing texts by the final editor, see my edition of the Eth.En. pp. 189, 260, 267, 268, 270, 274.

XIII. 1. *Mount Zion.* Mount Zion is the scene of the revelation in xiii.-xx.; of the prayer in xxi. 4-25 (cf. xiii. 1; xx. 6; xxi. 2); of the revelation in xxii.-xxx.; of the seven days' fast in xlvii. 2; and of the prayer and revelation that follow xlviii.-lii.

A voice. Cf. xxii. 1, note.

2. *Stand upon thy feet.* Ezek. ii. 1.

The mighty God. Cf. vi. 8; vii. 1; xiii. 4.

3. *Thou shalt therefore be assuredly preserved*, etc. This promise recurs twice again in B², *i.e.* in xxv. 1 and lxxvi. 2. Baruch is thus to be preserved as a testimony or a sign against the inhabitants of the earth in the last days (see also xiv. 2). This assumption and preservation of Baruch till the last judgment is the teaching of B². With the above passages compare also xlviii. 30 and xlvi. 7, where the last is due to the final editor. In B¹, on the other hand, Baruch is to die a natural death (lxxviii. 5; lxxxiv. 1); he is to go the way of all flesh (xliv. 2) and to forget all corruptible things and the affairs of mortals (xliii. 2). Thus we have two conflicting accounts touching the destiny of Baruch. It is noteworthy that we have in the text a transference of a distinct Enochic function to Baruch. For in Jubilees iv. 24 it is stated: "(Enoch) was set as a *sign* there (in Eden), and that he should *testify* against all the children of men;" and again in x. 17: "As a *testimony* to the generations of the world the office was ordained for Enoch of recounting all the deeds of generation unto generation till the day of judgment" (see also Slav. En. xl. 13; liii. 2; lxiv. 5).

that thou mayst be for a testimony. 4. So that, if ever those prosperous cities say: 'Why hath the mighty God brought upon us this retribution?' 5. Thou and those like thee may say to them (even) ye who have seen: 'This evil and (these) retributions which

This robbing of Enoch to benefit Baruch is a clear sign of Jewish hostility to Christianity, and a tribute to the influence that Enoch enjoyed in the Christian Church of the first century. Enoch's acceptance amongst Christians as a Messianic prophet was the ground for his rejection by the Jews. So thoroughgoing, indeed, was this rejection that, although he was the chief figure next to Daniel in Jewish Apocalyptic prior to 40 A.D., in subsequent Jewish literature his functions and achievements are assigned to others, such as Moses, Ezra, or Baruch, and, with the exception of two or three passages, his name in subsequent Jewish literature is henceforth studiously ignored. The observation of this tendency of Jewish thought becomes of practical value to us when we come to lix. 4-11, as we are thus enabled to conclude that a document which on other grounds is prior to 70 A.D., is posterior to the rise of Christianity because it manifests clear signs of this tendency.

Assuredly be preserved. The Syriac lit. = σωσθεὶς σωσθήσει, a familiar Hebraism שָׁמוֹר תִּשָּׁמֵר. This idiom recurs frequently in this book (see xxii. 7; xli. 6; xlviii. 30; l. 2; lvi. 2; lxxv. 6; lxxvi. 2; lxxxii. 2; lxxxiii. 1, 2, 3, 6; lxxxiv. 2). That we have herein indubitable evidence of a Hebrew original we have shown in the Introduction.

4. *Those prosperous cities.* The abruptness with which these cities are introduced, though not heretofore mentioned, and their complaints about the retribution that has befallen them, though no such retribution has as yet been recorded, shows either that the text preceding these words has been lost, or else that xiii. 3*b*-12 should be read after xxiv. 2-4. In fact, since in xiii. 3*b*-12 we have an answer to xxiv. 4, we must assume that xiii. 3*b*-12 originally followed after xxiv. 4, and since xiii. 4 presupposes that a statement about the retribution that is to come upon the prosperous enemies of Israel has already been made, and since no such statement is found, we must further assume the loss of such words immediately preceding xiii. 3*b* (see note on xxiv. 3, 4). It might be possible to explain xiii. 4 by xxv. 3, and accordingly regard xiii. 3*b*-12 as following originally upon xxiv. 2-xxv. But many difficulties beset this interpretation. The cities here spoken of are of course Gentile cities (cf. ver. 11).

Brought upon us this retribution. The same phrase practically is applied to Israel in lxxvii. 4, but here the "us" refers to the "prosperous cities." The *retribution* intended by the editor seems to be that threatened in xii. 4.

5. *Thou and those like thee who have seen it.* These words are hardly capable of interpretation as they stand. They clearly mean Baruch's contemporaries; observe "ye who have seen"; but as the time is that of the end, they cannot be his contemporaries; for only

are coming upon you and upon your people (are sent) in its time that the nations may be perfectly chastened.' 6. And then they will expect. 7. And if they say at that time: 'When?' 8. Thou wilt say to them: 'Ye who have drunk the strained wine, drink ye also of its dregs, the judgment of the Lofty One who has no respect of persons.' 9. On this account He had before no mercy on His own sons, but afflicted them as His enemies, because they sinned. 10. They were therefore chastened then that they might receive mercy. 11. But now, ye peoples and nations, ye are debtors. because all this time ye have trodden down the earth,

Baruch is to be preserved till that date. If, however, xiii. 3*b*-12 was originally preceded by xxiv. 2-4, we can trace the phrase back to xxiv. 2—"thou wilt see and many who are with thee."

That the nations may be perfectly chastened. That this chastisement is vindictive and not corrective is clear from verse 7; the nations are to "drink of the dregs, the judgment of the Lofty One"; and also from verses 10, 11, where the implication obviously is that, whereas Israel is punished with a view to its ultimate pardon, it is otherwise with the Gentiles. The vindictive punishment therefore of the Gentiles is dealt with in this chapter. But so far as I know ܪܕܐ = "chasten" is never used in the sense of vindictive punishment. This difficulty might be surmounted by supposing ܢܬܪܕܘܢ = "may be chastened," corrupt for ܢܬܒܕܪܘܢ = "may be dispersed" (cf. Isa. xxxiii. 3). In the next chapter, however, in xiv. 1, the retribution spoken of by God is to be of service to the Gentiles. But see note *in loc.* On the other hand, it might be possible to understand ܥܡܡ̈ܐ = "nations," "peoples," of Israel, as in xlii. 5 (if the text is right there). But in this case it would be better to emend ܢܬܪ̈ܕܘܢ into ܥܡܐ ܢܬܪܕܐ = "that the people may be chastened."

6. The Gentiles will wait for or look forward to the consummation of their chastisement. This verse might by a slight change be understood of Israel (cf. xiv. 3).

8. Cf. Ps. lxxv. 7, 8: "God is the judge. . . . For in the hand of the Lord there is a cup . . . surely all the wicked of the earth . . . shall drink them."

The Lofty One. Here only in this book (see 4 Ezra iv. 34; Isa. lvii. 15).

Has no respect of persons. Cf. xliv. 4.

10. *Chastened.* Cf. i. 5.

11. *Trodden down.* *I.e.* in the sense of oppressing it, a frequent meaning in the O.T.

and used the creation unrighteously. 12. For I have always benefited you, and ye have always denied the beneficence."

XIV. And I answered and said: "Lo! Thou hast shown me the method of the times, and that which will be after these things, and Thou hast said unto me, that the retribution, which has been spoken of by Thee, will be of advantage to the nations. 2. And now I know that those who have sinned are many, and they have lived in prosperity, and departed from the world, but that few

12. Cf. i. 4.

I have . . . benefited you. The Syriac is ܗܘܝܬ ܡܛܐܒ, but this order of the words, with this meaning, is highly irregular; for Syriac idiom all but universally requires the participle before the substantive and not as here, and in lxiii. 8, the converse order. This exceptional order may be due to the survival of the Hebrew order in the Syriac translation, *i.e.* הוית מטיב. For this seems to be the explanation of two out of the three instances where I have observed this irregularity in the Peshitto O.T., *i.e.* Gen. iv. 17 and 2 Sam. viii. 15. In the third (1 Sam. xviii. 13) I can offer no explanation, and the abnormality is there all the more striking, as three verses later the same phrase recurs in its right order. This irregularity (which is not noticed in Duval's Grammar, and only passingly mentioned in Nöldeke's) is not found, so far as I am aware, in the Peshitto N.T.

Ye have . . . denied. The Syriac is ܗܘܝܬܘܢ ܟܦܪܝܢ, which, according to Syriac idiom, is an imperative = "deny ye." The converse order = "ye have denied." This irregularity, as in the last instance, I would trace to a survival of the Hebrew idiom through the Greek.

XIV. 1. The final editor is again greatly to blame here. According to the text Baruch says: "Thou hast shown me the method of the times and that which will be after these things." Now this has not been done. In the preceding chapter instruction has been given as to the reason of the retribution which has come upon the cities of the Gentiles, and likewise as to the date when their chastisement will be consummated. "The method or scheme of the times" would imply such information as we find in xxiv. 2-xxv. taken in conjunction with xiii., or to xxvii.-xxx. In xx. 6 certain disclosures are promised regarding "the method of the times." The phrase is found also in xlviii. 1.

The retribution . . . spoken of by Thee. These words probably refer to xiii. 5, and yet the retribution in question is first mentioned, not by God but by the cities (xiii. 4), unless we suppose xxv. 8 to precede xiv.

Will be of advantage to the nations. In xiii. 5-11 the context is against the idea of a remedial chastisement of the Gentiles, which seems to be asserted here. Here, again something seems wrong.

nations will be left in those times, to whom those words shall be said which Thou didst say. 3. For what advantage is there in this, or what (evil), worse than what we have seen befall us, are we to expect to see? 4. But again I will speak in Thy presence: 5. What have they profited who confessed before Thee, and have not walked in vanity as the rest of the nations, and have not said to the dead: 'Give us life,' but always feared Thee, and have not left Thy ways? 6. And lo! they have been carried off, nor on their account hast Thou had mercy on Zion. 7. And if others did evil, it was

2. *Few nations will be left in those times to whom*, etc. Do these words refer back to xiii. 3? In that case Baruch complains that few of the Gentile nations will be alive to whom the words in xiii. 5, 7-11 are to be addressed.

3. These words seem to point to xiii. 6; cf. "they will expect" and "what . . . are we to expect to see?" But here they undoubtedly refer to Israel, whereas there they naturally refer to the Gentiles.

4-19. Of what profit has been the righteousness of the righteous? Of none; for it has helped neither them nor their city, though the last was at least their due (verses 4-7). Seeing this is so, man cannot understand Thy judgment (verses 8, 9), for he is but a breath; his birth is involuntary, and his end a mystery (verses 10, 11); for that end the righteous indeed may hope, for they have treasures in heaven, but for us there is only woe, here and hereafter (verses 12-14). Hence what Thou hast done on Thy servants' behalf Thou knowest, but we cannot discover. The world indeed Thou didst say was made for man. But how can this be? We pass away and the world abides (verses 15-19).

5. *Confessed before Thee.* I have here emended ܝܕܥܘ = "knew" into ܐܘܕܝܘ = "confessed."

Walked in vanity. Jer. ii. 5.

Have not said to the dead, etc. Cf. Isa. viii. 19*b*: "On behalf of the living should they seek unto the dead?"

6, 7. In these verses the destruction of Zion seems to be far in the background.

6. *Have been carried off.* Cf. lxxxv. 3. I have here followed Ceriani's emendation of ܐܬܚܛܦܘ into ܐܬܚܛܦܘܗ, who rightly compares xv. 2.

Nor on their account hast Thou had mercy on Zion. This was a great difficulty to the Jew. The presence of ten righteous men would have preserved Sodom; why then did Zion fall? Moreover, the preservation of the world, according to the Talmud (Weber, 201), depended on Israel. See xiv. 18, note.

7. We have here ideas which in some respects resemble those in Gen. xviii. 23-33. But whereas it

due to Zion, that on account of the works of those who wrought good works she should be forgiven, and should not be overwhelmed on account of the works of those who wrought unrighteousness. 8. But who, O Lord, my Lord, will comprehend Thy judgment, or who will find out the profoundness of Thy path? or who will think out the gravity of Thy way? 9. Or who will be able to think out Thy incomprehensible counsel? or who of those that are born has ever found

is taught there that God would spare a city because of the righteous *persons* in it, here and in ii. 2 it is the works of the righteous considered in themselves that are put forward as the ground of such mercy. On the question of good works the thought of the writers in this book, *i.e.* between 50 and 80 A.D., is to be described as follows: (*a*) The righteous are saved by their works (li. 7); they are justified by the law (li. 8); for righteousness is by the law (lxvii. 6). (*b*) Their works impart confidence to the righteous with respect to God when they pray for themselves or others. Thus Hezekiah trusted in his works and was hopeful in his righteousness, and so God heard him (lxiii. 3, 5); and the prophets also were heard because they trusted in their works (lxxxv. 2). (*c*) But the works of the righteous avail not themselves only; they are a defence also to the unrighteous among whom they dwell (ii. 2), and even after their death their works are regarded as a lasting merit on the ground of which mercy should be shown to Zion (xiv. 7; lxxxiv. 10). (*d*) Again these works are conceived as going before them to the next world, and being there guarded in the treasure chambers of God (xiv. 12), where they will be kept safely till the final judgment (xxiv. 1); hence the righteous hope for the end and leave the world without fear (xiv. 12). (On the teaching of this book as to faith, see note on liv. 21.) In 4 Ezra the doctrine of works as it is found in Baruch can hardly be said to exist. To (*b*) and (*c*) we find no parallels and only seeming parallels to (*a*), such as men "will be able to escape by their works or their faith in which they have believed" (ix. 7), and that "God will guard those who have works and faith in the Most Mighty" (xiii. 23). It will be observed that the doctrine of salvation by works is carefully guarded against by the addition of the words "and faith." To (*d*) we have good parallels in vii. 77, where Ezra is said to have "a treasury of works laid up with the Most High," and in viii. 33, where "the righteous are those who have many works laid up with Thee: from their own works will they receive reward."

Though the doctrine of justification as taught in Baruch should naturally be discussed here, we must refer the reader to the note on xxi. 9.

8. O Lord, *my Lord*. See iii. 1, note.

the beginning or end of Thy wisdom? 10. For we have all been made like a breath. 11. For as the breath ascends from the heart, and returning not is extinguished, such is the nature of men, who depart not according to their own will, and know not what will befall them in the end. 12. For the righteous justly hope for the end, and without fear depart from this habitation, because they have with Thee a store of works preserved in treasuries. 13. On this account also these without fear leave this world, and trusting with joy they hope to receive the world which Thou hast promised them. 14. But unto us there is woe, who also now are shamefully entreated, and at that time look forward

10. See references on next verse.

11. *Ascends from the heart, and returning not is extinguished.* Cf. Ps. lxxviii. 39: "a wind that passeth away, and cometh not again;" Ps. cxlvi. 4; Job vii. 7; James iv. 14. This rendering rests on a slight change of order in the text, *i.e.* ܡܢ ܠܒܐ ܘܕܠܐ ܗܦܟ instead of ܕܠܐ ܡܢ ܠܒܐ ܘܗܦܟ. Ceriani and Fritzsche render the text, "ascendit quin procedat de corde et restinguitur."

Depart not according to their own will. Man does not settle the hour of his departure from this life. Cf. xlviii. 15; 4 Ezra viii. 5, "convenisti enim obaudire" (read *nolens* with Syr. for *obaudire*) et profecta es nolens."

Know not what, etc. Cf. Slav. En. ii. 1; vii. 5.

12. *The righteous justly hope.* Eth. En. cii. 4.

A store of works, etc. The text reads ܚܝܠܐ ܕܥܒܕܐ = "a force or supply of works." But it also = "a store of works." Cf. 4 Ezra vii. 77, where we find "a treasure of works." In *Shabbath*, 31*b*, a man is spoken of as having אוצר זכיות, "a treasure of merits" in heaven. Cf. Matt. vi. 19, 20; Pss. Sol. ix. 9, ὁ ποιῶν δικαιοσύνην θησαυρίζει ζωὴν ἑαυτῷ παρὰ κυρίῳ. See note on verse 7.

13. *The world which Thou hast promised.* This is clearly the spiritual world. Thus in li. 3 the righteous after death are to "receive the world which does not die, which is then promised to them;" in xliv. 13, 15 "theirs is the inheritance of the promised time," "for unto them will be given the world to come;" and in xv. 7, 8 "the world which is to come" is said to be on their account. Cf. 4 Ezra ix. 13. It is referred to again in xxi. 25 and lxxxiii. 5 under the general name of something promised. Throughout B[2] there is no promise of an earthly felicity, but only of spiritual transmundane blessedness.

14. *There is woe.* Cf. for diction lxxxiv. 11; 4 Ezra xiii. 16.

(only) to evils. 15. But Thou knowest accurately what Thou hast made on behalf of Thy servants; for we are not able to understand by means of any good thing that Thou art our Creator. 16. But again I will speak in Thy presence, O LORD, my Lord. 17. When of old there was no world with its inhabitants, Thou didst devise and speak with a word, and forthwith the works of creation stood before Thee. 18. And Thou didst say that Thou wouldst make for Thy world man as the administrator of Thy works, that it might be known that he was by no means made on account of the world, but the world on account of him.

Evils. These words refer back to xiv. 3, and their subject is again touched upon in xv. 1. What these are is given in xliv. 15; lxxxv. 13.

15. *What Thou hast made* (*or done*) *on behalf of Thy servants. I.e.* ܡܕܡ ܕܥܒܕܬ ܥܠ ܥܒ̈ܕܝܟ. If my rendering is right, the entire verse appears to be in its wrong place, and should be read after verse 16. The sense then would be excellent: "Thou knowest what good things Thou hast created on behalf of Thy servants; but we know of none: yet Thou didst say that Thou didst make the world for man," etc. (verses 15, 17, 18). But the Syriac may be translated, "what Thou hast made out of Thy servants," or if we neglect the diacritic point, "what Thou has wrought out of Thy works." Ceriani translates the verse: "Tu autem recte nosti quid feceris de servis tuis: quia nos non possumus intelligere aliquid boni, quomodo tu sis fictor noster." Before aliquid we should read "per."

17. *Speak with a word*, etc. Cf. Gen. i. 6, 7; Ps. xxxiii. 6; Heb. xi. 3; 2 Peter iii. 5; Slav. En. xxiv. 5; xxv. 1; 4 Ezra vi. 38.

18. *Thou wouldst make for Thy world man*, etc. Cf. Gen. i. 26, 28; Ps. viii. 6; 4 Ezra vi. 54.

The world on account of him. So far as I am aware this exalted view of man's dignity in respect of the world is not found earlier than the first century of the Christian era. It recurs frequently in the literature of this time: cf. xiv. 19; xv. 7; xxi. 24 (this doctrine is thus confined to B[2] in this book); Assumpt. Mosis i. 12; 4 Ezra vi. 55, 59; vii. 11; viii. 44; ix. 13. In these passages the statement of the reason for the creation of the world assumes three forms: First, the world was created on account of man (Apoc. Bar. xiv. 18; 4 Ezra viii. 1, 44). But the writers of these books if pressed, would at once have withdrawn this statement in favour of two diverging statements: the one, that the world was created on account of Israel (4 Ezra vi. 55, 59; vii. 11; Assumpt. Mosis i. 12); the other that the world was created on account of the righteous in Israel

19. And now I see that as for the world which was made on account of us, lo! it abides, but we, on account of whom it was made, depart."

XV. And the Lord answered and said unto me: "Thou art rightly astonied regarding the departure of man, but thou hast not judged well regarding the evils which befall those who sin. 2. And as regards what thou hast said, that the righteous are carried off and the impious are prospered, 3. And as regards what thou hast said: 'Man knows not Thy judgment'— 4. On this account hear, and I will speak to thee, and hearken, and I will cause thee to hear My words. 5. Man would not rightly have understood My judgment, if he had not accepted the law, and if his fear

(Apoc. Bar. xiv. 19; xv. 7; xxi. 24). Either of the latter forms the real Jewish view from the Christian era onwards. Thus in the Talmud, it is either Israel, or the righteous in Israel, that were the cause of the world's creation and its subsequent preservation. Thus in *Bammidbar rabba*, ii., "if Israel were not, the world would not exist"; in the *Shemoth rabba*, xxviii., "The world was created owing to the merits of Israel, and upon Israel stands the world." See Weber, pp. 201, 202, for other passages of the same import. See also note on xv. 7.

19. See note on last verse. That the "us" and the "we" here are the righteous is clear from xv. 7. This verse shows that the writer believed in the view that the safety of the world was bound up with that of the righteous.

In *Pesikta* 200*b* God is said to have created the world on account of Abraham's merit (Weber, p. 295).

XV. 1. *Astonied regarding the departure of man.* These words refer to xiv. 19. The Syriac noun translated "departure" is derived from the verb translated "depart" in xiv. 19. In xiii. 3 Baruch was "astonied" about the fate of Jerusalem.

Not judged rightly regarding the evils, etc. See xiv. 3, 14.

2. See xiv. 6.

3. See xiv. 8, 9.

5. *The law.* The law was the centre round which Jewish thought and life revolved. To a limited extent the Messianic expectation was likewise a centre. Frequently we find that in proportion as the one is emphasised the other falls into the background. This will receive illustration as we proceed to examine the position assigned to the law and the Messiah respectively in the five main constituents of this book. Thus in B[1] (written after 70 A.D.) *where the restoration of Jerusalem is looked for, but no Messiah*, the law is spoken of as

had not been (rooted) in understanding. 6. But now,

follows: God gave the law to Israel (lxxvii. 3); for transgressing it they were sent into exile (lxxvii. 4; lxxxiv. 2); but let not Israel withdraw from the law (xliv. 3), but obey it (xlvi. 5); let them remember it (lxxxiv. 8); for if they do so, they will see the consolation of Zion (xliv. 7), and a son of the law will never be wanting (xlvi. 4), nor a lamp nor a shepherd (lxxvii. 16); for lamps and shepherds are from the law, and though these depart the law stands (lxxvii. 15); if they remember it, they will see the consolation of Zion (xliv. 7). In B² *where there is no Messiah and no expectation of the restoration of Jerusalem*, the law is still further glorified. Thus Moses brought the law to Jacob (xvii. 4); this conveyed a knowledge of the judgment of God (xv. 5), and entailed retribution on the consciously disobedient (xv. 6; xix. 3; xlviii. 40); it will exact all its rights (xlviii. 27), and repay the transgressor (xlviii. 47); apostates from it (xli. 3) will be specially dealt with (xlii. 4). On the other hand it will protect those who receive it in their hearts (xxxii. 1; xlviii. 24); by it they will be justified (li. 3), and in it will be the hope of the righteous (li. 7); the law is with Israel, and so long as they obey it they will not fall (xlviii. 22, 24). They have received one law from One (xlviii. 24). In B³ (which is akin to xiii. 2 in this respect) Israel has nothing save the Mighty One and the law (lxxxv. 3); they have one law by one (lxxxv. 14). When, however, we turn to the Messiah Apocalypses A¹ (= xxvii.-xxx. 1), A² (=xxxvi.-xl.), A³ (=liii.-lxxiv.), and to S. (=x. 6-12) which form more than a third of the entire book, we find no mention at all of the law in A¹ and S. In A² there is only one mention of it, *i.e.* God's law is life (xxxviii. 2). In A³ it naturally becomes more prominent, as A³ gives a brief history of God's dealings with Israel. The law and the tradition were observed by Abraham and his sons (lvii. 2). Thus, through the agency of Moses, its light shone on those in darkness (lix. 2). God imparted to Moses certain studies of the law (lix. 3). Josiah alone was faithful to it in his time (lxvi. 5). Such as loved it not perished (liv. 14). Righteousness comes by the law (lxvii. 6). Thus we observe that in purely eschatological descriptions such as A¹, there is not a single allusion to the law: the Messiah is the entire centre of interest. This is practically true in A² also; for the reference in xxxviii. 2 does not belong to the account of the last things. In A³ finally, most of the references are to historical incidents, though it is true that in A³ great store is set by the law. The law was the centre of Jewish life, the source of righteousness, and in fact its spiritual schoolmaster, till the advent of the Messiah had arrived. Thenceforward (lxx.-lxxiv.) there is not even an allusion to it. The same phenomena are observable in the various constituents of 4 Ezra. Thus in the three or four distinct Messiah Apocalypses in that book (according to Kabisch's critical analyses) the law is only mentioned two or three times. The only strong expression regarding it is in xiii. 38, and there the text is doubtful. In the groundwork of the book (*circ.* 100 A.D.) however, *where we find no hope of a Messiah nor of a restored Jerusalem*, the law, as might be expected, has a more important rôle to play. Thus God gave the law to Jacob (iii. 19). He sowed it in them that they might keep it (ix. 32), but it bare no fruit owing to

because he transgressed though he knew, yea, on account of this also, he shall be tormented because he knew. 7. And as regards what thou didst say touching the righteous, that on account of them has this world come, nay more, even that which is to come is on their account. 8. For this world is to them

the evil heart (iii. 20); they neglected it (vii. 20), did not keep it (ix. 32), rejected it (vii. 72), despised it (vii. 24; viii. 56), yet the law cannot perish (ix. 37.) Some did try to keep the law perfectly in this life (vii. 89), and God bore testimony to them because they did so (vii. 94); these acquired a store of good works (vii. 77; viii. 33), and from these they received their reward (viii. 33); and yet none can claim heaven purely as the reward of their righteousness, for all men have sinned (viii. 35).

It is obvious at a glance that the possession of the law by Israel is less a subject of self-gratulation in 4 Ezra than in Baruch. In the latter, especially in B[2] (written, like the groundwork in 4 Ezra, after 70 A.D., and having no expectation of the Messiah or a restored Jerusalem) the law is everything: it protects the righteous (xxxii. 1), justifies them (li. 3), is their hope (li. 7), and so long as it is with Israel, Israel cannot fall (xlviii. 22, 24). In Ezra, on the other hand, the law has begotten in the writer such a sense of sin that he trembles before it. Man needs mercy, not the award of the law; for all have sinned (viii. 35), and all but a very few would perish, but for the divine compassion (vii. 139).

5, 6. *If his fear had not been (rooted) in understanding. But now, because he transgressed though he knew*, etc. Here Ceriani followed by Fritzsche has mistranslated ܥܒܪ (= transgressus est) by "fecit," thus taking it for ܥܒܕ. This thought partially recurs in xix. 3; xlviii. 40, "Each of the inhabitants of the earth knew when he was committing iniquity" (see note *in loc.*), lv. 2; and almost a perfect parallel is found in 4 Ezra vii. 72: "Qui ergo commorantes sunt in terra hinc cruciabuntur quoniam sensum habentes iniquitatem fecerunt." Cf. Luke xii. 48.

7. *As regards . . . has this world come.* See note on xiv. 18. Nowhere in the present book are these words given as a divine utterance. The same statement is again made in xxi. 24. From a similar statement in 4 Ezra vi. 55, at the close of the short hexæmeron there, it is probable that some such statement was originally included in that hexæmeron in its independent form. On this hexæmeron see xxix. 4, note. Cf. 4 Ezra vi. 55; vii. 11.

Seeing that this world is "a trouble and a weariness" to the righteous, it is hard to understand such a belief unless we suppose that it was designed to be their discipline for the future life. Cf. lii. 6. On *the world which is to come*, see xiv. 13, note.

8. *This world is to them a trouble . . . with much labour.* Cf. xlviii. 50; li. 14; 4 Ezra vii. 3-14; Rom. viii. 18; 2 Cor. iv. 17. This world is evidently regarded by the

a trouble and a weariness with much labour; and that accordingly which is to come, a crown with great glory."

XVI. And I answered and said: "O Lord, my Lord, lo! the years of this time are few and evil, and who is able in this little (space) to acquire that which is measureless?"

XVII. And the Lord answered and said unto me: "With the Most High account is not taken of much time nor of a few years. 2. For what did it profit Adam that he lived nine hundred and thirty years, and transgressed that which he was commanded? 3. Therefore the multitude of time that he lived did not profit him, but brought death and cut off the years of those who were born from him. 4. Or wherein did Moses suffer loss in that he lived only one hundred and twenty years, and, inasmuch as he was subject to Him who formed him, brought the law to the

writer of B[2] but not of B[1] as a scene of trial and sorrow: a man must give himself to an ascetic life here if he is to attain blessedness hereafter. There is a more ascetic tone about 4 Ezra. In the Eth. En., however, still stronger statements are found. Thus in xlviii. 7 the Messiah "preserveth the lot of the righteous because they have hated and despised this world of unrighteousness," and in cviii. 7 God recompenses "the spirits of the humble and of those who afflict their bodies," and likewise those (cviii. 10) who, though "trodden under foot of wicked men," "loved heaven more than their life in this world."

Crown with great glory. Cf. 1 Pet. v. 4. We should expect "crown of great glory." Observe that if we retranslate these words into Hebrew, we have a paronomasia already familiar from Isa. lxii. 3; Ezek. xvi. 12; xxiii. 42, *i.e.* עֲטָרָה בתפארה רבה.

XVI. 1. *Years . . . few and evil.* Gen. xlvii. 9.

XVII. 1. *The Most High.* This title belongs to B[1], B[2], B[3], and A[3]. See xxv. 1; liv. 9, 17; lvi. 1; lxiv. 6, 8; lxvii. 4, 7; lxix. 2; lxx. 7; lxxvi. 1; lxxvii. 4, 21; lxxx. 1, 3; lxxxi. 2, 4; lxxxii. 2, 6; lxxxiii. 1; lxxxv. 8, 12.

3. *Brought death,* etc. See xxiii. 4, note.

4. *Brought the law,* etc. Cf. 4 Ezra iii. 19. "Give the law to the seed of Jacob, and the commandment to the race of Israel."

seed of Jacob, and lighted a lamp for the nation of Israel."

XVIII. And I answered and said: "He that lighted has taken from the light, and there are but few that have imitated him. 2. But those many whom he has lighted have taken from the darkness of Adam, and have not rejoiced in the light of the lamp."

XIX. And He answered and said unto me: "Wherefore at that time he appointed for them a covenant, and said: 'Behold I have placed before you life and death,' and he called heaven and earth to witness against them. 2. For he knew that his time was but short, but that heaven and earth endure always. 3.

Lighted a lamp. Cf. lix. 2, "lamp of the eternal law." The thought in both phrases is drawn from Ps. cxix. 105, "Thy word is a lamp," etc. Cf. xviii. 2.

XVIII. 1. *Has taken from the light*, *i.e.* has chosen the light. In the next verse the many are said to have chosen the darkness of Adam.

2. The law and Adam are in this passage symbolical names for the opposing powers of light and darkness. This thought is foreign to the O.T. though Gen. i.-iii. has prepared the way for it. Adam is here, as in the Slav. En., represented as the primary source of human transgression, whereas in the Eth. En. and Jubilees human depravity is traced mainly to the angels that sinned with the daughters of men. Again, as in the Slav. En., the writer does not teach the doctrine of original sin and inherited spiritual incapacities. He implies rather that man is left to determine his own destiny, to choose light or take darkness for his portion, just as in much later times it was said: "God does not determine beforehand whether a man shall be righteous or wicked, but puts this into the hands of the man himself" (*Tanchuma*, *Pikkude* 3). See Slav. En. xxx. 15, 16, notes. The same view is enforced in A^3, *i.e.* liv. 15, 16. See notes *in loc.*

XIX. 1, 2. Because few chose light and many chose darkness, Moses showed further that their choice of light or darkness was likewise a choice of life or death. xix. 1-3 looks like an addition of the final editor. The answer to xviii. seems to begin with xix. 4.

Behold I have placed, etc., Deut. xxx. 19. *Called heaven*, etc., Deut. iv. 26; xxx. 19; xxxi. 28. Cf. lxxxiv. 2; Ass. Mos. iii. 12.

Later times seem to have drawn from Deut. xxx. 19 the conclusion that the permanence of the law was bound up with that of heaven and earth. Cf. ver. 2; Matt. v. 18. Contrast Luke xvi. 17; Mark xiii. 31.

For after his death these sinned and transgressed (the covenant), though they knew that they had the law reproving (them), and the light in which nothing could err, also the spheres, which testify, and Me. 4. Now regarding everything that is it is I that judge, but do not thou take counsel in thy soul regarding these things, nor afflict thyself because of those which have been. 5. For now it is the consummation of time that is sought, whether of business, or of prosperity, or of shame, and not the beginning thereof. 6. Because if a man be prospered in his beginnings and shamefully entreated in his old age, he forgets all the prosperity that he had. 7. And again, if a man is shamefully entreated in his beginnings, and at his end is prospered, he remembereth not again his evil entreatment. 8. And again hearken: though each one were prospered all that time—all the time from the day on which death was decreed against those who transgress—and

3. *Transgressed.* This word recurs in the same connection (lxxxiv. 2) where it has as its object "the law." We must supply this or "the covenant" from ver. 1.

4. These words deal with Baruch's difficulties in xviii. 1, 2. Do not distress thyself with such problems; the end of all things is at hand.

5. Here only the end of all things is looked for—not an earthly felicity in a rebuilt Jerusalem.

6-8. The end of all things is at hand, and the only important question is: How does it find a man? will it bring him shame or honour? We are strongly reminded here of the well-known words of Solon in Herodotus i. 32 *σκοπέειν δὲ χρὴ παντὸς χρήματος τὴν τελευτήν, κῇ ἀποβήσεται. πολλοῖσι γὰρ δὴ ὑποδέξας ὄλβον ὁ θεὸς προρρίζους ἀνέτρεψε.* It was a familiar Hellenic theme. Cf. Soph. *Trach.* 1-3; *Oed. Rex*, 1494-97; Eurip. *Androm.* 100-103, etc.

8. *Though a man . . . vanity.* This seems the natural rendering of the passage. Ceriani renders: "Omne tempus istud a die quo decreta fuit mors contra eos qui praetereunt in isto tempore, si unusquisque prosperatus esset, et in fine suo in vanitatem corrumperetur, esset omne." Fritzsche quite wrongly writes "vanum" for "omne."

On which death was decreed, etc. See xxiii. 4, note.

in his end was destroyed, in vain would have been everything."

XX. Therefore, behold! the days will come, and the times will hasten more than the former, and the seasons will speed on more than those that are past, and the years will pass more quickly than the present (years). 2. Therefore have I now taken away Zion, in order that I may the more speedily visit the world in its season. 3. Now therefore hold fast in thy heart everything that I command thee, and seal it in the recesses of thy mind. 4. And then I will

XX. 1. *Therefore.* It is not clear that this word follows upon anything in xix. It could be taken closely with xviii. So far as I can see it is best to regard it as following directly on xiii. 3*a*. Jerusalem has fallen, therefore the years intervening before the judgment will be shortened. Cf. liv. 1, "Against the works of the inhabitants of the earth Thou dost hasten the beginnings of the times"; Matt. xxiv. 22. For the probable order of the text originally see pp. 20, 119.

The days will come. Cf. xxiv. 1; xxxi. 5; xxxix. 3; 4 Ezra vi. 18. A familiar O.T. phrase. Cf. Jer. xxiii. 7; xxx. 3, etc.

The times will hasten. Cf. lxxxiii. 1, 6, where almost the same thoughts and diction recur. Cf. liv. 1; 4 Ezra iv. 26.

2. The fall of Jerusalem is one of the steps preparatory for the final judgment. See xxi. 21. There is no hope here of a restored Jerusalem. See i. 4, note.

Speedily visit. The Syriac literally = σπεύσω καὶ ἐπισκέψωμαι, a Hebraism, אמהר ואפקד.

Visit. Cf. xxiv. 4; lxxxiii. 2. This word seems to be used in Baruch in a bad sense of the penal visitation of God, as in Exod. xx. 5; Ps. lxxxix. 32; Jer. vi. 15; ix. 25; xi. 22, etc.; also in 4 Ezra v. 56; vi. 18; ix. 2; Pss. Sol. xv. 14. The word (פקד = ἐπισκέπτεσθαι) has generally a good sense in the O.T., as in Gen. xxi. 1; Exod. iv. 31; Job x. 12; Pss. viii. 4; lxxx. 14; also in Ecclus. xlvi. 14; Wisdom vii. 7, 13; Pss. Sol. iii. 14; x. 5 (?); xi. 2, 7; always in the N.T., as in Luke i. 68, 78; vii. 16; xix. 44; Acts xv. 14; 1 Peter ii. 12. It is noteworthy that whereas in the N.T. the thought of God's visitation is one of joy, its associations in 4 Ezra and Baruch are fear and wrath to come.

3. *Everything that I command thee.* The relative is omitted in the Syriac, but both the sense and the Syriac idiom require it. If the text is right, we must take it as a Hebraism; for the Hebrew admits the omission of the relative. We must then suppose this Hebraism misunderstood by the Greek translator; for neither does the Greek allow of the omission of the relative.

show thee the judgment of My might, and My ways which are past finding out. 5. Go therefore and sanctify thyself seven days, and eat no bread, nor drink water, nor speak to any one. 6. And afterwards come to that place, and I will reveal Myself to thee, and speak true things with thee, and I will give thee commandment regarding the method of the times; for they will come and will not tarry.

The Prayer of Baruch the Son of Neriah

XXI. And I went thence and sat in the valley of Cedron in a cave of the earth, and I sanctified my

4. *Show thee the judgment of My might.* In lxxxiii. 7 we have a nearly related phrase, "The consummation . . . will show the great might of its ruler."

6. *That place.* See xiii. 1, note.

Method of the times. See xiv. 1, note.

Will come and will not tarry. Hab. ii. 3. Cf. xlviii. 39 of text.

The Fifth and Sixth Sections

XXI.-XLVI. This constitutes the fifth section of the book according to the present text, but in reality the fifth and sixth sections (see v. 7, note). For according to the scheme of the final editor, events proceed in each section in a certain order: thus first we find a fast, then generally a prayer or lamentation, then a divine message or disclosure followed by an announcement to the people. Thus we have here the fast of seven days in Cedron (xxi. 1); the prayer on Mount Zion (xxi. 4-26); the revelation (xxii.-xxx.); address to the people assembled in Cedron (xxxi.-xxxiv). At the close of xxxiv. there should follow a fast of seven days. The sixth section should open with this fast, but all mention of it has disappeared from the present text. After the fast comes a vision (xxxvi.-xl.) and a revelation regarding apostates and proselytes (xli. xlii.) with some further disclosures (xliii.); then the sixth section duly closes with an address to the people (xliv.-xlvi.)

It will be observed that xxi.-xlvi. embrace material from a variety of sources. Thus xxvi.-xxx. 1 = A^1, and xxxvi.-xl. = A^2 are independent Messiah apocalypses, and xliii, xliv. 7; xlv. xlvi. are derived from B^1. What remains of B^2 has been completely rearranged according to the views of the final editor. For what was probably the original order of B^2 see p. 119, and the Introduction, pp. lxi.-lxiii.

XXI. 1. *Cedron.* See v. 5. On the fasts of Baruch see notes on v. 7 and ix.

Cave. Cf. Assumpt. Mos. ix. 6.

soul there, and I eat no bread, yet I was not hungry, and I drank no water, yet I thirsted not, and I was there till the seventh day, as He had commanded me. 2. And afterwards I came to that place where He had spoken with me. 3. And it came to pass at sunset that my soul took much thought, and I began to speak in the presence of the Mighty One, and said: 4. "O Thou that hast made the earth hear me, that hast fixed the firmament in its fulness, and hast made firm the height of the heaven by the spirit, that hast called from the beginning of the world that which did not yet exist, and they obey Thee. 5. Thou that hast commanded the air by Thy nod, and hast seen those things which are to be as those things

2. *That place.* Probably Mount Zion. Cf. xx. 6 and xiii. 1; otherwise the temple, x. 5. But this and some other such place determinations may be due to the final editor. The scene of the fast, the prayer, and the revelation was probably the same. See xlvii. 1, note.

3. *The Mighty One.* This is the first time this title occurs. It is found in B[1], B[2], A[3], but not in A[1], A[2]. See xxv. 4; xxxii. 1, 6; xxxiv.; xliv. 3, 6; xlvi. 1, 4; xlvii. 1; xlviii. 1, 38; xlix. 1; liv. 1; lv. 6; lvi. 2, 3; lix. 8; lxi. 6; lxiii. 3, 5, 6, 8, 10; lxiv. 3, 4; lxv. 1; lxvi. 1, 5, 6; lxvii. 2; lxx. 2, 5; lxxvii. 11, 26; lxxxi. 4; lxxxii. 5; lxxxiv. 1, 6, 7, 10; lxxxv. 2, 3.

4. *By the spirit.* Have we here a reference to Gen. ii. 1, "The spirit of God," or does the whole phrase, "made firm . . . by the spirit," show a connection partly with the LXX. of Ps. xxxiii. 6, *τῷ λόγῳ κυρίῳ οἱ οὐρανοὶ ἐστερεώθησαν καὶ τῷ πνεύματι τοῦ στόματος κτλ.*

Hast called . . . that which did not yet exist. Cf. xlviii. 8, "with a word Thou quickenest that which was not." We seem to have here creation *ex nihilo.* On the other hand the words above are found in Philo, *de Justitia, τὰ γὰρ μὴ ὄντα ἐκάλεσεν εἰς τὸ εἶναι.* This may be accidental. At any rate the fundamental principles of the two writers are different; for, except in the *De Somno*, i. 13, Philo taught the formation of the world from pre-existent elements. See Slav. En. xxiv. 2; xxv. 1, notes. Such expressions as that in the text spring from the repeated "and God said," Gen. i. Cf. Ps. cxlviii. 5; Philo, *de sacrif. Abel et Cain, ὁ γὰρ θεὸς λέγων ἅμα ἐποίει, μηδὲν μεταξὺ ἀμφοῖν τιθείς.* In 2 Pet. iii. 5, "There were heavens from of old, and an earth compacted out of water . . . by the word of God," we have the same teaching, with the additional idea that the solid earth was made from the water, as in the Slav. En. xxviii. 2.

which Thou art doing. 6. Thou that rulest with great thought the powers that stand before Thee: (yea) rulest with indignation the holy living creatures, who are without number, which Thou didst make from the beginning, of flame and fire, which stand around Thy throne. 7. To Thee only does this belong that Thou shouldst do forthwith whatsoever Thou dost wish. 8. Who causest the drops of rain to rain by number upon the earth, and alone knowest the consummation of the times before they come: have respect unto my prayer. 9. For Thou alone art able to sustain all who are, and those who pass away, and those who are to be, those who sin, and those who are righteous [as

6. *Powers that stand before Thee.* Cf. xlviii. 10; 4 Ezra viii. 21*a*, "cui adstat exercitus angelorum."

Creatures, who are without number. lix. 11.

Which Thou didst make from the beginning. In Jub. ii. 2, the creation of the angels is assigned to the first day—evidently on the ground of Job xxxviii. 7. According to *Targ. Jer.* I. on Gen. i. 26, and *Shemoth rabba*, 15, God created the angels on the second day. So also Slav. En. xxix. 1.

7. Pss. cxv. 3; cxxxv. 6; Jonah i. 14.

8. *The drops of rain to rain by number.* Cf. lix. 5; Ecclus. i. 2; Slav. En. xlvii. 5, note.

Alone knowest the end of the times. Cf. liv. 1.

9. *Those who sin, and those who are righteous.* For "who are righteous" the Syriac reads here and in xxiv. 2 ܕܡܙܕܕܩܝܢ = "who are justified" = οἱ δικαιοῦνται, and in xxi. 11, 12; lxii. 7, ܐܙܕܕܩܘ = "have been justified" = δεδικαιωμένοι εἰσιν. In all these passages the Syriac is at fault, but its error is to be traced to the Greek Version; for the Greek translator mistranslated the Hebrew before him, which was in the former case הצדקים, and in the latter צדקו. The grounds for this conclusion are as follows: (i.) The antithesis to "those who sin" is not "those who are justified," but "those who do righteousness" or "are righteous." (ii.) If "those who are justified" was the true text, then its antithesis would not be "those who sin," as we find it in xxi. 9, 11, 12; xxiv. 2, but "those who are condemned," as in li. 1 and 4 Ezra iv. 18. (iii.) But since "those who sin" is undoubtedly original, the error must lie in the phrase "those who are justified." (iv.) Now this error is easy to explain. From the LXX. we know that צדק was generally rendered by δικαιοῦσθαι, and only in a few cases by δίκαιος εἶναι (Job ix. 2, 15; x. 15; xv. 14; xxv. 4; xxxiii. 12; xxxiv. 5;

living (and) being past finding out]. 10. For Thou alone dost live immortal and past finding out, and knowest the number of mankind. 11. And if in time many have sinned, yet others not a few have been righteous. 12. Thou knowest where Thou preservest

xxxv. 36). The Greek translator, not appreciating the right meaning of צדק in our Apocalypse, gave it the sense he was most familiar with, and so mistranslated it by *δικαιοῦσθαι*. (v.) The above conclusions receive confirmation from the fact that the antithesis in our emended text is actually found in Job x. 15 and xxxv. 36, 37. I have emended the text accordingly in xxi. 9, 11, 12; xxiv. 1, 2; lxvii. 2.

The doctrine of justification in this Apocalypse differs from that taught in 4 Ezra.

(1) In Baruch men are justified by the law: thus the text in li. 3 = *ἐδικαιώθησαν ἐν τῷ νόμῳ μου* (where *μου = τοῦ θεοῦ*), and in lxvii. 6 it = *ἡ δικαιοσύνη ἡ ἐκ τοῦ νόμου*, and in lxxxi. 7 it = *ἐσώθησαν ἐν τοῖς ἔργοις αὐτῶν*. In Ezra, on the other hand, the expression "salvation by works" is qualified by the addition of "and by faith." Cf. ix. 7; xiii. 23. In fact we do not find there either expressed or implied the doctrine of justification by works. (2) Quite in keeping with what precedes is the absolute assurance of salvation on the part of Baruch. He never personally dreads condemnation: he looks forward calmly to a life of future blessedness. Cf. xiii. 3; xxv. 1; xlvi. 7; lxxvi. 2. Ezra, on the other hand, continually assumes his future woe till assured otherwise in viii. 47-49, 51-54. 4 Ezra xiv. does not belong to the rest of the book. There is a pessimistic outlook in Ezra as there is an optimistic one in all Baruch save S (*i.e.* x. 6-xii.) The note on xiv. 7 of this book will confirm the view above taken.

In 4 Ezra "to justify" preserves its ordinary meaning of "to declare just" in iv. 18 and xii. 7. It is used in this sense also in Ecclus. i. 22; vii. 5; x. 29; xiii. 22; xviii. 22; xxxi. 5; xlii. 2. In 4 Ezra, however, we find another use: thus in x. 16 it = "to vindicate as just." So also in Ps. li. 4; Isa. xlii. 21 (?); Pss. Sol. ii. 16; iii. 5; iv. 9; viii. 7, 27, 31; ix. 3; Luke vii. 29; Apoc. Baruch lxxviii. 5. On the word *δικαιοῦν* the reader can consult with advantage Sanday and Headlam's *Romans*, pp. 28-31. On the teaching on faith in A^3, *i.e.* chaps. liii.-lxxiv., see liv. 25, note.

As living . . . out. This I bracket as a dittography. See next line.

10. *Knowest the number of mankind.* Gen. xxiii. 4, 5; xlviii. 4, 6.

11. Men many have sinned, but many also have been justified.

Others not a few have been righteous. This statement differs strongly from that given in 4 Ezra viii. 3, where it is said plainly that whereas "multi quidem creati sunt, pauci autem salvabuntur," and that the ratio of the saved to the lost is as the amount of gold in the earth to that of the clay in it (viii. 2). This optimism which we have observed already (see xxi. 9, note) differentiates Baruch from Ezra. The latter is in the main pessimistic both with regard to his own destiny (till otherwise reassured by God) and that of the vast bulk of mankind.

12, 13. But this life is not all; sin and righteousness have further

the end of those who have sinned, or the consummation of those who have been righteous. 13. For if there were this life only, which here belongs to all men, nothing could be more bitter than this. 14. For of what profit is strength that turns to weakness, or the food of plenty that turns to famine, or beauty that turns to a hateful (thing)? 15. For the nature of man is always changeable. 16. For we have by no means been from the beginning what we now are, and what we now are we shall not afterwards remain. 17. For if a consummation had not been prepared for all, in vain would have been their beginning. 18. But regarding everything that comes from Thee, do Thou inform me, and regarding everything about which I ask Thee, do Thou enlighten me. 19. How long will that which is corruptible remain, and how long will the time of

issues; else the life of the righteous here were a crowning bitterness.

13. This verse may be drawn from 1 Cor. xv. 19, or else both from a common source. Of what worth is life? for (1) it is subject to constant change (xxi. 14, 15); and (2) is likewise mortal (xxi. 16, 17, 22).

14. *Strength that turns*, etc. lxxxiii. 11.

Beauty that turns to a hateful (thing). lxxxiii. 12.

15. There is no fixity in the being of man: he is the creature of change. In ver. 22, which should follow verses 17, 18, man is by appointment mortal.

16. The text is corrupt. The above rendering rests on an emendation of the text. Thus for ܐܘ ܠܐ ܡܕܡ ܐܝܟ ܡܢܐ ܕܐܝܬܝܢ ܗܘܐ ܓܝܪ ܡܢ ܫܘܪܝܐ . ܗܫܐ ܠܐ ܐܝܬܝܢ. I have read ܠܐ ܡܕܡ ܓܝܪ ܐܝܟ ܡܢܐ ܕܐܝܬܝܢ ܗܫܐ ܗܘܝܢ ܡܢ ܫܘܪܝܐ. This restores, I believe, the original sense (cf. ver. 15). As the text stands it = "aut nihil, sicuti quod sumus, est enim ab initio, nunc non sumus" (Ceriani).

17. Ver. 22 may have originally followed this verse.

19. *How long will that which is corruptible remain?* If this question comes from the final editor, its answer will be found in xl. 3; lxxiv. 3. But if it belongs to B^{3}, its answer would naturally be found in xxiii. 7 - xxiv. 1; xxxi. 5. The writers of this book (particularly the writer of B^{2}) are greatly impressed with the corruptibility of the present world. The whole present world, the *olam hazzeh*, belongs

mortals be prospered, and until what time will those who transgress in the world be polluted with much wickedness? 20. Command therefore in mercy, and accomplish all that Thou saidst Thou wouldst bring, that Thy might may be made known to those who think that Thy long-suffering is weakness. 21. And show to those who know not, and let them see that it has befallen us and our city until now according to the long-suffering of Thy power, because on account of Thy name Thou hast called us a beloved people. 22. Every nature therefore from this onward is mortal.

to the sphere of corruption. Even so does the Messianic kingdom if it falls within the *olam hazzeh*, as it does in A[1], A[2], and A[3] in this book. Thus in A[2] the Messianic reign forms the end of the world of corruption (xl. 3), and in A[3], the end of corruption and the beginning of incorruption (lxxiv. 3). In B[2] all that has been is doomed to corruption (xxxi. 5); all that is corruptible will perish (xliv. 9); the new world that awaits them will not turn them to corruption (xliv. 12). In B[3] what the righteous have lost was corruptible, but what they will receive is incorruptible (lxxxv. 5). The only reference to this subject in B[1] is where Baruch is told that he will pass away from the earth and forget all that is corruptible (xliii. 2). As to the remaining passages where this word recurs, the text is doubtful in xlviii. 29, and probably interpolated in xxviii. 5. In 4 Ezra vii. 113, the day of judgment is the end of this period and the beginning of the next immortal period. See also iv. 11; vii. 111.

Who transgress. These words could be rendered "who pass away," as in verse 9.

20. This is a prayer for the hastening of the final judgment (cf. 2 Pet. iii. 4-9).

21. The text is unintelligible as it stands: "Show to those who know not, and they have seen what has befallen us and our city until now according to the longsuffering," etc. Merely by the emendation of ܘܚܙܘ = "and they have seen," into ܕܗܘܐ = "and that it has been," we arrive at a perfectly consistent text. The fall of Jerusalem was brought about in the mercy of God to hasten the final judgment. See verse 23; xx. 2.

But, if the text is correct, it = καὶ ἑωράκασιν = וראו. Have we here an instance of the Hebrew perfect with strong waw used as a continuation of the imperative? In that case the original may have been הודיע . . . וראו את אשר נקרה לנו = "Show . . . and let them see that it has happened to us." I have emended accordingly.

A beloved people. Cf. v. 1.

22. It is obvious that this verse breaks the connection of thought. It should be read after verse 17 as

23. Reprove therefore the angel of death, and let Thy glory appear, and let the might of Thy beauty be known, and let Sheol be sealed so that from this time forward it may not receive the dead, and let the treasuries of souls restore those which are enclosed in them. 24. For there have been many years like those that are desolate from the days of Abraham and Isaac and Jacob, and of all those who are like them, who sleep in the earth, on whose account Thou didst say that Thou hadst created the world. 25. And now quickly show Thy glory, and do not defer

suggested above. It is possible that ܗܟܐ is corrupt for ܗܢܐ. We should then translate, "Every one, therefore, according to this law is mortal" (cf. ver. 15).

23. The writer in 20, 21, urged God to bring on the final judgment, that His power might be made known, and that men might learn that Israel's calamities had befallen them in the mercy of God. With a view to this final judgment the writer prays to God to put an end to death, to let His glory appear, and the dead arise.

23. *The angel of death.* Cf. Rev. vi. 8. On the prominent *rôle* played by this angel in later Jewish writings, see *Testament of Abraham* (ed. James); Weber, 239-242, 244, 247 262, 321, 322, 378; Eisenmenger, *Entdecktes Jud.* i. 854, 855, 862-879.

Sheol. See xi. 6, note.

Be sealed. Cf. Isa. v. 14.

Treasuries of souls. Only the righteous souls were admitted to these treasuries or chambers. I have preserved the literal meaning of the original word. These are the places in which God *treasures* His righteous ones, or their righteous acts. After the death of a righteous man his soul was permitted during seven days to behold the seven ways of the righteous and the seven ways of the wicked. After so doing, the soul entered these chambers (4 Ezra vii. 101; iv. 35). These chambers were in Sheol (4 Ezra iv. 41); only righteous souls could enter them (4 Ezra vii. 80); they were guarded by angels, and were full of rest (Eth. En. c. 5; 4 Ezra vii. 95); at the final judgment they were to restore the souls committed to them (Apoc. Bar. xxi. 3; xxx. 2; 4 Ezra vii. 32, 80). It is to be observed that as there were treasuries of righteous souls, so there were treasuries of righteous works (see xxiv. 1).

It is strange that only the righteous souls are here mentioned. The reference to the wicked may be lost.

24. This verse should in all probability be read after ver. 19. It would there form a good link between vers. 19 and 20. If this is not so the text seems corrupt.

Sleep in the earth. See xi. 4, note.

On whose account, etc. See xv. 7, note; xiv. 18, note.

what has been promised by Thee." 26. And it came to pass that when I had completed the words of this prayer that I was greatly weakened.

XXII. And it came to pass after these things that lo! the heavens were opened, and I saw, and power was given to me, and a voice was heard from on high, and it said unto me: 2. "Baruch, Baruch, why art thou troubled? 3. He who travels by a road but does not complete it, or he who departs by sea but does not arrive at the port, can he be comforted? 4. Or he who promises to give a present to another, but does not fulfil it, is it not robbery? 5. Or he who sows the earth, but does not reap its fruit in its season, does he not lose everything? 6. Or he who plants a plant, unless it grows till the time suitable to it, does he who planted it expect to receive fruit from it? 7. Or a woman who has conceived, if she bring forth untimely, does she not assuredly slay her infant? 8. Or he who builds a house, if he does not roof it and com-

25. *What has been promised by Thee.* *I.e.* "the world which Thou hast promised them" (xiv. 13; cf. lxxxiii. 5). The new world would become the dwelling of the righteous after the judgment.

26. *I was greatly weakened.* This weakness follows again on the prayer in xlviii. 25; cf. 4 Ezra v. 14.

XXII. 1. *The heavens were opened and I saw.* Ezek. i. 1; cf. Matt. iii. 16; John i. 52; Rev. iv. 1; Acts vii. 56.

A voice was heard, etc., *i.e.* the *bath-qôl.* Cf. xiii. 1; Matt. iii. 17; xvii. 5; Rev. iv. 1.

3-8. In xxii. 3, 5, God rejoins that no man undertakes a work without hoping to enjoy its results, and that no work can be duly judged till it is completed (xxii. 8). Thus Baruch's depreciation of this life (xxi. 13-17, 22) is in some fashion answered. Things must be judged in the light of their consummation. Again, in reply to Baruch's request to hasten the period of judgment (xxi. 19, 24, 20, 21, 23, 25), God rejoins that, for the due accomplishment of any work, time is needed (xxii. 6, 7). Finally, to Baruch's plea for the fulfilment of the divine promise (xxi. 25), God acknowledges the obligation of that promise (xxii. 4).

7. *Does . . . assuredly slay.* A Hebraism. Text = הרוג יהרג. Cf. xiii. 3; xli. 6; xlviii. 30, etc.

plete it, can it be called a house? Tell me that first."

XXIII. And I answered and said: "Not so, O LORD, my Lord." 2. And He answered and said unto me: "Why therefore art thou troubled about that which thou knowest not, and why art thou ill at ease about things in which thou art ignorant? 3. For as thou hast not forgotten the people who now are and those who have passed away, so I remember those who are remembered, and those who are to come. 4. Because when Adam sinned and death was decreed against those who should be born, then

XXIII. 1, 2. Baruch having admitted the justice of the divine reasons, God rejoins in the words of xxii. 3, "Why therefore art thou troubled?" for Baruch thereby acknowledges his ignorance of the things in question.

3. It is hard to see the relevance of this verse to any of Baruch's representations. Baruch has never doubted the ultimate fulfilment of the divine promises.

Who are remembered and those who are to come. The Syriac here ܕܡܬܥܗܕܝܢ ܘܡܛܝܒܝܢ ܕܐܬܝܢ seems corrupted from ܕܡܛܝܒܝܢ ܕܢܐܬܘܢ = "who are appointed to come."

4. *When Adam sinned and death was decreed against*, etc. There are two different conceptions of man's original destiny and of the *physical* effect of Adam's sin upon it in two of the different constituents of this book. (1) Thus in B², *i.e.* in xvii. 3; xix. 8; xxiii. 4, Adam's sin brought in physical death, otherwise man would have been immortal. We find the same view in Ecclus. xxv. 24 ἀπὸ γυναικὸς ἀρχὴ ἁμαρτίας, καὶ δι' αὐτὴν ἀποθνήσκομεν πάντες, though this view cannot be reconciled with the main teaching and tendencies of that book, which are to the effect that man was mortal from the outset (cf. xiv. 17; xvii. 1, 2; xl. 11). The conditional immortality of man appears next in Eth. En. lxix. 11; Book of Wisdom i. 13, 14; ii. 23, 24; Slav. En. xxx. 16, 17 (see notes *in loc.*); in 4 Ezra iii. 7, "Et huic (*sc.* Adamo) mandasti diligentiam unam tuam: et praeterivit eam, et statim instituisti in eum mortem et in nationibus ejus." It is likewise the Pauline view (cf. Rom. v. 12; 1 Cor. xv. 21). In the Talmud this was the prevailing view; thus, according to the *Beresh. rabba*, c. 9, Adam was not originally destined for death (*Pesikta*, 76*a*); if Adam had not sinned he would have lived for ever (see Weber, 214, 215, 239). (2) In A³, *i.e.* in liv. 15; lvi. 6, Adam is said to have brought in only *premature* death. This seems to be the view underlying Gen. ii., iii., though many, it is true, take it to be conditional immortality. But such an interpretation is difficult in the face

the multitude of those who should be born was numbered, and for that number a place was prepared where the living might dwell and the dead might be guarded. 5. Unless therefore the number aforesaid is fulfilled, the creature will not live again [for My spirit is the creator of life], and Sheol will receive the dead. 6. And again it is given to thee to hear what things are to come after these times. 7. For truly My redemption has drawn nigh, and is not far distant as aforetime.

of Gen. iii. 19. (3) It may be well to add here that a third view is occasionally taught in the Talmud. Death came into the world in consequence of divine predestination (see Edersheim, *Life and Times, etc.*, i. 166; Weber, 238, 239). On the *spiritual* effects of Adam's sin on his posterity, see xlviii. 42, note. On the whole question, see Sanday and Headlam, *Romans*, 136-138.

The multitude of those who should be born was numbered. This was a secret known only to God (xxi. 10; xlviii. 46). How this number was fixed upon is not recorded. It could not be added to or diminished; for the judgment could not come till it was completed (xxiii. 5; 4 Ezra iv. 33-43).

For that number a place was prepared. Cf. Slav. En. xlix. 2: "There has not been even a man in his mother's womb, for whom a place has not been prepared for every soul"; and lviii. 5: "There is a special place for mankind for all the souls of men according to their number." So in the Tractate *Chagiga*, fol. 15, col. 1; *Torath Adam*, fol. 101, col. 3; *Avodath hakkodesh*, fol. 19, col. 1, it is said that a place is prepared for every man either in Paradise or hell (Eisenmenger, ii. 315).

The dead might be guarded. The righteous were in "the treasuries of souls" guarded by angels (Eth. En. c. 5; 4 Ezra vii. 85, 95); the wicked in places of punishment guarded likewise by "those who keep the keys and are the guardians of the gates of hades standing like great serpents, and their faces are like quenched lamps, and their eyes fiery" (Slav. En. xlii. 1).

5. Not till the secret number of mankind is fulfilled can the resurrection take place. In Rev. vi. 11 and 4 Ezra iv. 36 the consummation of the world will follow, not when the number of mankind, but of the saints, is fulfilled. According to the *Shemoth rabba*, c. 39 (cf. *Aboda Sara*, 5*a*), all the generations of mankind were contained in a register called the ספר תולדות of Adam. And (*Beresh. rabba*, c. 24; *Wajjikra rabba*, c. 15) not until all the souls still dwelling in the גוף הנשמות, and included in the above register, had been born in the flesh should the Messiah come (*i.e.* the end of the world). See Weber, 335.

Sheol will receive. Cf. xxi. 23; xi. 6, note.

7. Cf. lxxxii. 2; Luke xxi. 28; 1 Pet. iv. 7.

XXIV. "For behold! the days come and the books will be opened in which are written the sins of all those who have sinned, and again also the treasuries in which the righteousness of all those who have been

XXIV. 1. *Behold! the days come.* See xx. 1, note.

The books will be opened. Dan. vii. 10; Eth. En. xc. 20; Rev. xx. 12; 4 Ezra vi. 20. The books mentioned here contain only a record of the sins of sinners, as in Eth. En. xc. 20. This is probably the case also in Rev. xx. 12: "And books were opened." In the last passage the succeeding words have to do with the lot of the righteous: "And another book was opened which (is the book) of life." This book of life is mentioned also in Eth. En. xlvii. 3; cviii. 3. The books that are spoken of in Dan. vii. 10; 4 Ezra vi. 20, may be records both of the righteous and the wicked.

The treasuries in which, etc. See xxi. 23, note. Divine "treasuries" or "storehouses" are a familiar idea in the O.T. Thus we have treasuries of rain (Deut. xxviii. 12), of snow and hail (Job xxxviii. 22), of wind (Jer. x. 13; li. 16; Ps. cxxxv. 7), of the sea (Ps. xxxiii. 7); see also Eth. En. lx. 11, 19, 20, 21; 4 Ezra vi. 40. Again the idea of laying up spiritual things in store is found in the LXX. Thus in Prov. i. 18 *θησαυρίζουσιν ἑαυτοῖς κακά*, and still more clearly in Pss. Sol. ix. 9 *θησαυρίζει ζωὴν ἑαυτῷ παρὰ κυρίῳ.* The last passage belongs to a time when heaven had come to be regarded as the true home and destination of the righteous. Naturally, when this was the belief of the faithful, their highest thoughts, aspirations, and efforts would be directed thither, and thus Ezra is assured: "Tibi thesaurus operum repositus apud Altissimum" (4 Ezra vii. 77), and the righteous are those qui fidem thesaurizaverunt (vi. 5); they would lay up treasures in heaven (Matt. vi. 19, 20). By a faithless life, on the other hand, men "treasured up for themselves wrath against the day of wrath" (Rom. ii. 5). Finally, the deeds of the righteous were regarded as gathered in "treasuries," as in our text. The expression is found in another sense in xliv. 14. We should observe that אוצר and *θησαυρός* alike mean a treasure and the place where it is stored.

The righteousness of all, etc. As Dr. Sanday writes (*Romans*, p. 29): "For a Jew the whole sphere of righteousness was taken up by the Mosaic Law. His one idea of righteousness was that of conformity to this law. Righteousness was for him essentially obedience to the law." That these words are true of the conception of righteousness entertained by the writers of this book will be seen by a perusal of the note on xiv. 7. But naturally the conception of righteousness varied accordingly as it was used by the legalistic or the prophetical wing, if I may so speak, of Pharisaism. With the strict Legalists righteousness meant the fulfilment first and mainly of ceremonial observances, and secondly, but only in a very subordinate degree, of works of mercy. See, for instance, the Book of Jubilees. With the prophetical wing, from which emanated most of the Messianic Apocalypses, righteousness was taken in its large sense as the fulfilment of

righteous in creation is gathered. 2. For it will come to pass at that time that thou shalt see—and many that are with thee—the long-suffering of the Most High, which has been throughout all generations, who has been long-suffering towards all those born that sin and are righteous." 3. And I answered and said: "But, behold! O Lord, no one knows the number of those things which have passed nor yet of those things which are to come. 4. For I know indeed that which has befallen us, but what will happen to our enemies I know not, and when Thou wilt visit Thy works."

moral duties and only in a very secondary degree of ceremonial. The Ethiopic and Slavonic Books of Enoch are illustrations of the latter statement. In some books it is hard to determine the pre-eminence of either tendency.

Who have been righteous. See note on xxi. 9.

2. I have already shown on p. 20 that xxiv. 2-4 probably followed originally on xx.

Thou shalt see—and many, etc. See note on xiii. 5.

Sin and are righteous. Both verbs depend on the same subject.

3, 4. In the preceding verse God had just assured Baruch that he and many with him should ultimately see the long-suffering of God. Baruch rejoins when that time of recompense will be no man knows (ver. 3), but there is one thing he knows well, *i.e.* the present calamities of Israel. Hence he wishes to know (*a*) what fate is in store for the Gentiles who inflicted these, and (*b*) when will it take effect. The answer to (*a*) is given in xiii. 3*b*-12. Just before xiii. 3*b* some statement such as "retribution will come upon your enemies who are now prospering," has been lost. Then follows xiii. 3*b*-12, in which Baruch is told that a special *rôle* is assigned him in reference to the enemies of Israel. He is to be preserved till the end of the times to testify to these cities, when the threatened retribution has befallen them, the reason of such retribution, the thoroughness with which it will be carried out, and the time of its consummation. Then in xxv. comes the answer to Baruch's second question: "When wilt Thou visit Thy works?" Baruch is to be preserved to play a part in this respect also (xxv. 1).

Befallen us. For ܕܓܕܫܢܝ = "what has befallen me," I have read ܕܓܕܫܢ = "what has befallen us?" The same corruption of the suffix appears in this MS. in lxxviii. 3 over against the right text in nine MSS.

Visit Thy works. xx. 2, note. The reference here is to the final judgment.

XXV. And He answered and said unto me: "Thou too shalt be kept safely till that time till that sign which the Most High will work for the inhabitants of the earth in the end of days. 2. This therefore will be the sign. 3. When a stupor shall seize the inhabitants of the earth, and they shall fall into many tribulations, and again when they shall fall into great torments. 4. And it will come to pass when they will say in their thoughts by reason of their much tribulation: 'The Mighty One doth no longer remember the earth'—yea, it will come to pass when they abandon hope, that the time will then awake."

XXVI. = E.

XXVI. And I answered and said: "Will that tribulation which is to be continue a long time, and will that necessity embrace many years?"

XXVII.-XXX. 1 = A[1].

XXVII. And He answered and said unto me:

XXV. In this chapter we have an answer to Baruch's question: "When wilt Thou visit Thy works?"

XXV. 1. In xiii. 3*b* Baruch was to be preserved to testify against the Gentiles. He has also a further function: observe the "too."

Till that time till that sign which. The sign is the stupor that will come on the inhabitants of the earth.

The inhabitants of the earth. This phrase is always used in a bad ethical sense in Baruch. Cf. xxv. 2; xlviii. 32, 40; liv. 1; lv. 2; lxx. 2, 10: generally in 4 Ezra; cf. iii. 34, 35; iv. 39; v. 6; vi. 24; vii. 72; x. 59; xiii. 30; but in vi. 18, 26; xi. 5, 32, 34; xii. 24, the sense of the phrase is merely geographical. For the various meanings of this phrase in the Eth. En. and Rev., see Eth. En. pp. 43, 111.

3, 4. When stupor and despair have seized the inhabitants of the earth, the time of the judgment has come.

3. *Stupor.* Cf. lxx. 2. This is rendered *excessus mentis* in 4 Ezra xiii. 30. For the diction, cf. Jer. viii. 21.

4. At the end of the tribulation and torments of the inhabitants of the earth the time of the judgment has come (cf. xiii. 8). This leaves no room for the Messianic kingdom in xxix., which precedes the judgment.

XXVI. This chapter is an addition of the final editor in order to introduce xxvii.-xxx. 1. xxv. was originally followed by xiv.-xix.

XXVII.-XXX. 1. We have here a fragment of a Messiah Apocalypse which for convenience of reference we designate A[1]. Its (1) chief

"Into twelve parts is that time divided, and each one of them is reserved for that which is appointed for it. 2. In the first part there will be the beginning of commotions. 3. And in the second part (there will be) slayings of the great ones. 4. And in the third part (there will be) the fall of many by death. 5. And in the fourth part the sending of desolation. 6.

characteristics, (2) its date, and (3) its points of divergence from B^1 and B^2 are as follows:—(1) After a terrible period of tribulation (*i.e.* the travel pains of the Messiah) (xxvii.-xxviii. 1) which should imperil the salvation even of the elect (xxviii. 3), and should prevail over all the earth (xxviii. 7-xxix. 1), a glorious kingdom, accompanied with every possible blessing, was to be established under the Messiah (xxix. 3-8), who after a reign of indefinite duration should return in glory into heaven (xxx. 1*a*). Thereupon the resurrection was to follow (xxx. 1*b*). The outlook is hopeful and thoroughly optimistic. (2) The later limit of composition is easy to determine. (*a*) Since the kingdom is to be established in Palestine, and only those Jews who are found there are to share in it, it is clear that there has been no dispersion of the Jews; for had there been, as it was in the case of B^1, we should here be told of a return from exile. Hence this fragment was written before 70 A.D. (*b*) Again, since Palestine is the scene of the kingdom, Jerusalem must still be standing; for in case it had fallen, we should here be told of its restoration, as in B^1, or of the setting up of the new Jerusalem, as in 4 Ezra xiii. 36. The Messianic kingdom could not be set up over the ruins of the holy city. Hence, again, we conclude that A^1 was written before 70 A.D. (3) Its points of divergence from B^1 and B^2 are obvious. In the latter, Jerusalem is destroyed and its people in exile; whereas in A^1 Jerusalem is standing and the Jews are in their own land. Again, whereas the law is the centre of interest and expectation in B^2, and in a somewhat less degree in B^1 (see xv. 5, note), it is the Messiah that is such in A^1. Further, whereas there is not a single allusion to the Messiah in B^1 and B^2, there is not a single allusion to the law in A^1. This, indeed, may be partly due to the shortness of this fragment.

XXVII. 1. In A^3, *i.e.* liii.-lxxiv. and 4 Ezra xiv. 11, 12, there are similar twelvefold divisions; but in these it is the entire history of the world that is so divided, whereas in our text it is only the time of troubles preceding the advent of the Messiah. These troubles were popularly conceived as the travail pains of the Messiah חבלי המשיח. We find a list of such woes (ὠδῖνες, Matt. xxiv. 8) in xlviii. 31-37; lxx. 2-10; Matt. xxiv. 6-29, with synoptic parallels; 2 Tim. iii. 1; Jubilees xxiii. 13, 16-25; 4 Ezra v. 1-12; vi. 14-18, 20-24; *Orac. Sibyl.* iii. 796-807; see Weber, 336; Schürer, Div. II., vol. ii. 154-156. In the Gospels, however, these woes are to precede the second coming of Christ or the end of the world.

5. Cf. 4 Ezra v. 8; vi. 22. For *desolation* we might also render "the sword"; cf. 5 Ezra xv. 5.

And in the fifth part famine and the withholding of rain. 7. And in the sixth part earthquakes and terrors. 8. [Wanting.] 9. And in the eighth part a multitude of portents and incursions of the Shedim. 10. And in the ninth part the fall of fire. 11. And in the tenth part rapine and much oppression. 12. And in the eleventh part wickedness and unchastity. 13. And in the twelfth part confusion from the mingling together of all those things aforesaid. 14. For these parts of that time are reserved, and will be mixed one with another and will minister one to another. 15. For some will of themselves be of service, and they will receive from others, and from themselves and others they will be perfected, so that those may not understand who are upon the earth in those days of this consummation of the times.

XXVIII. "Nevertheless, whosoever shall understand will then be wise. 2. For the measure and reckoning of that time are two parts weeks of seven weeks." 3. And I answered and said: "It is good for a man

6. *Famine.* As a sign of the end, cf. lxx. 8; Matt. xxiv. 7; Mark xiii. 8; Luke xxi. 11.

7. *Earthquakes.* Cf. lxx. 8; Matt. xxiv. 7; Mark xiii. 8; Luke xxi. 11.

9. *Portents.* Cf. 4 Ezra vi. 21: "Et anniculi infantes loquentur vocibus suis, et praegnantes immaturos parient infantes, etc." But owing to the next words it would perhaps be better to render ܦܢܛܣܝܐ = φαντασίαι as "spectres."

The Shedim. See x. 8, note.

10. *The fall of fire.* Cf. lxx. 8; 4 Ezra v. 8. If with the reviser of the MS. we delete the ܘ before ܢܘܪܐ we should render "the fire will fall."

15. These verses are obscure. They are possibly corrupt. For "of this . . . times" we can equally well render "that this is the consummation of the times."

XXVIII. 1. This verse recalls Dan. xii. 10: "the wise shall understand."

2. I cannot interpret this verse.

3. This verse expresses the difficulty of faithfulness in the times just described. Cf. 4 Ezra xiii. 16-20: "Vae qui derelicti fuerint in diebus illis, et multo plus vae his

to come and behold, but it is better that he should not come lest he fall. 4. [But I will say this also. XXVIII. 4-5 =E.
5. 'Will he who is incorruptible despise those things which are corruptible, and whatever befalls in the case of those things which are corruptible, so that he might look only to those things which are not corruptible?']
6. But if, O Lord, those things shall assuredly come to pass which Thou hast foretold to me; if, moreover, I have found grace in Thy sight, show this also unto me. 7. Is it in one place or in one of the parts of the earth that those things are to come to pass, or will the whole earth experience (them)?"

XXIX. And He answered and said unto me: "Whatever will then befall will belong to the whole earth; therefore all who live will experience (them). 2. For at that time I will protect only those who are found in those self-same days in this land. 3. And it

qui non sunt derelicti! Qui enim non sunt derelicti, tristes erunt, intelligentes quae sunt reposita in novissimis diebus et non occurrentes eis . . . adtamen facilius est periclitantem venire in haec quam pertransire . . . et non videre quae contingent in novissimo." Only the righteous, the fittest survive. Cf. xli. 1; lxxv. 5; 4 Ezra vii. 46, 47; Matt. xxiv. 22; Mark xiii. 21. This verse looks forward to the blessings described in xxix. 4-8.

4, 5. I have bracketed these verses as an interpolation of the final editor. They break the connection of thought. Further, no account is taken of them either by Baruch to whom they are assigned, or by God to whom they are addressed. They are unreasonable and out of place in the presence of the sensuous picture of Messianic bliss which meets us in the next chapter. The real answer to Baruch's question here can be gathered from xliii. 2.

6. *If I have found grace*, etc. A familiar O.T. phrase (Gen. vi. 8; xix. 19, etc.; 4 Ezra v. 56; vii. 102; viii. 42; xii. 7).

XXIX. 2. *I will protect*, etc. Here God protects His people who are found in the Holy Land, whereas in A^2 it is the Messiah (xl. 2) in A^3 the Holy Land itself (lxxi. 1). In B^2 it is the law that protects the faithful, irrespective of their place of habitation (xxxii. 1; cf. 6 Ezra vii. 122).

Found . . . in this land. Cf. xl. 2; lxxi. 1; 4 Ezra xiii. 48, 49. A special blessing attached to residence in Palestine. It alone was to escape the woes that should befall

will come to pass when all is accomplished that was to come to pass in those parts, that the Messiah will then

all the earth besides. But this thought is found only in the sections of this book written prior to 70 A.D. Such ideas as to the sacrosanct and inviolable character of Palestine seem to have disappeared for a time from Jewish speculation with the desecration and destruction of Jerusalem by the Romans, unless where the Messiah was expected. Hence in B^2 it is the law that protects the faithful (xxxii. 1), and in 4 Ezra vii. 122 it is the glory of God; and this protection avails them irrespective of their place of dwelling. The special privileges attaching to the Holy Land reappear in the Talmud, but in another form. Thus three will inherit the world to come: he who dwells in the land of Israel, he who brings up his sons to the study of the law, and he who repeats the ritual blessing over the appointed cup of wine at the close of the Sabbath (*Pesachim*, fol. 113*a*). Again the merits of the fathers will not avail a man who leaves the land of Israel for an outside land (*Baba bathra*, fol. 91*a*). Further, those who died in the Holy Land should rise first in the resurrection (Weber, pp. 64, 352); hence it is called "the land of the living" (*Beresh. rab.* 74); if the righteous died in any other land their bodies would have to roll (מתגלגלים) through underground passages (מחילות) till they came to Palestine before they could be raised (Weber, 352; Eisenmenger, ii. 920, 921). It was for this reason that Jacob and Joseph (Eisenmenger, ii. 925) and the Rabbis, who were specially honoured (Weber, 64), were buried in Canaan. Nay more, residents in the land of Israel could procure the resurrection of their relatives who died among the Gentiles (Eisenmenger, ii. 900). That the righteous who were buried outside the limits of Palestine should rise is also stated (Weber, 352).

3. The *rôle* here assigned to the Messiah is a passive one like that in Eth. En. xc. 37, 38; 4 Ezra vii. 28, 29. In this respect it differs from that represented in A^2 and A^3, *i.e.* xxxvi.-xl.; lii.-lxxiv.; and in Eth. En. xxxvii.-lxx.; Pss. Sol. xvii., xviii.; 4 Ezra xii. 32-34; xiii. 32-50, where the Messiah fights either with spiritual or material weapons on behalf of Israel, destroys its enemies, and sets up the Messianic kingdom.

The Messiah will then begin to be revealed. The phrase "begin to be revealed" seems corrupt. We should perhaps have "the principate of the Messiah will be revealed," as in xxxix. 7. We can get this by reading ܫܘܠܛܢܗ ܢܬܓܠܐ ܕܡܫܝܚܐ instead of ܢܫܪܐ ܕܢܬܓܠܐ ܡܫܝܚܐ. Cf. xli. 3. Or by simply reading ܢܫܝܐ ܕ instead of ܢܫܪܐ ܕ we have "Messiah the prince will be revealed." In this case the phraseology might be due to Dan. ix. 25. From a comparison of this verse and xxx. 1 the Messiah appears to be in heaven and is to be revealed from thence; but in other passages the implication of such language as "will be revealed" is merely that the Messiah may be already on earth and yet be unknown.

This emergence of the Messiah from concealment was a current view. Thus we find it in 4 Ezra vii. 28; xiii. 32; also in John vii. 27: "When the Christ cometh, no man knoweth whence he is." This concealment of the Messiah is mentioned also in Targum Jon. on Zech-

begin to be revealed. 4. And Behemoth will be revealed from his place, and Leviathan will ascend from

ariah iii. 8; vi. 12. In the Targum on Micah iv. 8 it is said to be due to the sins of the people. From Justin's *Dial. c. Tryph.* 8, it appears that though the Messiah may be already born, yet He may be unknown, and not even know His own calling till Elijah anoints and reveals Him. *Χριστὸς δέ, εἰ καὶ γεγένηται καὶ ἔστι που, ἄγνωστός ἐστι καὶ οὐδὲ αὐτός πω ἑαυτὸν ἐπίσταται οὐδὲ ἔχει δύναμίν τινα, μέχρις ἂν ἐλθὼν Ἠλίας χρίσῃ αὐτὸν καὶ φανερὸν πᾶσι ποιήσῃ.* Cf. also c. 110.

According to the Talmud, the Messiah was born at Bethlehem on the day of the destruction of the temple, was named Menahem, and afterwards suddenly carried away by a storm (*Hieros. Berachoth*, p. 5). His temporary abode, according to later writers, was to be Rome (*Sanhedrin*, 98*a*). On this subject see Lightfoot's *Horae* on Matt. ii. 1; Oehler's *Messias* in Herzog's *R.E.* ix. 668; Drummond, *The Jewish Messiah*, 293, 294; Schürer's *N.T. Times*, Div. II., vol. ii. 163, 164; Weber, 342, 343; Wünsche, *Die Leiden des Messias*, 57-59.

4. *And Behemoth will be revealed*, etc. The full form of this myth is given in 4 Ezra vi. 49-52: "Et tunc conservasti duo animalia, nomen uni vocasti Behemoth et nomen secundi vocasti Leviathan, Et separasti ea ab alterutro, non enim poterat septima pars ubi erat aqua congregata capere ea. Et dedisti Behemoth unam partem quae siccata est tertio die, ut inhabitet in ea, ubi sunt montes mille; Leviathan autem dedisti septimam partem humidam: et servasti ea ut fiant in devorationem quibus vis et quando vis." From a comparison of verse 4 with the verses just cited, it is clear that the words "from his place" and "from the sea" imply the account in these verses of Ezra. This is confirmed by the fact that not only is the thought the same, but also almost word for word the diction in the Syriac Versions of the two clauses: "Servasti ea ut fiant in devorationem" (4 Ezra vi. 52) and "kept them until that time and then they will be for food." Thus so far 4 Ezra would seem to be the source of our text. But if in these respects Baruch presupposes 4 Ezra, 4 Ezra in turn presupposes Baruch in the clauses: "Quibus vis et quando vis" (4 Ezra vi. 52) over against "for all that are left" in verse 4—the words "those who are left" being a technical phrase to express those who should survive to participate in the Messianic kingdom. We are thus led to assume that a short hexaemeron, closely resembling that found in 4 Ezra vi. 38-54, existed at one time independently, and that the writers of Ezra vi. 30-vii. 25 and Bar. xxvii.-xxx. laid it under contribution for their own purposes. (For a probable additional fragment of this hexaemeron, see xv. 7, note.) This assumption gains confirmation from the facts (1) that this hexaemeron cannot originally have proceeded from the writer of the Salathiel Apocalypse (*i.e.* the groundwork of 4 Ezra); for the latter looked for no Messianic kingdom, whereas the writer of this hexaemeron did as is obvious from vi. 52 compared with xxix. 4 of our text; and (2) that whereas A^1 of Baruch was written prior to the fall of Jerusalem, the Salathiel Apocalypse was written subsequently to it.

4. *Behemoth . . . and Leviathan.* In addition to the references in the preceding note, see Eth. En. lx. 7-9, 24, notes; Targ. Jon. on Gen.

the sea, those two great monsters which I created on the fifth day of creation, and I kept them until that time; and then they will be for food for all that are left. 5. The earth also will yield its fruit ten thousand-fold, and on one vine there will be a thousand branches,

i. 21: "And God created great beasts Leviathan and his wife which were prepared for the day of consolation;" see also the Targum on Ps. l. 10; Weber, 156, 195, 370, 384; Buxtorf, *Lexicon Chald. rabb. Talmud*, and Levy, *Chaldäisches Wörterbuch* and *Neuhebräisches Wörterb. in loc.*

All that are left. This is in fact "the remnant" that survives to share in the Messiah's kingdom. This remnant is frequently referred to in this sense (cf. xl. 2; 4 Ezra vi. 25; vii. 28; ix. 7; xii. 34; xiii. 48).

5. We have here another fragment of an old Apocalypse, of which we find a Latin version in Irenaeus, v. 33. This Apocalypse Papias, according to Irenaeus, assigned to our Lord. It is recounted in the fourth book of his Λογίων κυριακῶν ἐξήγησις. The passage in question is: "Venient dies, in quibus vineae nascentur, singulae decem millia palmitum habentes, et in uno palmite dena millia brachiorum, et in uno vero palmite dena millia flagellorum, et in unoquoque flagello dena millia botruum, et in unoquoque botro dena millia acinorum et unumquodque acinum expressum dabit vigintiquinque metretas vini. Et quum eorum apprehenderit aliquis sanctorum botrum, alius clamabit: Botrus ego melior sum, me sume, per me Dominum benedic." Scholars have taken our text to be the original of this passage. That this is unlikely, and that both may be derived from the same original source, I will now proceed to show. In the first place, the passage in Irenaeus contains two additional sentences: "Dena millia brachiorum . . . palmite," and "Et quum eorum . . . benedic." Hence a fuller text is presupposed than we have in Bar. xxix. 5. In the next place, immediately after the words just cited, the text in Irenaeus proceeds: "Similiter et granum tritici decem millia spicarum generaturum, et unamquamque spicam habituram decem millia granorum, et unumquodque granum quinque bilibres similae clarae mundae." With these words compare the Eth. En. x. 19, where, in an account of Messianic bliss, we find "The vine that is planted thereon will yield wine in abundance, and of all the seed which is sown thereon will each measure bear ten thousand." From this we conclude that for a long time prior to Christianity there existed either in tradition or in writing a sensuous description of Messianic felicity. In this description not only the fruitfulness of the vine was dwelt upon, but also of all seeds and fruit-bearing trees. Of this description the largest survival is in Irenaeus, v. 33, preserved through the agency of Papias; the fragmentary survivals in the Eth. En. x. 19 (see above) and in our text form complimentary portions of this tradition.

Finally, the text presents a syncretistic appearance. In xxix. 4 one description of food—a flesh diet—is provided for the members of the Messianic kingdom; and in the next verse quite another—a vegetable diet; and in xxix. 8 a heavenly food, *i.e.* manna. The second is a more ancient view than the first and

and each branch will produce a thousand clusters, and each cluster will produce a thousand grapes, and each grape will produce a cor of wine. 6. And those who have hungered will rejoice: moreover, also, they will behold marvels every day. 7. For winds will go forth from before Me to bring every morning the fragrance of aromatic fruits, and at the close of the day clouds distilling the dew of health. 8. And it will come to pass at that self-same time that the treasury of manna will again descend from on high, and they will eat of it in those years, because these are they who have come to the consummation of time.

the most reasonable, being a return to the food of Adam in Paradise.

As to the origin of the 10,000-fold yield of the corn and wine, etc., Mr. Rendel Harris (*Expositor*, 1895, pp. 448, 449) offers a most ingenious and probable suggestion. He derives it from the blessing of Isaac (Gen. xxvii. 28), where he conjectures that in the statement רֹב דָּגָן וְתִירֹשׁ = "plenty of corn and wine," the word רֹב was taken as רִבּוֹ = 10,000. He points out that the context in Irenaeus (see above), in which the story of Papias and the elders is given, supports his contention; for that it follows a discussion of the blessing in question.

Each branch . . . each cluster . . . each grape. Instead of "each" the Syriac in all three cases gives "one." But the sense requires "each," and in the Latin Version of this passage preserved in Irenaeus (see above) "each" is found in the three phrases, *i.e.* "unoquoque flagello, unoquoque botro, unumquodque acinum." The explanation is not far to seek. The Hebrew אחד which = εἷς, one, occasionally also = ἕκαστος, each. The former meaning was wrongly followed by the Greek translator. Hence the wrong turn in the Syriac.

A cor. This represents κόρος which in turn is a translation of כֹּר or חֹמֶר. The cor was equal to about 120 gallons. Cf. Joseph. *Ant.* xv. 9, 2 ὁ δὲ κόρος δύναται μεδίμνους ἀττικοὺς δέκα.

6. *Rejoice.* This is a characteristic of the members of the kingdom. Cf. 4 Ezra vii. 28; xii. 34.

Behold marvels. The belief that the Messiah would signalise His advent by marvels was general. Cf. 4 Ezra vii. 27; xiii. 50; Matt. xi. 4-6; Luke vii. 22, 23; John vii. 31.

8. *The treasury of manna will again descend,* etc. In Ps. lxxviii. 25 manna is called angels' food. In *Or. Sibyl.* vii. 149 it is to be the food of the members of the Messianic kingdom Μάννην τὴν δροσερὴν λευκοῖσιν ὀδοῦσι φάγονται, and in Rev. ii. 17 the idea is spiritualised: the faithful are to receive "hidden manna."

These are they, etc. These are "the remnant" of verse 4.

Consummation of time. This

XXX. "And it will come to pass after these things, when the time of the advent of the Messiah is fulfilled, and He will return in glory, then all who have
XXX. 2-XXXV. = B^2. fallen asleep in hope of Him shall rise again. 2. And it will come to pass at that time that the treasuries will be opened in which is preserved the number of the souls of the righteous, and they will come forth, and a multitude of souls will be seen together in one assemblage of one thought, and the first will rejoice and the last will not be grieved. 3.

phrase is found in xxvii. 15. The Messianic age forms the "consummation of the time or times" = ἡ συντελεία τοῦ αἰῶνος or τῶν αἰώνων. We should observe that this phrase has a different meaning in xxx. 3; but there we have the work of B^2.

XXX. 1. *When the time of the advent of the Messiah is fulfilled*, etc. This can have only one meaning, and this is that, at the close of His reign, the Messiah will return in glory to heaven. The word translated "advent" is ܡܐܬܝܬܗ which in turn was an ordinary rendering of παρουσία. Now παρουσία can mean not only "coming" or "advent," but also "presence" (cf. 2 Cor. x. 10; 2 Macc. xv. 21, and probably 2 Cor. vii. 6, 7; 2 Thess. ii. 9). Hence we should render: "When the time of the presence of the Messiah is fulfilled."

Return in glory. These words imply that the Messiah pre-existed in heaven before His advent. He returns whither He had come. This is also the teaching of Eth. En. xlvi. 1, 2; xlviii. 3 (see note); lxii. 7; 4 Ezra xii. 32; xiii. 26 (?); xiv. 9. This seems also to be the legitimate interpretation of Pss. Sol. xviii. 6 εἰς ἡμέραν ἐκλογῆς ἐν ἀνάξει χριστοῦ αὐτοῦ. In 4 Ezra vii. 29, 30, the Messiah and the righteous die at the close of the Messianic kingdom.

Then all who have fallen asleep in hope of Him shall rise again. The resurrection follows immediately on the return of the Messiah into heaven; on his death in 4 Ezra vii. 29, 30. The words "of him" cannot be original. The text was probably "those who have fallen asleep in hope." Cf. LXX. of Ps. xvi. 9 ἡ σάρξ μου κατασκηνώσει ἐπ' ἐλπίδι. The corruption could have arisen easily in the Syriac by a change of ܒܣܒܪܐ into ܒܣܒܪܗ.

Fallen asleep. Cf. xi. 4, note. As A^1 is fragmentary, we are not told what befalls the living righteous. In the following verses of B^2 only the destinies of *souls* are dealt with. The complementary half of this doctrine is given in l., li.

2. With this verse we return to B^2, resuming the text that ended with xxiv. 1. We have here an account of the general resurrection (cf. xlii. 8; l. 2).

Treasuries. See xxi. 23, note; xxiv. 1, note.

For he knows that the time has come of which it is said, that it is the consummation of the times. 4. But the souls of the wicked, when they behold all those things, shall then waste away the more. 5. For they will know that their torment has come and their perdition has arrived."

XXXI. And it came to pass after these things that I went to the people and said unto them: "Assemble unto me all your elders and I will speak

3. *The consummation of the times.* This phrase means here the final judgment; in A[1] it means the Messianic age (cf. xxvii. 15; xxix. 8).

4. *Waste away.* Cf. li. 5; 4 Ezra vii. 87.

5. This verse does not mean that the wicked souls have not hitherto suffered, but that their suffering hitherto is as nothing compared to the torments they shall now endure. Similarly, the righteous have in the treasuries of souls had rest and peace, but they too (cf. ver. 3) know that their real blessedness has now come. See xxxvi. 10.

XXXI.-XXXV. Baruch assembles and addresses the elders of the people (xxxi. 1-3); he exhorts them not to forget the anguish of Zion (xxxi. 4), and announces the coming end of all that is corruptible (xxxi. 5); and, in case they observe the law, their safety amid the convulsions which will accompany the renewal of the entire creation (xxxii. 1); they are not to grieve so much for the past as for the coming time; for then the strife and stress will exceed all that has been before when God renews creation (xxxii. 1, 5, 6). Thereupon, when Baruch seeks to dismiss the people (xxxii. 7), they remonstrate against his forsaking them (xxxii. 8 - xxxiii.) Baruch rejoins that he is not forsaking them, but only going to the Holy Place to get light from God (xxxiv.) He then proceeds thither and laments over Zion (xxxv.) A fast of seven days should follow here.

The subject on which Baruch addresses the people is to be found in each instance in the previous divine revelation (see v. 5; x. 4); but it will be observed that this address (xxxi. 3-xxxii. 6) is wholly out of relation to all that has gone before. There is therefore something wrong. The gist of this address is: (*a*) The end of all things corruptible is at hand; (*b*) if ye prepare your hearts to obey the law ye will then be safe in this time of crisis; (*c*) for the entire creation must be shaken, and give place to a new and incorruptible creation. Now these questions are discussed later in the dialogues between God and Baruch. Thus, for (*a*), see xlii. 6-8; for (*b*), see xlviii. 22-24, 38-41; for (*c*), see xlviii. 49; lii. 3, 8-9, 16. We therefore hold that xxxi.-xxxv. was read after lii. originally. Finally, xliv. 8-15 really forms the conclusion of Baruch's address in xxxi., xxxii.; it should be read immediately after xxxii. 6 (see p. 69).

XXXI. 1. *All your elders.* See xliv. 1, note.

words unto them." 2. And they all assembled in the valley of the Cedron. 3. And I answered and said unto them: "Hear, O Israel, and I will speak to thee, and give ear, O seed of Jacob, and I will instruct thee. 4. Forget not Zion, but hold in remembrance the anguish of Jerusalem. 5. For lo! the days come, when everything that exists will become the prey of corruption and be as though it had not been.

XXXII. "But ye, if ye prepare your hearts, so as to sow in them the fruits of the law, it will protect you in that time in which the Mighty One is to shake the whole creation. [2. Because after a little time the building of Zion will be shaken in order that it

XXXII. 2-4 = E.

2. *Cedron.* See v. 5, note.

3. *Hear, O Israel . . . and give ear, O seed of Jacob.* Cf. xvii. 4; xlvi. 4; 4 Ezra ix. 30. For the combination "hear . . . and give ear," see Isa. i. 2.

5. *Will become the prey of.* Literally = "will be taken to corruption." See xxi. 19, note.

XXXII. 1. *Prepare your hearts.* An O.T. phrase (cf. 1 Sam. vii. 3; Job xi. 13; Ps. lxxviii. 8). It is a favourite expression in B^1 and B^2 of this book; cf. xlvi. 5; lii. 7; lxxxiii. 8; lxxxv. 9, 11.

The fruits of the law. Cf. 4 Ezra iii. 20; ix. 32; see note on xv. 5.

It will protect. See xxix. 2, note. These words point back to xlviii. 22-24; cf. xliv. 13, 14; xlviii. 38-41.

Shake the whole creation. *I.e.* with a view to a new heavens and a new earth (see ver. 6). The thought comes originally from Haggai ii. 6; cf. Heb. xii. 26.

2-4. I have bracketed these verses as an interpolation; for in verse 2 it is announced that the temple will be destroyed after a little time; but, according to all B^2 as well as B^1, the temple has already been destroyed, and this is the presupposition of xxxi. 4. Again, verses 2-4 break the connection of thought in the text. Observe the awkwardness of "Because after a little time," etc., following on verse 1; and, on the other hand, how appropriately verse 5 follows on xxxi. 4-xxxii. 1. We should observe that there is nothing inconsistent in the idea of a heavenly Jerusalem being established on a new and incorruptible earth. Indeed, it is not impossible that iv. 2-7 originally followed xxxii. 6. We have a close parallel to xxxii. 2-4 in *Beresh rab.* 2, and *Pesikta,* 145*a*, where it is said that the temple was built in glory, destroyed, again rebuilt, but in mean fashion; finally, it should again be rebuilt in glory.

2. *Zion will be shaken.* *I.e.* in 588 by Nebuchadnezzar; but according to xxxi. 4; xxxii. 5; xxxiii. 2, 3; xxxv. 1, this is already in the past.

may again be built. 3. But that building will not remain, but will again after a time be rooted out, and will remain desolate until the time. 4. And afterwards it must be renewed in glory, and it will be perfected for evermore.] 5. Therefore we should not be distressed so much over the evil which has now come as over that which is still to be. 6. For there will be a greater trial than these two tribulations when the Mighty One will renew His creation. 7. And now do not draw near to me for a few days, nor seek me till I come to you." 8. And it came to pass when I had spoken to them all these words, that I, Baruch, went my way, and when the people saw me setting out, they lifted up their voice and lamented and said:

In order that it may again be built. *I.e.* by Ezra and Nehemiah.

3. *Again . . . be rooted out.* *I.e.* by the Romans in 70 A.D.

4. On the heavenly Jerusalem. See iv. 3, note.

5. *We should . . . be distressed.* I have here followed Bensly's emendation of ܢܟܡܪܢ into ܢܬܟܡܪܢ. Otherwise, we should render with Ceriani, "Non ergo debet nos contristare hoc omne super malo quod supervenit," etc.

The evil which has now come. The fall of Jerusalem.

6. *Two tribulations.* *I.e.* those accompanying the destruction of Jerusalem and the renewal of creation. But the more natural rendering is: "For there will be a greater trial than the two tribulations when," etc. If we must accept this, the words "than the two tribulations" are an addition of E, and without them the text would run: "For the trial will be great when," etc.

Renew His creation. This signifies an incorruptible world which was to take the place of the corruptible (cf. xxxi. 5; xliv. 12; lvii. 2). It was a current expectation from the times of the captivity (cf. Isa. lxv. 17; lxvi. 22; Eth. En. xlv. 4, note; lxxii. 1; xci. 15, 16; 4 Ezra vii. 75; Matt. xix. 28; 2 Pet. iii. 13; Rev. xxi. 1). This announcement of Baruch is the presupposition of li., lii., and the truth correlative to the renewal and transformation of the righteous in li.

7. *Do not draw near*, etc. 4 Ezra v. 19. This verse was preceded originally by xliv. 8-15 (see p. 69).

For a few days. These words refer to the interval in which the next fast of seven days should take place. The mention of this fast at the beginning or close of xxxv. has through some accident been omitted (see v. 7, note; ix. 2, note).

9. "Whither departest thou from us, Baruch, and forsakest us as a father who forsakes his orphan children, and departs from them?

XXXIII. "Are these the commands which thy companion, Jeremiah the prophet, commanded thee, and said unto thee: 2. 'Look to this people till I go and confirm the rest of the brethren in Babylon, against whom has gone forth the sentence that they should be led into captivity?' 3. And now if thou also forsakest us, it were good for us all to die before thee, and then that thou shouldst withdraw from us."

XXXIV. And I answered and said unto the people: "Far be it from me to forsake you or to withdraw from you, but I will only go unto the Holy of Holies to enquire of the Mighty One concerning you and concerning Zion, if in some respect I should receive more illumination: and after these things I will return to you."

XXXV. And I, Baruch, went to the holy place, and sat down upon the ruins and wept, and said: 2. "Become ye springs, O mine eyes, and ye, mine eyelids, a fount of tears. 3. For how shall I lament

9. *Cf.* 4 Ezra v. 18.

XXXIII. 1, 2. See x. 2, note, where I have shown that, according to B[1], Jeremiah does not seem to have gone to Babylon.

3. For another form of the same thought, cf. 4 Ezra xii. 44.

XXXIV. *Far be it from me to forsake you.* Cf. 4 Ezra xii. 48: "Si ergo tu nos dereliqueris, quanto erit nobis melius, si essemus succensi et nos in incendio Sion."

Holy of Holies. This is practically the same place as is mentioned in x. 5; in xxxv. 1 it is simply called the holy place. It is where the altar stood. See xxxv. 4.

XXXV. 1. *The holy place, and sat down upon the ruins.* See preceding note, and x. 5, note.

2. From Jer. ix. 1; cf. Eth. En. xcv. 1.

for Zion, and how shall I mourn for Jerusalem? 4. Because in that place where I am now prostrate, the high priest of old used to offer holy sacrifices, and to place thereon the smoke of the incense of fragrant odours. 5. But now our glorying has been made into dust, and the desire of our soul into sand."

XXXVI. And when I had said these things I fell XXXVI.-XL. $=A^2$.

THE SIXTH SECTION

XXXVI.-XLVI. This in reality forms the sixth part of this book. For the symmetry of the book as constructed by the final editor requires, as we have already shown (see v. 7, note, introduction to the fifth section, p. 36, and xxxii. 7, note), the insertion of a seven days' fast after xxxv., or possibly even before it. The omission of this fast may have been an original oversight of the editor, or may have been due to a careless copyist. The structure of this part is as follows:—First, the omitted fast, then a Messiah vision and its interpretation (xxxvi.-xl.), with further disclosures regarding apostates and proselytes (xli. 2-xlii. 8), and the announcement of Baruch's coming death (xliii.) Finally, Baruch's address to the people (xliv.-xlvi.)

This section is of very composite origin. Thus xxxvi.-xl. is a Messiah Apocalypse written prior to 70 A.D.; xliii.-xliv. 8; xlv.-xlvi. 6 belongs to B^1; the rest of the section mainly to B^2.

XXXVI.-XL. We have here the second Messiah Apocalypse A^2. (*a*) *Date of A^2 and its Relation to B^1 and B^2.* A^2 is quite distinct in its world-view and date from B^1 and B^2. We shall first establish the difference of date. Now whereas we have seen that B^1 and B^2 were written subsequent to the fall of Jerusalem, it is clear that A^2 was written prior to that event. For whereas, in a short historical outline from the rise of Babylon to the reign of the Messiah (xxxix. 2-xl. 2), the first destruction of Jerusalem is mentioned (xxxix. 3), there is not even a hint given as to its destruction by Rome, although the Roman oppression of Palestine is clearly indicated (xxxix. 5, 6). Again the Messiah makes Zion His capital (xl. 1). If it were in ruins, its restoration would of necessity be mentioned. Finally, as there is no allusion in A^2 to the second destruction of Jerusalem, so there is none to the subsequent dispersion after that event, and none to a return of the exiles. Consequently, as we find, the remnant of Israel is still in Palestine (xl. 2). It is wholly otherwise in B^1 and B^2.

As regards their difference of world-view, it will be sufficient here to remark that whereas there is no Messiah in B^1 and B^2, the Messiah is the centre of expectation and the stay of Israel in A^2. And whereas B^2 is pessimistic as regards this world, A^2 is optimistic. And whereas in B^2, and in a less degree in B^1, the law is the centre and the end of life, in A^2 this place is occupied by the Messiah.

(*b*) *Relation of A^2 to A^1.* The two writings come from different authors. In A^1 the Messiah has only a passive *rôle* assigned to Him; He does not appear till the enemies

asleep there, and I saw a vision in the night. 2. And lo! a forest of trees planted on the plain, and lofty mountains surrounded it and precipitous rocks, and that forest occupied much space. 3. And lo! over against it arose a vine, and from under it there went forth a fountain peacefully. 4. Now that fountain came to the forest and was (stirred) into great waves, and those waves submerged that forest, and suddenly they rooted out the multitude of (the trees) of that forest, and overthrew all the mountains which were round about it. 5. And the height of the forest began to be made low, and the top of the mountains was made low, and that fountain prevailed greatly, so that it left nothing of that great forest save one cedar only. 6. Also when it had cast it down and had destroyed and rooted out the multitude of (the trees of) that forest, so that nothing was left of it, nor could its place be recognised, then that vine began to come with the fountain in peace and great tranquillity, and it came to a place which was not far from the cedar, and they brought the cedar which had been cast down to it. 7. And I beheld and lo! that vine opened its mouth and spake and said to that cedar: "Art thou not that cedar which was left of the forest of wickedness, and by whose means wickedness persisted, and was wrought all those years, and goodness never. 8.

of Israel are destroyed. In A^2, on the other hand, the destruction of the wicked and the vindication of Israel is the sole work of the Messiah.

XXXVI. 1. It will be remarked that these visions are only found in A^2 and A^3. Elsewhere we have direct revelations.

I fell asleep. Cf. lii. 8.

And thou didst keep conquering that which was not thine, and to that which was thine thou didst never show compassion, and thou didst keep extending thy power over those who were far from thee, and those who drew nigh thee thou didst hold fast in the toils of thy wickedness, and thou didst uplift thyself always as one that could not be rooted out! 9. But now thy time has sped and thy hour is come. 10. Do thou also therefore depart, O cedar, after the forest, which departed before thee, and become dust with it, and let your ashes be mingled together. 11. And now recline in anguish and rest in torment till thy last time come, in which thou wilt come again, and be tormented still more."

XXXVII. And after these things I saw that cedar burning, and the vine growing, itself and all around it, the plain full of unfading flowers. And I indeed awoke and arose.

XXXVIII. And I prayed and said: "O LORD, my Lord, Thou dost always enlighten those who are led by understanding. 2. Thy law is life, and Thy

8. *Rooted out.* This phrase is constantly used in the Talmud with reference to the future fate of Rome. The word is עקר.

11. *In anguish,* etc. See xxx. 5, where as here the intermediate state is one involving certain degrees of happiness or pain.

XXXVII. *Unfading flowers.* Cf. Apoc. Pet. τὴν γῆν αὐτὴν ἀνθοῦσαν ἀμαράντοις ἄνθεσι.

XXXVIII. 1. *O LORD, my Lord.* See note on iii. 1. It is God Himself who interprets this vision for Baruch, but Ramiel who does so in A[3] (see lv. 3).

2. *Thy law is life.* Cf. xlv. 2; Ecclus. xlv. 5 νόμον ζωῆς καὶ ἐπιστήμης (also xvii. 11). With this sentiment cf. Hillel's words (*Aboth.* ii. 7): "The more law the more life . . . he who gains a knowledge of the law gains life in the world to come." As correlative expressions might be cited (John vii. 49), "This people, which knoweth not the law, is accursed," and Hillel's saying: "An unlearned man cannot be

wisdom is right guidance. 3. Make known to me therefore the interpretation of this vision. 4. For Thou knowest that my soul hath always walked in Thy law, and from my (earliest) days I departed not from Thy wisdom."

XXXIX. And He answered and said unto me: "This is the interpretation of the vision which thou hast seen. 2. As thou hast seen a great forest which lofty and precipitous mountains surrounded, this is the word. 3. Behold! the days come, and this kingdom will be destroyed which once destroyed Zion, and it will be subjected to that which comes after it. 4. Moreover, that also again after a time will be destroyed, and another, a third, will arise, and that also will have dominion for its time, and will be destroyed. 5. And after these things a fourth kingdom will arise, whose power will be harsh and evil far beyond those which were before it, and it will rule many times as the forests on the plain, and it will hold fast the times, and will

pious" (לא עם הארץ חסיד). He was even excluded from the resurrection (see Weber, 42-44). The words in the text, however, are far from being as strong as these statements. So we infer from the parallel, "Thy wisdom, etc."

Thy wisdom is right guidance. This is based upon the Massoretic text of Ecclesiastes x. 10, where the Versions take directions of their own. Thus the Heb. is יתרון הכשיר חכמה. The LXX. *καὶ περισσεία τοῦ ἀνδρείου σοφία*, and the Syr. = "et sapientia sollertibus emolumentum."

4. *From my (earliest) days.* This is the Hebrew idiom מִיָּמַי. Cf. 1 Kings i. 6; 1 Sam. xxv. 28.

XXXIX. 3-5. Of the four world empires here mentioned there can be no doubt as to the first and fourth. The first is of course the Babylonian, for it is that which effected the first destruction of Jerusalem in 588 (see ver. 3). The fourth (in verses 5-7; cf. xxxvi. 5-10) is just as clearly Rome. The second and third empires are probably the Persian and the Græco-Egyptian and Syrian. The fourfold division of world empires in the text is due no doubt to Dan. vii. On these four empires, see *Tanchuma, Terumah*, 7.

exalt itself more than the cedars of Lebanon. 6. And by it the truth will be hidden, and all those who are polluted with iniquity will flee to it, as evil beasts flee and creep into the forest. 7. And it will come to pass when the time of his consummation that he should fall has approached, then the principate of My Messiah will be revealed, which is like the fountain and the vine, and when it is revealed it will root out the multitude of his host. 8. And that which thou hast seen, the lofty cedar, which was left of that forest, and with regard to this fact, that the vine spoke those words with it which thou didst hear, this is the word.

XL. "The last leader of that time will be left alive, when the multitude of his hosts will be put to the sword and be bound, and they will take him up to Mount Zion, and My Messiah will convict him of all his impieties, and will gather and set before him all the works of his hosts. 2. And afterwards he will put

6. *The truth will be hidden.* Cf. 4 Ezra v. 1, where, in connection with Rome, the same statement is made: "abscondetur veritatis via."

7. *The principate of My Messiah,* etc. See xxix. 3, note.

XL. 1. Who this last leader is we cannot determine; it may be any emperor or general from 70 A.D. back till Pompey's time. Since the personal wrong-doings of this leader are dwelt upon, it is possible that it is actually Pompey that is here referred to. The words "his impieties" = ܪ̈ܘܫܥܘܗܝ, might favour this view (cf. Pss. Sol. ii. 24-35).

According to the Talmud, a single leader was to "unite in himself all hatred and hostility against God's people. He was to be called Armilus, and to be the רשיעא κατ' ἐξοχήν." See Weber, 348, 349.

My Messiah. As we have already remarked (pp. 52, 61), the Messiah here plays an active part as compared to the Messiah in A^1, *i.e.* xxvii.-xxx. 1. The protection of the remnant of Israel and the destruction of their enemies, which are here the work of the Messiah, are there assigned to God Himself, and the Messiah does not appear till these tasks are completed (see xxix. 3).

Will convict . . . of . . . impieties. So 4 Ezra xii. 32; xiii. 37.

him to death, and protect the rest of My people which shall be found in the place which I have chosen. 3. And his principate will stand for ever, until the world of corruption is at an end, and until the times aforesaid are fulfilled. 4. This is thy vision, and this is its interpretation."

XLI.-XLII. = B².

XLI. And I answered and said: "To whom will these things be, and how many (will they be)? or who will be worthy to live at that time? 2. For I will speak before Thee everything that I think, and I will ask of Thee regarding those things which I meditate. 3. For lo! I see many of Thy people who have withdrawn from Thy covenant, and cast from them the yoke of Thy law. 4. But others again I

2. *Protect the rest*, etc. See xxix. 2, note.

3. *Until the world of corruption is at an end.* The Messianic kingdom is only of temporary duration; it belongs to the *olam hazzeh* (see xxi. 19, note).

XLI., XLII. These two chapters appear to belong to B², and to have followed originally after xxx. The same world-view is presented as in B². Thus the times (xlii. 6) are hastened, as in xx., in order to usher in the end, when corruption will disappear and the life of incorruption set in through the resurrection (xlii. 7, 8).

The chief topics discussed in these chapters are two: First, the ultimate destiny of the apostates; and secondly, that of the proselytes.

Thus hitherto the portions of this book derived from B², and their original order, appear to have been ix. 2-xii. (?); xiii. 1-3*a*; xx.; xxiv. 2-4; xiii. 3*b*-12; xxv.; xiv.-xix.; xxi.-xxiv. 1; xxx. 2-5; xli.-xlii.

XLI. 1. Baruch's question goes back to xxx. 2-5, with which they originally stood in connection in B². For a similar question, cf. lxxv. 5.

To live. The life referred to here is the spiritual life subsequent to the resurrection (cf. xlix. 2; lxxvi. 5; 4 Ezra xiv. 22).

3. The apostates here dealt with may be Christians.

Yoke of Thy law. On the "law" see xv. 5, note. The term "yoke" as expressing "obligation" is common in Jewish writings (cf. Ecclus. li. 26), *τὸν τράχηλον ὑμῶν ὑπόθετε ὑπὸ ξυγόν* (Pss. Sol. vii. 8; xvii. 32; Acts xv. 10; Gal. v. 1). In later Judaism such expressions as "yoke of the law," "yoke of the precept," "yoke of the kingdom of heaven," are frequent. See Schöttgen, *Hor. Hebr.* i. 115-120. Contrast Matt. xi. 29, 30.

4. The proselytes, *i.e.* the גרים. Cf. 4 Ezra vii. 133: "Et miserator

have seen who have forsaken their vanity, and fled for refuge beneath Thy wings. 5. What therefore will be to them? or how will the last time receive them? 6. Or perhaps the time of these will assuredly be weighed, and as the beam inclines will they be judged accordingly?"

XLII. And He answered and said unto me: "These things also I will show unto thee. 2. As for what thou didst say—'To whom will these things be, and how many (will they be)?'—to those who have believed there will be the good which was spoken of aforetime, and to those who despise there will be the contrary of these things. 3. And as for what thou didst say regarding those who have drawn near and those who have withdrawn, this is the word. 4. As for those who were before subject, and afterwards withdrew and mingled themselves with the seed of mingled peoples,

in eo quod miseretur illis qui conversionem faciunt in lege ejus."

Their vanity. *I.e.* their idols (cf. Deut. xxxii. 21).

Fled for refuge beneath Thy wings. Exactly the sense of Ps. xxxvi. 8, בצל כנפיך יחסיון; and of lvii. 1, where in both cases the LXX. renders חסה by ἐλπίζειν and the Syr. by two different words meaning "to hide." This tends to show that the writer used the Hebrew text independently. For other instances of the same metaphor, cf. Ps. xvii. 8; lxiii. 8; Deut. xxxii. 11.

But in our text the above phrase is technically used of proselytes גרים. This technical sense is derived from Ruth ii. 12, where, in reference to Ruth, it is said: "The God of Israel under whose wings thou art come to take refuge" (לחסות תחת-כנפיו). In the *Aboda Sara*, 13*b*, *Shabbat*, 31*a*, the proselyte is said to have come under the wings of the Shekinah; and in the *Jer. Sanh.* ii. 20*c*, it is stated that "Solomon loved many strange women in order to bring them under the wings of the Shekinah."

5. *The last time.* *I.e.* that described in xxx. 2-5.

XLII. 2. *Those who believed.* See liv. 5, note, also xxi. 9, on the doctrine of justification in Baruch.

4. The sense seems to be that the apostates have only this world.

Mingled peoples. This is a rendering of עֵרֶב (cf. Jer. xxv. 20, 24). The Greek translation of it is found in Pss. Sol. xvii. 17 ἐθνῶν συμμίκτων.

the time of these is the former, and I am meditating deep things. 5. And as for those who before knew not but afterwards knew life, and mingled (only) with the seed of the people which had separated itself, the time of these (is) the former, I am meditating deep things. 6. And time will succeed to time and season to season, and one will receive from another, and then with a view to the consummation will everything be compared according to the measure of the times and the hours of the seasons. 7. For corruption will take those that belong to it, and life those that belong to it. 8. And the dust will be called, and there will be said to it: 'Give back that which is not thine, and raise up all that thou hast kept until its time.'

XLIII.-XLIV. 7 = B^1.

XLIII. "Moreover, do thou, Baruch, strengthen thy

5. *Of the people.* The text ܕܥܡ̈ܡܐ = "of the peoples" I have emended into ܕܥܡܐ, for it would be strange to speak of Israel as "the peoples" or "the nations."

Which had separated itself. I.e. the legalistic Israel by means of the "fence" of the law (cf. xlviii. 23). The "separatists" are the Pharisees, the פרושין.

The former. This seems corrupt, and probably, as Kabisch proposes, we should have "the latter." This would admit the proselytes to all the blessings of the world to come. On the treatment of "proselytes" in the Talmud, see Weber, 55, 73 f., 98, 107, 183, 254, 257 f., 282 f., 368 f.

6. This verse is obscure. Cf. 4 Ezra iv. 37.

7. Cf. xxxi. 5. See note on xxi. 19.

8. *Give back*, etc. Cf. l. 2. The earth gives back the body; Sheol gives back the soul.

XLIII.-XLVI. Of these chapters *xliii.-xliv. 7; xlv.-xlvi. 6 belong to* B^1. Not to B^2, for (1) in xliii. 2; xliv. 2, as in lxxviii. 5; lxxxiv. 1, Baruch is to die an ordinary death and go the way of all the earth and forget all the concerns of mortals, whereas in B^2 he is not to die an ordinary death, but to be taken up and preserved till the last day; he is not to forget human affairs, for he is in the last days to testify against the Gentile oppressors of Israel (xiii. 3, note; xxv. 1; xlviii. 30). (2) The people are assured of good tidings in store for them (xlvi. 6) just as in lxxvii. 12; they are bidden to look for the consolation of Zion (*i.e.* its restoration), as we infer from lxxxi. 1, 4, taken together with i. 4; vi. 9, whereas in B^2 there is no consolation of any kind to be looked for *in this world.* (3) In

heart for that which has been said to thee, and understand those things which have been shown to thee; for there are many eternal consolations for thee. 2. For thou wilt depart from this place, and thou wilt pass from the regions which are now seen by thee, and thou wilt forget whatever is corruptible, and wilt not again recall those things which happen among mortals. 3. Go therefore and command thy people, and come to this place, and afterwards fast seven days, and then I will come to thee and speak with thee."

XLIV. And I, Baruch, went from thence, and

xliv. 7 and xlviii. 38 the same phrase, *i.e.* as to a "change of the times," is found; in the former with an optimistic, in the latter with a pessimistic reference. (4) xliv. 5 vividly recalls the scene depicted in vi.-viii. As all the intervening chapters deal with questions of the school, xliii.-xlvi. probably stood originally in close juxtaposition with vi.-viii.

The fragment xliv. 8-15 belongs to B², for just as in B² expectation is fixed not on an earthly felicity but only on the world to come (xliv. 15), the inheritance of the promised time (xliv. 13), the time that passeth not away (xliv. 11), the new world which turneth not to corruption those who enter it (xliv. 12), (2) the whole present world, the entire *olam hazzeh* is hopeless; it is defiled with evil (xliv. 9), and with its corruption it will pass away (xliv. 8). (3) In xliv. 9 the present world is to be committed to oblivion. This is in flat contradiction to iv. 1.

The original position of xliv. 8-15. This seems easy to determine. The main statements in this address of Baruch to the people really presuppose xlviii.-lii. as their background. They express shortly some of the main conclusions of these chapters. It is not reasonable to suppose that Baruch makes known to the people the very truths which, according to the present order of the book, are revealed to him later by God. We have already seen that xxxi.-xxxv. were originally subsequent to xlviii.-lii. (see p. 57). Since therefore both these passages form the address or part of the address of Baruch that was based upon previous disclosures of God, it is obvious that xliv. 8-15 followed originally on xxxii. 6 and formed the natural sequel to the closing words of that verse.

XLIII. 1. These words have no reference to the preceding chapters. They refer probably to some lost passage of B¹.

2. *Thou wilt depart.* Both the context and the word "depart" point to an ordinary death here. See xiii. 3, note. The word rendered "depart" is ܫܢܐ. It is found also in xiv. 19; xv. 1; xliv. 2.

Whatever is corruptible. Cf. xxi. 19, note.

3. Parts of this verse relating to the fast, etc., are probably due to the final editor. See xlvii. 1, note.

came to my people, and I called my first-born son and the Gedaliahs my friends, and seven of the elders of the people, and I said unto them: 2. "Behold, I go unto my fathers according to the way of all the earth. 3. But withdraw ye not from the way of the law, but guard and admonish the people which remain, lest they withdraw from the commandments of the Mighty One. 4. For ye see that he whom we serve is just, and our Creator is no respecter of persons. 5. And see ye what hath befallen Zion, and what hath happened to Jerusalem. 6. For the judgment of the Mighty One will (thereby) be made known, and His ways, which, though past finding out, are right. 7. For if ye endure and persevere in His fear, and do not forget His law, the times will change over you for good, and ye will see

XLIV. 8-15 = B[2]. the consolation of Zion. 8. Because whatever is now

XLIV. 1. *My first-born son.* Elsewhere mentioned only in xlvi. 1.

The Gedaliahs—possibly a corruption for Gedaliah. Cf. v. 1. Gedaliah is mentioned only in B[1].

Seven of the elders of the people. In v. 5 Baruch assembled all the elders or honourable amongst the people. This is natural, as it is prior to the destruction of the city. That seven should be summoned now that the bulk of the population is carried into exile is equally fitting. We must bear in mind that in xxxii. 1 we have the work of a different author, else the writer might seem to have been guilty of an inconsistency.

2. Cf. iii. 2. See xiii. 3, note. The text is drawn from Gen. xv. 15 and Joshua xxiii. 14; 1 Kings ii. 2.

3. *Way of the law.* See xv. 5, note. *Commandments of the Mighty One.* Cf. xlviii. 38; lxxxiv. 7.

4. *No respecter of persons.* Cf. xiii. 8.

5. These words as we have observed above (p. 69) vividly recall vi.-viii., and seem to show that these chapters followed much more closely on vi.-viii. than they do now.

6. *Which, though . . . right.* The text = *which are past finding out and right.*

7. *The times will change over you for good.* Contrast the use of this phrase in xlviii. 38.

The consolation of Zion. *I.e.* its restoration; cf. lxxxi. 1, 4; for the temple was to be rebuilt (i. 4; vi. 9) according to B[1]. The announcement of this future in store for Zion is called good tidings in xlvi. 6; lxxvii. 12; lxxxi. 1.

is nothing, but that which will be is very great. 9. For everything that is corruptible will pass away, and everything that dies will depart, and all the present time will be forgotten, nor will there be any remembrance of the present time, which is defiled with evils. 10. For that which runs now runs unto vanity, and that which prospers will quickly fall and be humiliated. 11. For that which is to be will be the object of desire, and on that which will come afterwards do we place our hope; for it is a time that will not pass away. 12. And the hour comes which will abide for ever, and the new world which does not turn to corruption those who depart to its blessedness, and has no mercy on those who depart to torment, and will not

8-15. These verses should be read after xxxii. 6 (see p. 69).

8. In xxxii. 6 God has declared His purpose to renew creation; the reason is given here; for all things that now are are nothing.

9. *Corruptible.* Cf. xxi. 19, note; xxxi. 5.

All the present time will be forgotten. In iv. 1 this is denied, but iv. 1 is from B[1] (cf. Isa. lxv. 17).

11. *A time that will not pass away.* This is set over against xlviii. 50: "this world which passeth away."

12. *The new world*, etc., implied in the new creation (xxxii. 6). In li. 3 it is the world which dies not, nor ages those who come to it (lii. 9, 16).

Who depart to its blessedness. The text here ܕܒܪܫܗ ܐܙܠܝܢ = "who depart on its beginning" is corrupt. This clause should describe the destination of the righteous, as the antithetical clause in the next line, "those who depart to torment," describes that of the wicked. The error thus lies in the words "in its beginning." In the next place, we can reason back to what should stand here instead of these words. For the corresponding phrase in the other clause, *i.e.* "to torment," requires as its antithesis, not the meaningless "on its beginning," but "to blessedness." That is, over against "those who depart to torment," the sense needs "those who depart to blessedness." This conclusion as to the original text is confirmed by the fact that the erroneous text can be explained by the transposition of a single letter in the Hebrew original. Thus "in its beginning" = בראשו, but this arose from a false transcription of באשרו, *i.e.* by wrongly transposing the ר. Now באשרו = "to its blessedness," I have emended accordingly.

lead to perdition those who live in it. 13. For these are they who shall inherit that time which has been spoken of, and theirs is the inheritance of the promised time. 14. These are they who have acquired for themselves treasures of wisdom, and with them are found stores of understanding, and from mercy have they not withdrawn, and the truth of the law have they preserved. 15. For to them will be given the world to come, but the dwelling of the rest who are many will be in the fire.

XLV.-XLVI. 6=B[1].

XLV. "Do ye therefore so far as ye are able instruct the people, for that labour is ours. 2. For if ye teach them, ye will quicken them."

XLVI. And my son and the elders of the people answered and said unto me: "Has the Mighty One humiliated us to such a degree as to take thee from us quickly? 2. And truly we shall be in darkness, and there will be no light to the people who are left. 3. For where again shall we seek the law, or who will distinguish for us between death and life?" 4. And I said unto them: "The throne of the Mighty One I cannot resist: nevertheless, there shall not be wanting to Israel

13. *The inheritance . . . time*= "the world to come" in verse 15.

14. This verse presupposes li. 3, 7. The "treasures" here mentioned differ from those in xxiv. 1.

15. Those described in the preceding verse are to receive the world to come, just as those who are similarly described in li. 3 are to receive the world that dies not. On the contrast of this world and the world to come, see xv. 8, note.

In the fire. Cf. xlviii. 39, 43; lix. 2; lxiv. 7; lxxxv. 13.

XLV. B[1] reappears here. The connection with xliv. 7 is all that could be desired. There it is said, "If ye keep faithful to the law ye will see the consolation of Zion"; "do ye therefore . . . instruct the people . . . for if ye teach them ye will quicken them."

2. *If ye teach*, etc. Cf. xxxviii. 2; Ps. cxix. 50, 93. This is the work of the true scribe. Pharisaism teaches obedience to the law, God will do the rest (cf. xliv. 7).

XLVI. 2. For similar diction, cf. lxxvii. 14; 4 Ezra xiv. 20.

a wise man nor a son of the law to the race of Jacob. 5. But only prepare ye your hearts, that ye may hear the law, and be subject to those who in fear are wise and understanding; and prepare your soul that ye may not depart from them. 6. For if ye do these things, good tidings will come unto you, which I before told you of; nor will ye fall into the torment, of which I testified to you before."
[7. But with regard to the word that I was to be taken, XLVI. 7 = E.
I did not make (it) known to them or to my son.]

XLVII. And when I had gone forth and dismissed XLVII.-LII. = B².
them, I went thence and said unto them: "Behold! I go to Hebron: for thither the Mighty One hath sent me."

4. *There shall not be wanting . . . a son of the law.* This is really an answer to the question put in iii. 6. The expression "son of the law" seems to occur here first in existing literature. Its earliest occurrence elsewhere in the Talmud appears to be in *Baba Mezia*, 96*a*. See Levy, *Neuhebräisches Wörterbuch*, i. 258. The term בר מצוה was used in the Middle Ages as a designation of a full-grown Israelite. See Schürer, Div. II., vol. ii. 51 (note). For the parallelism *Israel . . . Jacob*, cf. xvii. 4; xxxi. 3.

5. *Prepare ye your hearts.* See xxxii. 1, note.

Obedience to the law and the Rabbis is here enforced.

6. Here the promise in xliv. 7 is enforced anew.

Good tidings. Cf. lxxvii. 12.

7. This verse is an addition of the final editor in order the better to adapt the fragment of B[1] just given to its new context. It belongs in spirit to B².

I was to be taken. Cf. xiii. 3, note; xlviii. 30. In lxxxv. 9 the phrase has a different meaning. ܐܬܕܒܪ is a rendering of *ἀναλαμβάνειν* (also of *μετατιθέναι* in Gen. v. 24). The former is the usual word in the sense of the text. The idea of the ascension into heaven of great heroes in Jewish history was a familiar one. Thus it is told of Elijah in the LXX. of 2 Kings ii. 11, *καὶ ἀνελήμφθη . . . εἰς τὸν οὐρανόν*: Ecclus. xlviii. 9, *ὁ ἀναλημφθεὶς ἐν λαίλαπι πυρός*: also in Eth. En. lxxxix. 52; xciii. 8; 1 Macc. ii. 58; of Enoch in Ecclus. xliv. 16; Eth. En. lxx. 1; lxxxvii. 3, 4; Slav. En. lxvii. 2; Jubilees, iv. 24; of Moses, Assumpt. Mos. x. 12; of Baruch, Apoc. Bar. xiii. 3; xxv. 1; xlvi. 7; xlviii. 30; lxxvi. 2; of Ezra, 4 Ezra viii. 20; xiv. 49; of many unnamed heroes, 4 Ezra vi. 26. *ἀναλαμβάνειν* is well-known in the N.T. in this sense (cf. Mark xvi. 19; Acts i. 2, 11, 22; 1 Tim. iii. 16). The substantive *ἀνάληψις* is rare. Ryle and James (Pss. Sol.) take iv. 20 of those Pss. to be the first known instance of its use; see also Luke ix. 51, and Test. Levi xviii. In the last passage it is a late Christian interpolation.

2. And I came to that place where the word had been spoken to me, and I sat there, and fasted seven days.

Prayer of Baruch

XLVIII. And it came to pass after the seventh day, that I prayed before the Mighty One and said: 2. "O my Lord, Thou summonest the advent of the times, and they stand before Thee; Thou causest the power of the ages to pass away, and they do not resist Thee; Thou arrangest the method of the seasons, and they obey Thee. 3. Thou alone knowest the goal of the generations, and Thou revealest not Thy mysteries to many. 4. Thou makest known the multitude of the fire, and Thou weighest the lightness of the wind.

The Seventh Section

XLVII.-LXXVII. First we have Baruch's fast of seven days (xlvii. 2), followed by his prayer (xlviii. 2-24). Then in the dialogue that ensues various revelations are made to Baruch touching the coming woes and the judgment (xlviii. 26-41), and the resurrection (l.-lii.) On these revelations follows a Messiah Apocalypse (liii.-lxxiv. = A^3). In lxxvi. Baruch is told of his approaching translation, and in lxxvii. he calls the people together and addresses them.

This section is composite: xlviii.-lii. being derived from B^2; liii.-lxxiv. from A^3; lxxv., lxxvi. from B^2; and lxxvii. from B^1.

XLVII. 1. The purposeless journey to Hebron spoken of here must be derived from an original source. According to the scheme of the final editor it has no business here. Further, no such command has been given to Baruch in the existing text. Hence this entire verse must be regarded as drawn from B^1 or B^2, and the next verse, which conflicts with it, as due to the final editor, as also xliii. 3. It is noteworthy, too, that the words "and dismissed them" must be corrupt; for "and when I had gone forth and dismissed them, I went thence and said unto them" is absurd. Baruch goes forth from some place (here undefined) and dismisses the people; then he departs thence and speaks to them. It is possible then that "when I had gone forth" refers to "the cavern in the earth" in xxi. 1. It will be remembered that of chapters xxi.-xlvi., xxi.-xxiv. 1, xxx. 2-5, xli., xlii. belong to B^2. These form in some sense a whole, and the scene with which they are connected may be the "cavern" in xxi. 1. If this is so, xlvii. 1 belongs to B^2.

2. Cf. xliii. 3; v. 7, note; ix., note; xxi. 2, note.

XLVIII. 2. *Method of the seasons.* Cf. xiv. 1, note; xx. 6.

5. Thou explorest the limit of the heights, and Thou scrutinisest the depths of the darkness. 6. Thou carest for the number which pass away that they may be preserved, and Thou preparest an abode for those that are to be. 7. Thou rememberest the beginning which Thou hast made, and the destruction that is to be Thou forgettest not. 8. With nods of fear and indignation Thou givest commandment to the flames, and they change into spirits, and with a word Thou quickenest that which was not, and with mighty power Thou holdest that which has not yet come. 9. Thou instructest created things in the understanding of Thee, and Thou makest wise the spheres so as to minister in their orders. 10. Armies innumerable stand before Thee and minister in their orders quietly at Thy nod. 11. Hear Thy servant and give ear to my petition. 12. For in a little time are we born, and in a little time do we return. 13. But with Thee hours are as a time, and days as generations. 14. Be not therefore wroth with man; for he is nothing, and take not account of our works. 15. For what are we? for lo! by Thy gift do we come

6. See xxiii. 4, note.

Thou carest . . . preserved. The text which here = "Thou commandest the number which passes away and it is preserved" is nonsense as it stands, but, if retranslated into Hebrew, it supplies us at once with the true text. Retranslated it = אתה פֹּקֵר את־המספר העובר וְיִשָּׁמֵר. Here clearly the Greek translator followed the wrong meaning of פקר, and mistranslated the weak vav with the voluntative imperfect. The translation required by the context is given above.

8. *With a word . . . which was not.* Cf. xxi. 4, note; 4 Ezra iv. 37. *Flames . . . spirits.* Cf. Ps. civ. 4; Heb. i. 7.

9. *The spheres . . . in their orders.* Cf. Eth. En. ii. 1; Slav. En. xxx. 2, 3; Pss. Sol. xix. 2, 3.

10. Cf. Slav. En. xvii.; Test. Levi iii. *In their orders.* There were ten orders of angels according to the Jews; nine according to the Christians (see Slav. En. xx. 1, 3, note).

13. We should expect rather: "time is as a (few) hours, and generations as days."

into the world, and we depart not of our own will. 16. For we said not to our parents, 'Beget us,' nor did we send to Sheol and say, 'Receive us.' 17. What therefore is our strength that we should bear Thy wrath, or what are we that we should endure Thy judgment? 18. Protect us in Thy compassions, and in Thy mercy help us. 19. Behold the little ones that are subject unto Thee, and save all that draw nigh unto Thee, and destroy not the hope of our people, and cut not short the times of our aid. 20. For this is the nation which Thou hast chosen, and these are the people, to whom Thou findest no equal. 21. But I will speak now before Thee, and I will say as my heart thinketh. 22. In Thee do we trust, for lo! Thy law is with us, and we know that we shall not fall so far as we keep Thy statutes. 23. In this at least we are always blest that we have not mingled with the Gentiles. 24. For we are all named one people, who have received one law from One, and the law which is amongst us will aid us, and the surpassing wisdom which is in us will help us." 25.

15. *Depart not*, etc. In xiv. 11 men are said to "come not of their own will"; in 4 Ezra viii. 5 the two statements are combined.

16. *Sheol*. See xi. 6, note.

18. See lxxv. 6.

19. *That are subject to Thee*. Cf. xlii. 4.

All that draw nigh. Are these proselytes? (see xli. 4; xlii. 3).

20. Cf. xxi. 21; 4 Ezra v. 27. *The nation*. So I have emended by reading ܐܘܡܬܐ for the unmeaning ܥܕܡܐ. This gives a good parallel to "people" (ܥܡܐ). Ceriani proposes ܥܒܕܐ = "servant."

21. *Say as my heart thinketh*. Cf. xli. 2.

22. See xv. 5, note.

23. Cf. xlii. 5.

24. *One law from One*. lxxxv. 14. This is directed polemically against the Christians.

The law . . . will aid us. Cf. xxix. 2, note; xxxii. 1; xv. 5, note; cf. *De singularitate cler*. 15 (Cyprian, Ed. Hartel. ii. 190), "sicut Esaias ait, legem inquit in adjutorium dedit."

And when I had prayed and said these things, I was greatly weakened. 26. And He answered and said unto me: "Thou hast prayed simply, O Baruch, and all thy words have been heard. 27. But My judgment exacts its own and My law exacts its rights. 28. For from thy words I will answer thee, and from thy prayer I will speak to thee. 29. For this is as follows: he that is corrupted is not at all; he has both wrought iniquity so far as he could do anything, and has not remembered My goodness, nor been grateful for My long-suffering. 30. Therefore thou shalt surely be taken up, as I before told thee: and the time is coming of which I told thee. 31. For that time will arise which brings affliction; for it will come and pass by with quick vehemence, and it will be turbulent coming in the heat of indignation. 32. And it will come to pass in those days that all the inhabitants of the earth will be moved one against another, because they know not that My judgment has drawn nigh. 33. For there will not be found many wise at that time, and the intelligent will be but a few: moreover,

25. *I was greatly weakened.* Cf. xxi. 26. The same phenomenon accompanies the visions in Dan. vii. 28; viii. 27; x. 8, 16.

27. Cf. v. 2; lxxxv. 9.

29. *For this . . . is not at all.* The text which is unintelligible runs: ܗܝ ܗܝ ܡܚܒܠ ܗܘܐ ܕܠܐ ܗܘܐ ܡܕܡ ܗܘ ܕܥܛܡܒܠ.

30. See xlvi. 7, note.

31-41. The last woes and the final judgment. Cf. xxvii.-xxix. 1; lxx. 2-10.

32. *The inhabitants of the earth.* See xxv. 1, note.

Will be moved one against another. The text ܢܬܬܢܝܚܘܢ = "will rest" is meaningless. It seems corrupted from ܢܬܬܚܪܘܢ or ܢܬܬܙܝܥܘܢ, either of which can be rendered as above.

33. Cf. lxx. 5. This verse seems to be the source of the following words which Cyprian (*Testim.* iii. 29) quotes as from Baruch: "erit enim sapientia in paucis vigilantibus et taciturnis."

even those who know will most of all be silent. 34. And there will be many rumours and tidings not a few, and the works of portents will be shown, and promises not a few will be recounted, (and) some of them (will prove) idle, and some of them will be confirmed. 35. And honour will be turned into shame, and strength humiliated into contempt, and probity destroyed, and beauty will become a scorn. 36. And many will say to many at that time: 'Where hath the multitude of intelligence hidden itself, and whither hath the multitude of wisdom removed itself?' 37. And whilst they are meditating these things, then zeal will arise in those of whom they thought not, and passion will seize him who is peaceful, and many will be roused in anger to injure many, and they will rouse up armies in order to shed blood, and in the end they will perish together with them. 38. And it will come to pass at the self-same time, that a change of times will manifestly appear to every man, by reason of which in all those times they were polluted and practised oppression, and walked every man in his own works, and remembered

34. Joseph, *Ant.* xx. 5. 1; 8. 6, tells of many impostors who so deceived the people (cf. Matt. xxiv. 11, 24). This verse seems to be the source of Cyprian's (*Testim.* iii. 29) quotation from Baruch: "alii autem sapientes ad spiritum erroris et pronuntiantes sicut Altissimi et Fortis edicta."

35. Cf. lxx. 3. It is remarkable that if we retranslate this verse into Hebrew we have a series of paronomasiae. Thus "honour will be turned into shame" = כבוד יהפך לקלון, "strength humiliated into contempt" = עז יורד אל בוז, and "beauty will become a scorn" = יופי יהיה לדפי.

36. Cf. 4 Ezra v. 9-11. This seems the source of Cyprian's quotation from Baruch (*Testim.* iii. 29): "Quaeretis me et vos et qui post vos venerint audire verbum sapientiae et intellectus et non invenietis."

37. Cf. lxx. 6.

38. *A change of times.* Cf. xliv. 7. *Walked every man*, etc. Cf. 4 Ezra iii. 8.

not the law of the Mighty One. 39. Therefore a fire will consume their thoughts, and in flame will the meditations of their reins be tried; for the Judge will come and will not tarry. 40. Because each of the inhabitants of the earth knew when he was committing iniquity, and they have not known My law by reason of their pride. 41. For many will then assuredly weep, yea, over the living more than over the dead."
42. And I answered and said: "O Adam, what hast thou done to all those who are born from thee?

Remembered not the law of the Mighty One. Cf. xliv. 3, 7; lxxxiv. 7.

39. *A fire will consume*, etc. Cf. verse 43; xliv. 15; lix. 2, note.

The Judge will come and will not tarry. Cf. xx. 6, note.

40. *Knew when he was committing*, etc. See xv. 6, note; lv. 2. Cf. Ep. Barn. v. 4 δικαίως ἀπολεῖται ἄνθρωπος ὃς ἔχων ὁδοῦ δικαιοσύνης γνῶσιν ἑαυτὸν εἰς ὁδὸν σκότους ἀποσυνέχει. In xv. 6 men are to be tormented because, though knowing the law, they transgressed it. In that passage the words, therefore, may be limited to Israel, but here they are obviously descriptive of the Gentiles: "the inhabitants of the earth" (see xxv. 2, note). The writer thus holds that all men alike possessed a conscience or faculty for moral judgment. We have, therefore, in this verse a statement in some degree parallel to Rom. ii. 14, 15: "For when Gentiles, which have no law, do by nature the things of the law, these, having no law, are a law unto themselves: in that they shew the work of the law written in their hearts, their conscience bearing witness therewith, etc."

Have not known My law by reason of their pride. These words seem to point to the rejection of the law by the Gentiles; for according to an oft-repeated statement in the Talmud (see Weber, 19, 56, 57, 65), the law was originally designed for all nations, but the Gentiles rejected it (see 4 Ezra vii. 72, 73).

41. Since the sin of the world is intensified towards its close, so naturally the sinners then surviving will meet with severer judgment than the less guilty of earlier times.

42-50. What havoc Adam and Eve have wrought by the spiritual death and torments which they have brought upon their posterity. Yet God knows all that is in man, for He created him; He knows likewise the number of men that are to be, and their sins (verses 42-46). But since the law will give all these their due in the judgment, let inquiry be made rather after the blessedness of the righteous; for though they have endured much weariness in this passing world, in the world to come they shall have abundant light.

42. Spiritual death is here traced to Adam and Eve, but in xvii. 3; xxiii. 4; liv. 15 it is only physical death. See notes on xxiii. 4; liv. 15-19. In 4 Ezra both spiritual

and what will be said to the first Eve who hearkened to the serpent? 43. For all this multitude are going to corruption, nor is there any numbering of those whom the fire devours. 44. But again I will speak in Thy presence. 45. Thou, O LORD, my Lord, knowest what is in Thy creature. 46. For Thou didst of old command the dust to produce Adam, and Thou knowest the number of those who are born from him, and how far they have sinned before Thee, who have existed and not confessed Thee as their Creator. 47. And as regards all these their end will convict them, and Thy law which they have transgressed will requite them on Thy day. [48. But now let us dismiss the wicked and enquire about the righteous. 49. And I will recount their blessedness and not be silent in celebrating their

death and physical are always traced to Adam (iii. 21, 22; iv. 30; vii. 118-121).

43. *Fire devours.* Cf. verse 39; xliv. 15; lxiv. 7.

46. *Command the dust to produce Adam.* 4 Ezra iii. 4, 5; vii. 116.

The number of those who are born. See xxiii. 5, note.

47. *Thy law . . . will requite.* See v. 2, note.

48-50. These verses were used originally in B[2] by Baruch in addressing the people, or by God in addressing Baruch, but not by Baruch in addressing God as the present text implies. That they could not have been addressed by Baruch to God is clear; for Baruch could not say to God, "In this world . . . in which ye live" (ver. 50). Two facts are in favour of their being God's words to Baruch: (1) The very same contrast between the two worlds is found in God's reply to Baruch in xv. 7; and (2) the very same change of subject is enjoined and the same word "inquire" used in reference to the righteous in 4 Ezra ix. 13: "tu ergo adhuc noli curiosus esse quomodo impii cruciabuntur sed inquire quomodo justi salvabuntur." But the plural in verse 48 is against this view; and secondly, the words "I will not be silent in celebrating, etc.," while hardly conceivable on the divine lips, are appropriate on Baruch's. Hence we must regard xlviii. 48-50 as a fragment of an address delivered by Baruch to the people. Another fragment of this same address which originally preceded xlviii. 48-50 is to be found in liv. 16-18, and yet another which followed it in liv. 16-18.

49. *Will not be silent in celebrating.* A Hebrew idiom = לא אחרל לשבח.

glory, which is reserved for them. 50. For assuredly as in a little time in this world which passeth away, in which ye live, ye have endured much labour, so in that world to which there is no end, ye shall receive great light."]

XLIX. "Nevertheless, I will again ask from Thee, O Mighty One, yea, I will ask mercy from Him who made all things. 2. 'In what shape will those live who live in Thy day? or how will the splendour of those who (are) after that time continue? 3. Will they then resume this form of the present, and put on these entrammeling members, which are now involved in evils, and in which evils are consummated, or wilt Thou perchance change these things which have been in the world as also the world?'"

L. And He answered and said unto me: "Hear,

50. Cf. xv. 8 for the same contrast and largely the same diction.

Light. This does not seem the right word.

XLIX. 2. *In what shape*, etc. Cf. 1 Cor. xv. 35: "How are the dead raised? and with what manner of body do they come?"

Live. See xli. 1, note.

The splendour of those who (are) after that time. For "splendour" we might perhaps render "appearance." The text is ܐܣܟܡܗܘܢ ܕܡܢ ܒܬܪ ܗܝܕܝܢ.

3. *Entrammeling members*, lit. members of bonds.

L.-LI. *The nature of the resurrection body.* The teaching here as to the nature of the resurrection proceeds on the line suggested in xlix. 3: "Wilt thou perchance change these things (*i.e.* man's material body) which have been in the world as also the world?" The world was to be renewed (xxxii. 6), and in this renewal from being transitory and verging to its close (xlviii. 50; lxxxv. 10), it becomes undying (li. 3) and everlasting (xlviii. 50); from being a world of corruption (xl. 3; lxxiv. 2; xxi. 19; xxxi. 5, etc.) it becomes incorruptible (lxxiv. 2) and invisible (li. 8). As these conceptions are in germ and principle as old as Isa. lxv. 17-lxvi., the same doctrine of renewal and transformation that was taught touching the world was naturally applied in due course to those destined to live in it. This is done partially in Isa. lxv. 17-25, but the developed form appears in Dan. xii. 2, where the risen righteous are to shine as the stars for ever and ever; in Eth. En. they are to joy as the angels (civ. 4)

Baruch, this word, and write in the remembrance of thy heart all that thou shalt learn. 2. For the earth will then assuredly restore the dead, which it now receives, in order to preserve them, making no change in their form, but as it has received, so will it restore them, and as I delivered them unto it, so also shall it raise them. 3. For then it will be necessary to show to the living that the dead have come to life again, and that those who had departed have returned (again). 4. And it will come to pass, when they have severally

and to become angels in heaven (li. 4) and companions of the heavenly hosts (civ. 6), and to be clad in garments of life (lxii. 15, 16) and in raiment of light (cviii. 12); see also xc. 38. We thus see that long before the time of the writers of Baruch the Pharisees were familiar with the idea of the spiritual transformation of the body after the resurrection; and that *to some extent* the Pauline teaching on the resurrection in 1 Cor. xv. 35-50 was not an innovation, but an able and developed exposition of ideas that were current in the Judaism of the time. 1 Cor. xv. 35-50 is in one of its aspects the logical sequel of Isa. lxv. 17.

Over against this spiritual view of the future life we must remember that a materialistic one prevailed not only popularly, but also in Rabbinic circles. According to the latter the blessed should beget children and eat the flesh of the Leviathan. See Weber, 383, 384.

L. 2. Cf. xi. 4, note; xlii. 8, note; Eth. En. li. 1, note. In the resurrection soul and body were to be united. On the scene of the resurrection see xxix. 2, note. The soul's abode was Sheol (see xxi. 23 note); the body rested in the earth (xlii. 8). According to the text the body was to be restored in exactly the same form in which it had been committed to the earth. The following speculations of later Judaism on this subject are instructive. According to the *Othioth*, 17c, of R. Akiba (Weber, 352, 353), God was to sound a trumpet seven times at the end of the world. At the first blast the whole world was to be moved, at the second the dust was to be separated, at the third the bones of the dead were to be gathered together, at the fourth their limbs were to be warmed, at the fifth they were to be covered with skin, at the sixth the souls and spirits were to enter their bodies, in the seventh they were to become living and stand upon their feet, clad in their clothes. According to another account (*Beresh. rab.* 28) the resurrection body was built up from a small fragment of the backbone which was in all cases indestructible. This was called לוז. See Levy, *Neuhebräisches Wörterb.* ii. 481; see verse 4, note.

L. 3. Those who are to be judged are the living righteous, and sinners, and the risen dead.

4. The object with which the dead are raised is for common recognition.

recognised those whom they now know, then judgment will grow strong, and those things which before were spoken of will come.

LI. " And it will come to pass, when that appointed day has gone by, that then shall the aspect of those who are condemned be afterwards changed, and the glory of those who are justified. 2. For the aspect of those who now act wickedly will become worse than is that of such as suffer torment. 3. Also (as for) the glory of those who have now been justified in My law, who have had understanding in their life, and who have planted in their heart the root of wisdom, then their splendour will be glorified in changes, and the form of their face will be turned into the light of their beauty, that they may be able to acquire and receive the world which does not die, which is then promised to them. 4. For

There is nothing corresponding to this in the N.T. In later Judaism the resemblance of the risen was to be so carefully preserved that they were to be raised in the same clothes in which they were buried. This was proved *Sanhedrin*, 90*b* (Weber, 353) by the analogy of a grain of corn which comes up from the earth, not naked but clothed. The Rabbis, therefore, on the approach of death, gave careful directions as to their grave-clothes. According to the *Beresh. rab.* 95 (Weber, 353), men were to be raised with all their bodily defects, such as blindness, lameness, etc., in order that their identity might be established. Thereupon, in the case of the righteous these infirmities were healed.

LI. 1. This transformation of the living is mentioned in 1 Cor. xv. 51.

Aspect. I have here followed Ceriani's emendation of ܪܡܘܬܗܘܢ into ܕܡܘܬܗܘܢ.

Condemned . . . justified. See xxi. 9, note. The word "justify" has here its ordinary meaning of "to declare righteous."

3. *Justified in My law.* See xv. 5, note; xxi. 9, note.

Root of wisdom. lix. 7; Ecclus. i. 6, 20, ῥίζα σοφίας; Wisdom iii. 15.

Their splendour, etc. The righteous will undergo successive transformations till their bodies are assimilated to their new environment, or to use the words of the text, "that they may be able . . . to receive the world that does not die."

The world that does not die. Cf. xlviii. 50; li. 8; lxxiv. 2, for various characteristics of the *olam habba* or future world.

Then promised. See xiv. 13, note.

over this above all will those who come then lament, that they rejected My law, and stopped their ears that they might not hear wisdom or receive understanding. 5. When therefore they see those, over whom they are now exalted, (but) who will then be exalted and glorified more than they, they will respectively be transformed, the latter into the splendour of angels, and the former will mainly waste away in wonder at the visions and in the beholding of the forms. 6. For they will first behold and afterwards depart to be tormented. 7. But those who have been saved by their works, and to whom the law has been now a hope, and understanding an expectation, and wisdom a confidence, to them wonders will appear in their time. 8. For they will behold the world which is now invisible to them, and they will behold the time which is now hidden from them. 9. And again time will not age them. 10. For in the heights of that world shall they dwell, and they shall be made like unto the angels, and be made

4. The wicked here include not only the faithless Israelites, but also the Gentiles.

Stopped their ears that they might not hear. Zech. vii. 11. The LXX. renders differently: τὰ ὦτα αὐτῶν ἐβάρυναν κτλ.

5. *The splendour.* This word ܙܝܘܐ here, and in xlix. 2; li. 3, might also be rendered by "appearance."

Will waste away, or *will be dissolved.* Cf. xxx. 4; 4 Ezra vii. 87. The latter reference as well as our text show that the writer here was not thinking of annihilation, though this view is found later. Cf. Weber, 374, 375.

7. *Saved by their works.* See xiv. 7, note.

9. Cf. verse 3, note, and the phrase in verse 16: "The world which ages not those." After this verse we should probably read verses 13 and 14. Verse 12 would then form a fitting close and climax to li. 1-9, 13, 14, 10, 11.

10. The condition of the risen righteous is very spiritually conceived. Thus they have passed from a world of tribulation (li. 14) and enter a world that is everlasting (li. 3), invisible (li. 8); they live in the high places thereof (li. 10); they are made equal to the stars (li. 10),

equal to the stars, and they shall be changed into every form they desire, from beauty into loveliness, and from light into the splendour of glory. 11. For there will be spread before them the extents of Paradise, and there will be shown to them the beauty of the majesty of the living creatures which are beneath the throne, and all the armies of the angels, who [are now held fast by My word, lest they should appear, and] are held fast by a command, that they may stand in their places till their advent comes. 12. Moreover, there will then be excellency in the righteous surpassing that in the angels. 13. For the first will receive the last, those whom they were expecting, and the last those of whom they used to hear that they had passed away. 14. For they have been delivered from this world of tribulation, and laid down the burthen of anguish. 15. For what then have men lost their life, and for what have those who were on the earth exchanged their soul? 16. For then they chose (not) for themselves that time, which, beyond the reach of

and their glory is greater than that of the angels (x. 12).

Made equal to the stars. Cf. 4 Ezra vii. 97, 125.

11. *Living creatures which are beneath the throne.* Cf. Rev. iv. 6.

Armies of the angels who . . . are held fast, etc. These angels are probably the armed host mentioned in lxx. 7; Slav. En. xvii.; and in Test. Lev. 3: ἐν τῷ τρίτῳ εἰσὶν αἱ δυνάμεις τῶν παρεμβολῶν, οἱ ταχθέντες εἰς ἡμέραν κρίσεως, ποιῆσαι ἐκδίκησιν ἐν τοῖς πνεύμασι τῆς πλάνης καὶ τοῦ Βελίαρ. I have bracketed one of the clauses in this verse as a gloss.

13, 14. These two verses seem to be wrongly transposed from their place after verse 9.

13. Cf. 4 Ezra v. 42: "Coronae adsimilabo judicium meum; sicut non novissimorum tarditas, sic nec priorum velocitas"; also Matt. xix. 30.

14. See xv. 8, note.

15. Cf. Matt. xvi. 26.

16. I have added a negative in the first clause as the sense requires it. In lvi. 14 there is a similar loss of the negative, as Ceriani has already observed. *Which ages not*, etc. (cf. ver. 9).

anguish, could not pass away, and they chose for themselves that time, whose issues are full of lamentations and evils, and they denied the world which ages not those who come to it, and they have rejected the time and the glory, so that they shall not come to the honour of which I told thee before."

LII. And I answered and said: "How do those forget for whom woe is then reserved? 2. And why therefore again do we mourn for those who die? or why do we weep for those who depart to Sheol? 3. Let lamentations be reserved for the beginning of that coming torment, and let tears be laid up for the advent of the destruction of that time. 4. But even in the face of these things I will speak. [5. And as for the righteous, what will they do now? 6. Rejoice ye in the suffering which ye now suffer: for why do ye look for the decline of your enemies? 7. Make ready your soul for that which is reserved for you, and prepare your souls for the reward which is laid up for you."]

LIII. And when I had said these things I fell asleep there, and I saw a vision, and lo! a cloud was

LII. 1, 2. Considering the terrible destiny in store for the wicked after the resurrection, our grief should be reserved for those who shall suffer its torments, and not for those who depart to Sheol. And yet there is a certain degree of pain and torment in Sheol as we have seen (cf. xxx. 5; xxxvi. 10).

5-7. These verses cannot have been addressed by Baruch to God. Like xlviii. 48-50, they are part of his address to the people. They would form an appropriate sequel to xlviii. 48-50 (see note on liv. 16-18).

6. Cf. lxxviii. 6. These words recall James i. 2: "Count it all joy, my brethren, when ye fall into manifold temptations." The sentiment looks Christian.

7. *Make ready . . . prepare your souls.* See xxxii. 1, note. One half of this verse seems to be a gloss on the other.

8. Cf. xxxvi. 1.

LIII.-LXXIV. This constitutes

ascending from a very great sea, and I kept gazing upon it, and lo! it was full of waters white and black, and there were many colours in those self-same waters, and as it were the likeness of great lightning was seen at its summit. 2. And I saw that cloud passing swiftly in quick courses, and it covered all the earth. 3. And it came to pass after these things

the third Messiah Apocalypse = A^3 embodied by the final editor in this book. It will be sufficient here to indicate (*a*) its date; (*b*) its relation to the other constituents of the book; and to touch on (*c*) the question of its integrity; (*d*) and of its author.

(*a*) *Its date.* It was written prior to 70 A.D. (see lxviii. 5, note), and subsequent to 50 A.D. (see lix. 5-11, note).

(*b*) *Relations of A^3 to B^1, B^2, A^1, A^2.* It is distinct from B^1, and B^2 in date, as these were composed subsequently to the fall of the temple. It is distinct in character from B^1 and B^2; for whereas in the latter there is no expectation of the Messiah, in A^3 the Messiah is the centre of interest. Other points of difference will be dealt with in the notes. A^3 is distinct from A^1. In the latter the Messiah does not appear till the enemies of Israel are destroyed; in A^3, on the other hand, the Messiah is the agent of their destruction. A^3 may be distinct from A^2; contrast lxxi. 1 with xl. 2. If xl. 1, 2 refers to Pompey, it was written prior to his death, and A^2 would in that case be much earlier than A^3, which was composed between 50 and 70 A.D.

(*c*) *Integrity.* A^3 is handed down in tolerable preservation. liv. 17, 18 is an interpolation, and possibly lxx. 9. The text has been badly tampered with in lxxii. 1 and lxxxiv. 4 by the final editor.

(*d*) *The author.* A^3 is of extreme interest, as it is the oldest writing in which full justice is done alike to the claims of the Messiah and those of the law in moulding the world's history. The author belongs to the Rabbinical school, and assigns to certain elements of the law and tradition (cf. lvii., notes) the pre-Mosaic origin attributed to them in Jubilees. On the other hand, he recognises the popular aspiration for God's kingdom on earth as a legitimate outcome of prophecy, and gives it complete development in his forecast of history. Thus A^3 is the oldest literary evidence of the fusion of early Rabbinism and popular Messianic expectation.

LIII. In this vision a cloud is seen coming up from the sea and covering the whole earth with its summit crowned with lightning. And soon it began to discharge black waters, and then clear, and again black waters, and then clear, and so on till this succession of black and bright waters had occurred six times. And at the end of these twelve showers there was yet another shower of black waters, blacker than had been all before. Thereupon the lightning on the summit of the cloud flashed forth and healed the earth, and twelve streams came up from the sea and were subject to that lightning.

1. *A very great sea.* Cf. Dan. vii. 2.

that that cloud began to pour upon the earth the waters that were in it. 4. And I saw that there was not one and the same likeness in the waters which descended from it. 5. For in the first beginning they were black exceedingly for a time, and afterwards I saw that the waters became bright, but they were not many, and after these things again I saw black (waters), and after these things again bright, and again black and again bright. 6. Now this was done twelve times, but the black were always more numerous than the bright. 7. And it came to pass at the end of the cloud, that lo! it rained black waters, and they were darker than had been all those waters that were before, and fire was mingled with them, and where those waters descended, they wrought devastation and destruction. 8. And I saw after these things that lightning which I had seen on the summit of the cloud, that it held it fast and made it descend to the earth. 9. Now that lightning shone exceedingly, so as to illuminate the whole earth, and it healed those regions where the last waters had descended and wrought devastation. 10. And it took hold of the

6. For the twelvefold division of history see 4 Ezra xiv. 11, 12: "XII enim partibus divisum est saeculum, et transierunt ejus X jam et dimidium Xmae partis, Superant autem ejus duae post medium decimae partis." Cf. Hilgenfeld, *Mess. Jud.* 104.

7. These black waters are interpreted in lxix., lxx. They symbolise the travail pains of the Messiah.

8. The lightning on the cloud symbolises the Messiah. The imagery is derived from Dan. vii. 13. It was from the last passage that the Messiah was named ענני = "the cloud-man," or בר נפלי = "the son of the cloud." See Levi, *Neuhebräisch. Lex.* iii. 271, 422.

9. *Lightning shone . . . so as to illuminate the whole earth.* Cf. Matt. xxiv. 27: "For as the lightning cometh forth from the east, and is seen even unto the west, so shall be the coming of the Son of man."

whole earth and had dominion over it. 11. And I saw after these things, and lo! twelve rivers were ascending from the sea, and they began to surround that lightning and to become subject to it. 12. And by reason of my fear I awoke.

[Prayer of Baruch]

LIV. And I besought the Mighty One, and said: "Thou alone, O Lord, knowest of aforetime the deep things of the world, and the things which befall in their times Thou bringest about by Thy word, and against the works of the inhabitants of the earth Thou dost hasten the beginnings of the times, and the end of the seasons Thou alone knowest. 2. For whom nothing is too hard, but Thou doest everything easily by a nod. 3. To whom the depths as the heights are accessible, and the beginnings of the ages minister to Thy word. 4. Who revealeth to those who fear Him what is prepared for them, that He may thereby console them. 5. Thou showest great acts to those

10. We have here symbolised the Messiah's reign.

11. Do these twelve rivers symbolise the Gentile nations submitting themselves to the Messiah, or the twelve tribes of Israel?

LIV. 1. *Against the works*, etc. ... *hasten the beginnings of the times.* See xx. 1, note.

The end of the seasons Thou alone knowest. Cf. xxi. 8.

2. *For whom nothing is too hard.* This is a rendering of the phrase found in Gen. xviii. 14; Jer. xxxii. 17, 27. By comparing the text with the Peshitto of Luke i. 37, we see that the Greek was here *παρ' ᾧ ῥῆμα οὐκ ἀδυνατεῖ.* This is the LXX. of Gen. xviii. 14 *μὴ ἀδυνατεῖ παρὰ τῷ θεῷ ῥῆμα,* but not of Jer. xxxii. 17, 27, where we find (xxxix. 17, 27 in LXX.) *οὐ μὴ ἀποκρυβῇ ἀπὸ σοῦ οὐθέν.* This is the rendering of the Peshitto also in Gen. xviii. 14 and Jer. xxxii. 17, 27. From this verse in itself, therefore, we cannot conclude for or against the influence of the LXX. on the writer.

5. *Great acts* or "wonders."

who know not; Thou breakest up the enclosure of those who are ignorant, and lightest up what is dark, and revealest what is hidden to the pure, who in faith have submitted themselves to Thee and Thy law. 6. Thou hast shown to Thy servant this vision; reveal to me also its interpretation. 7. For I know that as regards those things wherein I besought Thee, I have received a response, and as regards what I besought, Thou didst reveal to me, and didst show me with what voice I should praise Thee, or from what members I should cause praises and hallelujahs to ascend to Thee. 8. For if my members were mouths, and the hairs of my head voices, even so I could not give Thee the meed of praise, or laud Thee as is befitting, nor could I recount Thy praise, nor tell the glory of Thy beauty, 9. For what am I amongst men, or why am I reckoned amongst those who are more excellent than I, that I should have heard all those marvellous things from the Most High, and good tidings numberless from Him who created me? 10. Blessed be my mother amongst those that bear, and praised among women be she that bare me. 11. For I will not be silent in praising the Mighty One, and with the voice of praise I will recount His marvellous deeds. 12. For who doeth like unto Thy marvellous deeds, O God, or who comprehendeth Thy deep thought of

In faith. See note on liv. 21.

8. In the *Shir ha-Shirim rabba*, i. 3 we find the hyperbolic statements of this verse far outdone: "R. Eliezer said: 'if all the seas were ink, and all the reeds were pens, and heaven and earth were rolls, and all men were scribes, yet the law could not be written down which I have taught.'"

10. An interpolation? it breaks

life? 13. For with Thy counsel Thou dost govern all the creatures which Thy right hand has created, and Thou hast established every fountain of light beside Thee, and the treasures of wisdom beneath Thy throne hast Thou prepared. 14. And justly do they perish who have not loved Thy law, and the torment of judgment will await those who have not submitted themselves to Thy power. 15. For though Adam

the connection. Cf. Luke i. 42; xi. 27; Judges v. 24.

13. *Thou dost govern.* Cf. verse 22.

14. A deliberate rejection of the law of God is here implied as in xlviii. 40, see note.

15, 19. In xxiii. 4 the *physical* effects of sin are referred to; in xlviii. 42 the *spiritual* effects. The former consisted according to B[2] (see xxiii. 4, note) in man's subjection to physical death. According to A[3] (see liv. 15; lvi. 6), however, man was already subject to physical death, and the penalty of sin consisted in premature death.

The main question, however, which concerns us here is that of predestination and free will. In order to understand the position of the writers of this book, it will be helpful to draw attention to the chief statements which appear on these subjects in Jewish non-canonical literature. In Ecclesiasticus these antinomies are stated unconditionally, not indeed in immediate contrast, but in distinct passages. Thus in xv. 11, 12, 14, 15, 17, 20, we have the freewill of man strongly affirmed: *μὴ εἴπῃς ὅτι διὰ κύριον ἀπέστην . . . μὴ εἴπῃς ὅτι αὐτός με ἐπλάνησεν· οὐ γὰρ χρείαν ἔχει ἀνδρὸς ἁμαρτωλοῦ . . . αὐτὸς ἐξ ἀρχῆς ἐποίησεν ἄνθρωπον, καὶ ἀφῆκεν αὐτὸν ἐν χειρὶ διαβουλίου αὐτοῦ. ἐὰν θέλῃς, συντηρήσεις ἐντολάς. . . ἔναντι ἀνθρώπων ἡ ζωὴ καὶ ὁ θάνατος καὶ ὃ ἐὰν εὐδοκήσῃ δοθήσεται αὐτῷ. . . . καὶ οὐκ ἐνετείλατο οὐδενὶ ἀσεβεῖν.* Cf. also xvii. 6. The doctrine of predestination is absolutely maintained in xxxvi. 10, 12, 13, *καὶ ἄνθρωποι πάντες ἀπὸ ἐδάφους καὶ ἐκ γῆς ἐκτίσθη Ἀδάμ· ἐξ αὐτῶν εὐλόγησεν καὶ ἀνύψωσεν . . . ἀπ' αὐτῶν κατηράσατο καὶ ἐταπείνωσεν καὶ ἀνέστρεψεν αὐτοὺς ἀπὸ στάσεως αὐτῶν. ὡς πηλὸς κεραμέως ἐν χειρὶ αὐτοῦ, πᾶσαι αἱ ὁδοὶ αὐτοῦ κατὰ τὴν εὐδοκίαν αὐτοῦ· οὕτως ἄνθρωποι ἐν χειρὶ τοῦ ποιήσαντος αὐτοὺς ἀποδοῦναι αὐτοῖς κατὰ τὴν κρίσιν αὐτοῦ.* Cf. also xxiii. 20; xxxix. 20, 21. These two doctrines which are thus separately affirmed in Ecclus., are given by Josephus as co-ordinate articles of the Pharisaic creed. Thus in *Bell. Jud.* ii. 8, 14, he says: *Φαρισαῖοι . . . εἱμαρμένῃ τε καὶ θεῷ προσάπτουσι πάντα καὶ τὸ μὲν πράττειν τὰ δίκαια καὶ μὴ κατὰ τὸ πλεῖστον ἐπὶ τοῖς ἀνθρώποις κεῖσθαι, βοηθεῖν δὲ εἰς ἕκαστον καὶ τὴν εἱμαρμένην.* *Ant.* xiii. 5, 9: *οἱ μὲν οὖν Φαρισαῖοι τινὰ καὶ οὐ πάντα τῆς εἱμαρμένης εἶναι λέγουσιν ἔργον, τινὰ δ' ἐφ' ἑαυτοῖς ὑπάρχειν, συμβαίνειν τε καὶ μὴ γίνεσθα* (*Ant.* xviii. 1. 3) *πράσσεσθαί τε εἱμαρμένῃ τὰ πάντα ἀξιοῦντες, οὐδὲ τοῦ ἀνθρωπείου τὸ βουλόμενον τῆς ἐπ' αὐτοῖς ὁρμῆς ἀφαιροῦνται, δοκῆσαν τῷ θεῷ κρᾶσιν γενέσθαι καὶ τῷ ἐκείνης βουλευτηρίῳ καὶ τῶν ἀνθρώπων τῷ θελήσαντι προσ-*

first sinned and brought untimely death upon all, yet of those who were born from him each one of them has

χωρεῖν μετ' ἀρετῆς ἢ κακίας. The same paradoxical creed appears in the *Pirke Aboth.* iii. 24 (ed. Taylor p. 73): "Everything is foreseen; and freewill is given. And the world is judged by grace: and everything is according to work"; and possibly also in the Pss. Sol. ix. 7 τὰ ἔργα ἡμῶν ἐν ἐκλογῇ καὶ ἐξουσίᾳ τῆς ψυχῆς ἡμῶν τοῦ ποιῆσαι δικαιοσύνην καὶ ἀδικίαν (see Ryle and James's edition, pp. 95, 96).

This co-ordination of fate and freewill as articles of faith was nothing more or less than an attempt on the part of the Pharisees to embody in their creed the two O.T. doctrines of God's omnipotence and man's responsibility. That theoretically such a creed was current may reasonably be concluded from the passages just cited, as well as from the attestation it receives in Pauline teaching in Rom. ix.-xi. (see Sanday and Headlam's *Romans*, pp. 347-350). Its acceptance, too, would, no doubt, be furthered by the pressure of the rival creeds of the Sadducees and the Essenes, who were the champions, respectively, of freewill and of fate (Joseph. *Bell. Jud.* ii. 8. 14; *Ant.* xiii. 5. 9). With the disappearance of Sadduceeism, however, the paradoxical character of Pharisaic belief seems to have disappeared also. Henceforth the Rabbinic schools teach mainly man's freedom of the will and limit God's predestinating action to his external lot.

The two doctrines of fate and freewill, though seen to be mutually exclusive, were, as we have already remarked, accepted *theoretically* as equally imperative by the Pharisees. The only instance where these two doctrines are developed into irreconcilable fulness and results and applied to religious questions in the first century is to be found in St. Paul's teaching (see above). In every other attempt to grapple with these problems a compromise is effected which results either in a vigorous or else in a very attenuated doctrine of freewill. Of this wavering attitude among the Pharisees in the first century we have sufficient evidence. Thus man's freewill is maintained in the Slav. En. xxx. 15: "And I gave him his will, and I showed him the two ways, the light and the darkness . . . that I should know whether he has love for Me or hate"; though in the next verse it is recognised that his freewill is hampered by his incorporation in the body, and his ignorance of its good and evil impulses. But the best evidence in this direction is furnished by the Apocalypse of Baruch and 4 Ezra. From our comparative study hitherto of these two works (see notes on xiv. 7; xxi. 9; xlviii. 42), we should expect that man's freewill and capacity for doing God's will, despite Adam's sin, would be emphasised in the former, and that man's helplessness and practical incapacity for righteousness in consequence of his original defects or Adam's sin would be conspicuous in the latter, and this we do find as a matter of fact. First as to 4 Ezra. In 4 Ezra the bulk of mankind was predestined to destruction (viii. 1-3); for from the beginning there was in man a wicked element (*i.e.* יצר רע) called here *granum seminis mali* (4 Ezra iv. 30): "Quoniam granum seminis mali seminatum est in corde Adam ab initio, et quantum impietatis generavit usque nunc et

prepared for his own soul torment to come, and again each one of them has chosen for himself glories to come.

generabit usque cum veniat area"; through Adam's yielding to this evil element a hereditary tendency to sin was created and the *cor malignum* developed (iii. 21, 22). Cor enim malignum baiolans primus Adam transgressus et victus est, sed et omnes qui ex eo nati sunt. Et facta est permanens infirmitas, et lex in corde populi cum malignitate radicis, et discessit quod bonum est, et mansit malignum. We should observe that *baiolans* in iii. 21 just cited represents *φορέσας*: for both the Syriac and Ethiopic Versions=*cum vestivit*. Hence Adam "clothed himself" with a wicked heart by yielding to the evil impulse which was in him when created. Adam was created with two impulses: "the good impulse" (יצר הטוב) implied in the words *discessit quod bonum est* (iii. 22), and "the evil impulse" already referred to. This subject is further pursued in iii. 25, 26: "Et deliquerunt qui habitabant civitatem, In omnibus facientes sicut fecit Adam et omnes generationes ejus, utebantur enim et ipsi cor malignum." As a result of Adam's transgression, the evil impulse having been developed into the *cor malignum*, and having thus obtained the mastery over man, the writer of vii. 118 naturally charges Adam with being the cause of the final perdition of mankind: "O tu quid fecisti Adam? si enim tu peccasti, non est factum solius tuus casus sed et nostrum qui ex te advenimus." Naturally in the face of such a hopeless view of man's condition no real doctrine of freewill could be maintained. In fact, in 4 Ezra only sufficient freewill is accorded to man to justify his final condemnation. Cf. 4 Ezra viii. 56, 58-60, "Nam et ipsi accipientes libertatem spreverunt Altissimum et legem ejus contempserunt. . . . Et dixerunt in corde suo non esse deum, et quidem scientes sciunt quoniam moriuntur. . . . Non enim Altissimus voluit hominem disperdi; Sed ipsi qui creati sunt coinquinaverunt nomen ejus qui fecit eos." vii. 72, "Qui ergo commorantes sunt in terra hinc cruciabuntur, quoniam sensum habentes iniquitatem fecerunt et mandata accipientes non servaverunt ea et legem consecuti fraudaverunt eam quam acceperunt." ix. 11, Fastidierunt legem meam cum adhuc erant habentes libertatem.

Turning now to the present Apocalypse, we find in all its sections, even in the gloomiest, B[2], a view of man's present capacities and future destiny that is optimistic when set side by side with 4 Ezra. Whereas in A[3], according to liv. 15, 19, the effects of Adam's sin are limited to physical results; his descendants must die prematurely. On the nature of these physical results in other sections see xxiii. 4, note. As to spiritual results, each man is the Adam of his own soul, and can choose for himself either bliss or torment; he can work out his own salvation and even make God his debtor (see xiv. 7, note). Only in xlviii. 42 is spiritual death traced to Adam.

The view set forth in the text as to man's condition is exactly that which prevails in the Talmud. In fact, Weber's summing up on this question would serve admirably for an exposition of the text: "Der freie Wille auch in Bezug auf das Verhalten gegen Gott ist dem Menschen auch nach dem Fall geblieben. Es

LIV. 16-18 = B². [16. For assuredly he who believeth will receive reward. 17. But now, as for you, ye wicked that now are, turn ye to destruction, because ye will speedily be visited, in that from time to time ye have rejected the understanding of the Most High. 18. For His works have not taught you, nor has the skill of His creation which is at all times persuaded you.] 19. Adam is

gibt eine Erbschuld, aber keine Erbsünde: der Fall Adam's hat dem ganzen Geschlecht den Tod, nicht aber die Sündigkeit im Sinne einer Nothwendigkeit zu sündigen verursacht; die Sünde ist das Ergebnis der Entscheidung jedes Einzelnen, erfahrungsgemäss allgemein, aber an sich auch nach dem Fall nicht schlechthin nothwendig" (*Lehren d. Talmud*, p. 217).

Only one statement in this citation seems untrustworthy, *i.e.* *Es gibt eine Erbschuld.* I can see nothing in Weber's learned work to justify this statement, but everything to show that there was neither hereditary sin nor hereditary guilt. Moreover, on p. 240 this statement is actually made: "Wenn die Sünde und Schuld nicht erblich ist, kann dann die Strafe erblich sein? . . . Diese Antinomie hat die jüdische Theologie durch drei Sätze auszugleichen versucht."

15. *Untimely*. See note on xxiii. 4. The phrase rendered "untimely" is ܕܠܐ ܒܙܒܢܗ. It recurs in lvi. 6 and lxxiii. 3.

16-18. These verses are clearly an interpolation for the same reasons as xlviii. 48-50 and lii. 5-7. These three passages seem to have been addressed by Baruch to the people, and to have formed part of one and the same discourse. The original order appears to have been: first, liv. 17, 18, where the wicked are menaced with the final judgment; then xlviii. 48-50, in which the destiny of the wicked is dismissed and that of the righteous described; next, lii. 5-7, where a line of conduct is prescribed to the righteous on the ground of that destiny, and a preparation of their souls for the reward laid up for them; and finally, liv. 16, where the faithful are assured of that reward.

It will be observed (1) that these verses break the sense of the context; (2) that a direct address to the wicked could not occur in a prayer to God.

18. In liv. 14 it is implied that the wicked there described knew the law. This is intelligible from the standpoint of the Jewish belief that the Gentiles were offered the law but refused it. But in this verse no such view is implied. Their knowledge of God could only arise from reflection on His works in nature. The same argument is found in Rom. i. 20. This argument "is as old as the Psalter, Job, and Isaiah (Pss. xix. 1; xciv. 9; cxliii. 5; Isa. xlii. 5; xlv. 18; Job xii. 9; xxvi. 14; xxxvi. 24; Wisdom ii. 23; xiii. 1, 5). It is common to Greek thought as well as Jewish (Arist. *De Mundo*, 6; Philo, *De Praem. et Poen.* 7" (Sanday and Headlam, Rom. p. 43).

19. See note on verse 15. The real force of this verse is that a man's guilt and sin are not derived

therefore not the cause, save only of his own soul, but each one of us has been the Adam of his own soul. 20. But do Thou, O Lord, expound to me regarding those things which Thou hast revealed to me, and inform me regarding that which I besought Thee. 21. For at the consummation of the world there will be vengeance taken upon those who have done wickedness according to their wickedness, and Thou wilt glorify the faithful according to their faithfulness. 22. For those who are amongst Thine own Thou rulest, and those who sin Thou blottest out from amongst Thine own."

LV. And it came to pass when I had finished speaking the words of this prayer, that I sat there under a tree, that I might rest in the shade of the branches. 2. And I wondered and was astonied, and pondered in my thoughts regarding the multitude of goodness which sinners who are upon the earth

from Adam, but are due to his own action. The evil impulse (יצר הרע) does not constitute guilt or sin unless man obeys it. As the Talmudists say, it was placed in man to be overcome (Weber, 210).

21. *The faithful according to their faith.* Faith in this passage is contrasted with unrighteousness (ܥܘܠܐ = ἀνομία). Hence we should take it here as equivalent either to "righteousness" or "fidelity to the law." In liv. 16 the verb "believe" may mean "to be faithful." But the context is doubtful. Elsewhere in Baruch faith = "belief." Thus in lix. 2 those who "believe" are opposed to those who "deny"; in xlii. 2 to those who "despise." This is the meaning also in liv. 5; lvii. 2; lxxxiii. 8. In 4 Ezra vi. 5 faith seems to mean "righteousness," the result of fidelity to the law (as in Apoc. Bar. liv. 21); for the righteous are those *qui fidem thesaurizaverunt;* possibly also in v. 1; vi. 28; it means fidelity to the law in vii. 34, as *incredulitas* in vii. 114 = "disloyalty." In ix. 7, 8; xiii. 23, faith and works are combined and appear nearly synonymous. For a most instructive note on the various meanings of "faith," see Sanday and Headlam's *Romans*, pp. 31-34.

Faith in the Talmud is in one of its aspects regarded as a work which as the fulfilment of the law produces merit. In the *Beresh. rabba*, lxxiv. the merit arising from faith and the merit arising from the law are co-ordinated. See Weber, pp. 292, 295, 298.

have rejected, and regarding the great torment which they have despised, though they knew that they should be tormented because of the sin they had committed. 3. And when I was pondering on these things and the like, lo! the angel Ramiel who presides over true visions was sent to me, and he said unto me: 4. "Why does thy heart trouble thee, Baruch, and why does thy thought disturb thee? 5. For if by the hearsay which thou hast only heard of judgment thou art so moved, what (wilt thou be) when thou shalt see it manifestly with thine eyes? 6. And if with the expectation wherewith thou dost expect the day of the Mighty One thou art so overcome, what (wilt thou be) when thou shalt come to its advent? 7. And, if at the word of the announcement of the torment of those who have done foolishly thou art so wholly distraught, how much more when the event will reveal marvellous things? 8. And if thou hast heard tidings of the good and evil things which are then coming and art grieved, what (wilt thou be) when thou shalt behold what the majesty will reveal, which will convict these and cause those to rejoice?

LV. 2. *Despised, though they knew.* See xv. 6, note; xlviii. 40, note.

3. *Ramiel.* Cf. lxiii. 6; this angel is mentioned in the Eth. En. xx. 7 (Greek) Ῥεμειὴλ ὁ εἷς τῶν ἁγίων ἀγγέλων ὃν ἔταξεν ὁ Θεὸς ἐπὶ τῶν ἀνισταμένων: also in 4 Ezra iv. 36, where the Syriac Version = "And the angel Ramiel answered and said unto them" (*i.e.* the righteous souls in the soul-treasuries); for "Ramiel" the Latin gives *Hieremihel.* Finally, in *Or. Sibyl.* ii. 215-217, Ramiel is one of the five angels appointed by God to bring the souls of men to judgment: Ἀρακιὴλ Ῥαμιὴλ Οὐριὴλ Σαμιὴλ Ἀζαὴλ τε . . . ἀνθρώπων ψυχὰς . . . ἐς κρίσιν ἄξουσιν πάσας. The function of Ramiel in the text agrees to some extent with that assigned to him in 4 Ezra.

5. *And art so moved.* I have followed Ceriani's suggestion here in supplying ܘ before ܗܟܢܐ.

LVI. "Nevertheless, because thou hast besought the Most High to reveal to thee the interpretation of the vision which thou hast seen, I have been sent to say to thee. 2. And the Mighty One hath assuredly made known to thee the methods of the times that have passed, and of those that are destined to pass in His world from the beginning of its creations even unto its consummation, of those things which (are) deceit and of those which (are) in truth. 3. For as thou didst see a great cloud which ascended from the sea, and went and covered the earth, this is the duration of the world (= αἰών) which the Mighty One made when He took counsel to make the world. 4. And it came to pass when the word had gone forth from His presence, that the duration of the world had come into being in a small degree, and was established according to the multitude of the intelligence of Him who sent it. 5. And as thou didst previously see on the summit of the cloud black waters which descended previously on the earth, this is the transgression wherewith Adam the first man transgressed. 6. For owing to his transgression untimely death came into being, and grief was named

LVI. 2. *And the Mighty.* We should expect *That the Mighty.*

3. *A great cloud . . . this is the duration of the world.* This cloud is divided into thirteen parts: the first twelve parts of alternate black and bright waters (see liii. 5, 6), and the thirteenth of the blackest waters of all (see liii. 7). These symbolise the thirteen periods into which the history of the world is divided prior to the Messiah's kingdom. This kingdom is foreshadowed by the lightning that shone on the extremity or summit of the cloud.

4. *Was established.* I have followed Ceriani here in reading ܘܐܬܬܩܢ instead of ܘܐܬܩܢ.

6. *Owing to his transgression.* The text literally = "when he transgressed."

Untimely. See liv. 15, note.

and anguish was prepared, and pain was created, and trouble perfected, and boasting began to be established, and Sheol to demand that it should be renewed in blood, and the begetting of children was brought about, and the passion of parents produced, and the greatness of humanity was humiliated, and goodness languished. 7. What therefore can be blacker or darker than these things? 8. This is the beginning of the black waters which thou hast seen. 9. And from these black (waters) again were black derived, and the darkness of darkness produced. 10. For he was a danger to his own soul: even to the angels was he a danger. 11. For, moreover, at that time when he was created, they enjoyed liberty. 12. And some of them descended, and mingled with women. 13. And then those who did so were tormented in chains. 14. But the rest of the multitude of the angels, of which there is no number, restrained themselves. 15. And those who dwelt on the earth perished together (with them) through the waters of the deluge. 16. These are the black first waters.

Sheol to demand, etc. For this hunger of Sheol, cf. Prov. xxvii. 20; Isa. v. 14. On Sheol, see note on xi. 6.

10. *He was a danger*, etc. This must mean that man's physical nature was a danger to his spiritual; for it was the physical side of man that proved a danger to the angels who fell through lust. Man's physical nature was dangerous; for in it resided the "evil impulse" (see note on liv. 15, 19).

11-13. *They enjoyed liberty*, *i.e.* the angels. This liberty, according to the ancient myth, they abused by taking to themselves wives of the daughters of men (see Eth. En. vi. 2, note; Slav. En. xviii. 4-6; Jubilees v. 1-11; x. 1-13).

14. *No number*. The MS. omits the negative, but wrongly, as Ceriani has already observed (cf. xxi. 6; lix. 11). For a still more obvious loss of the negative see li. 16, though strangely enough it has not hitherto been remarked.

LVII. "And after these (waters) thou didst see bright waters: this is the fount of Abraham, also his generations and advent of his son, and of his son's son, and of those like them. 2. Because at that time the unwritten law was named amongst them, and the works of the commandments were then fulfilled, and belief in the coming judgment was then generated, and hope of the world that was to be renewed was then built up, and the promise of the life that should come hereafter was implanted. 3. These are the bright waters, which thou hast seen.

LVIII. "And the black third waters which thou

LVII. 1. The first bright period embraces human history from the time of Abraham to that of the twelve sons of Jacob and their righteous contemporaries or immediate successors.

2. *The unwritten law.* This statement proceeds from the same spirit which animates the entire Book of Jubilees, and which seeks to trace traditionalism and its observances to the times of the patriarchs. In later Judaism there were manifold attempts of this nature. Thus in the *Avoda-sara*, 36*b*, according to Gen. xxxviii. 24, impurity was forbidden by the Rabbinic tribunal of Shem; in the *Beresh. rabba*, xciv., Shem and Eber are said to have handed on certain traditions to Jacob; in the *Joma*, 28*b*, Abraham is said to have observed the whole Torah and the traditional or unwritten law. To Abraham, Isaac, and Jacob the three daily times of prayer are traced back in the *Berachoth*, 26*b*. The above statements are drawn from Herzfeld, *Geschichte Israels*, p. 226. For a detailed description of the traditional law from the earliest times down to Hillel, see *op. cit.* iii. 226-263; Weber, 255.

Works of the commandments were then fulfilled. See preceding note.

Belief. See note on liv. 21.

Hope of the world to be renewed. See note on xxxii. 6. In the earlier Messiah-Apocalypses in this book, *i.e.* in A^1 and A^2, the renewal of the world is to take place at the close of the Messianic kingdom, for in these writings this kingdom belongs to this world *ὁ αἰὼν οὗτος* (Matt. xii. 82) = הָעוֹלָם הַזֶּה; whereas in A^3 with which we are at present dealing it is said (lxxiv. 2) to form the close of the present world and the beginning of the next (*i.e. ὁ αἰὼν ὁ μέλλλων* or *ὁ ἐρχόμενος* = הָעוֹלָם הַבָּא). If we are to take (lxxiv. 2) literally, then the renewal of the world is to take place during the Messiah's reign. But this is unlikely. In 4 Ezra vii. 28-30; xii. 32-34, the Messiah's kingdom belongs to this world. In xiii. 32-50 to the next, if xiii. 36 is genuine. In the older literature the Messianic kingdom belongs to the next world (cf. Eth. En. xxxvii.-lxx.)

hast seen, these are the mingling of all sins, which the nations afterwards wrought after the death of those righteous men, and the wickedness of the land of Egypt, wherein they did wickedly in the service wherewith they made their sons to serve. 2. Nevertheless, these also perished at last.

LIX. "And the bright fourth waters which thou hast seen are the advent of Moses and Aaron and Miriam and Joshua the son of Nun and Caleb and of all those like them. 2. For at that time the lamp of the eternal law shone on all those who sat in darkness, which announced to them that believe the promise of their reward, and to them that deny, the torment of fire which is reserved for them. 3. But also the heavens at that time were shaken from their place, and those who were under the throne of the Mighty One were perturbed, when He was taking Moses unto Himself. 4. For He showed him many admonitions together with the principles of the laws and the consummation of time, as also to thee, and likewise the pattern of Zion and its measures, which was to be

LVIII. 1. *The service wherewith they made their sons to serve.* Exod. i. 14 is here closely followed: בל־עבדתם אשר־עבדו בהם. As the LXX. has here *πάντα τὰ ἔργα ὧν καταδουλοῦντο αὐτούς*, it is clear that the original writer had the Hebrew text and not the LXX. before him.

LIX. 2. *The eternal law.* Cf. xvii. 6. See xv. 5, note.

The lamp . . . darkness—a Rabbinic application of Isa. ix. 2. Isa. ix. 2 was a favourite passage in N.T. times (cf. Matt. iv. 16; Luke i. 79).

That believe. See liv. 21, note.

Torment of fire. Cf. xliv. 15; xlviii. 39; lxxxv. 13. It will be observed that these passages suggest a material fire in which the wicked are to be tormented after the resurrection, *i.e.* after they have resumed their bodies.

4. *The pattern of Zion and its measures.* Cf. Exod. xxv. 40; xxvi. 30; Heb. viii. 5.

Which was to be made, etc. A very slight change in the Syriac would give a good text: "In the

made in the pattern of the sanctuary of the present time. 5. But then also He showed to him the measures of the fire, also the depths of the abyss, and the weight of the winds, and the number of the drops of rain. 6. And the suppression of anger, and the multitude of long-suffering, and the truth of judgment. 7. And the root of wisdom, and the riches of understanding, and the fount of knowledge. 8. And the height of the air, and the greatness of Paradise, and

pattern of which the sanctuary of the present time was to be made."

5-11. It is of importance to observe, with a view to determining the date of A[3], that in these verses we have a transference of Enoch's functions to Moses, and that the revelations hitherto attributed to Enoch are here for the first time assigned to Moses. It is noteworthy that another of Enoch's chief functions is ascribed to Ezra in 4 Ezra xiv. 50. This opposition to Enoch is unswervingly pursued in the Talmud. Thus, whereas in pre-Christian Judaism, Enoch, and Enoch only, is described as the scribe of the deeds of men (Jub. iv. 23; x. 17; Slav. En. xl. 13; liii. 2; lxiv. 5), this office is assigned to various Jewish heroes in later Judaism. Thus according to *Ruth rabba*, 33*a*, it is Elijah; according to *Esther rabba*, 86*d*, it is the angels; according to *Jalkut Shim.*, *Beresh.* 141, it was formerly the prophets, but now it is only Elijah and the Messiah (Weber, 272). We have already drawn attention to this phenomenon in the note on xiii. 3, and have there pointed out that this hostility to Enoch is the outcome of Jewish hostility to Christianity as a whole; for as we know from manifold evidence the writings of Enoch enjoyed a singular influence on early Christianity. This aggressive attitude of Judaism could hardly have originated before the open rupture of Christianity with the Synagogue and the Pauline controversy. Hence this writing was not earlier than A.D. 50. From lxviii. 5 it is clear that it is prior to A.D. 70. Therefore the limits of its composition are A.D. 50-70.

5. *The depths of the abyss.* A frequent subject in both books of Enoch: Eth. En. xviii. 11; xxi. 7-10, etc.; Slav. En. xxviii. 3.

The weight of the winds. The weighing of the winds is described in the Slav. En. xl. 11; cf. also Eth. xli. 4.

The number of the drops of rain. Slav. En. xlvii. 5; Ecclus. i. 2.

7. *Root of wisdom.* See li. 3, note.

Riches of understanding. lxi. 4.

The fount of knowledge. Bar. iii. 12; 4 Ezra xiv. 47.

8. *The height of the air.* Slav. En. xl. 12: "I have written down the height from the earth to the seventh heaven."

The greatness of Paradise. The measures of Paradise are taken by the angels for Enoch. Cf. Eth. En. lxi. 1-4; lxx. 3, 4.

the consummation of the ages, and the beginning of the day of judgment. 9. And the number of the offerings, and the earths which have not yet come. 10. And the mouth of Gehenna, and the station of vengeance, and the place of faith, and the region of hope. 11. And the likeness of future torment, and the multitude of innumerable angels, and the powers of the flames, and the splendour of the lightnings, and the voice of the thunders, and the orders of the chiefs of the angels, and the treasuries of light, and the changes of the times, and the investigations of the law. 12. These are the bright fourth waters which thou hast seen.

LX. "And the black fifth waters which thou hast

The consummation of the ages. This subject is discussed in every section of the Enochic literature.

The beginning of the day of judgment. This date is fixed according to a definite reckoning in the Slav. En. xxxii. 2-xxxiii. 2; lxv. 7-10; according to certain indefinite measures in Eth. En. lxxxiii.-xc.; xci.-civ.

10. *The mouth of Gehenna.* Eth. En. xxvii. 2, 3; liv.; lxii. 12; xc. 26, 27.

The station of vengeance. Many places of vengeance are described in the two books of Enoch: Eth. En. xviii. 12-16; xix.; xxi.; xxii. 10-13; liv. 1-6; xc. 24-27; Slav. En. x.; xl. 12.

The place of faith, and the region of hope. These seem to be the places of intermediate bliss. Cf. Eth. En. xxii. 5-9.

11. *The likeness of future torment.* Slav. xl. 12.

The multitude of innumerable angels. See lvi. 14, note. Of early Jewish literature, it is only in Enoch that the angels are described at length.

The splendour of the lightnings, and the voice of the thunders. Eth. En. xli. 3; xliii. 1, 2; xliv.; lix.; lx. 13-15; Slav. En. xl. 9.

The orders of the chiefs of the angels. I have here read the plural ܪ̈ܫܐ instead of the singular ܪܫܐ. Ceriani renders the text: "ordines principatus angelorum." The Jews believed in ten orders of angels, the Christians in nine. These orders are mentioned and in part enumerated in the Slav. En. xx. 1, 3 (see note); cf. also Eth. lxi. 10; lxxi. 7-9.

The treasuries of light. This expression is unexampled.

The changes of the times, i.e. the seasons. Slav. En. xiii. 5; xl. 6; Eth. En. lxxxii. 11-20.

seen raining are the works which the Amorites wrought, and the spells of their incantations which they wrought, and the wickedness of their mysteries, and the mingling of their pollution. 2. But even Israel was then polluted by sins in the days of the judges, though they saw many signs which were from Him who made them.

LXI. "And the bright sixth waters which thou didst see, this is the time in which David and Solomon were born. 2. And there was at that time the building of Zion, and the dedication of the sanctuary, and the shedding of much blood of the nations that sinned then, and many offerings which were offered then in the dedication of the sanctuary. 3. And peace and tranquillity existed at that time. 4. And wisdom was heard in the assembly, and the riches of understanding were magnified in the congregations. 5. And the holy festivals were fulfilled in goodness and in much joy. 6. And the judgment of the rulers was then seen to be without guile, and the righteousness of the precepts of the Mighty One was accomplished with truth. 7. And because the land was then beloved at that time, and because its inhabitants sinned not, it was glorified beyond all lands, and the city Zion ruled then over all lands and regions. 8. These are the bright waters which thou hast seen.

LX. 1. *Mingling of their pollution.* Cf. Pss. Sol. ii. 14, ἐν φυρμῷ ἀναμίξεως.

2. *Of the judges.* I here follow Ceriani in correcting ܕܕܝܢܐ (="of judgment") into ܕܕܝ̈ܢܐ.

LXI. 4. *Riches of understanding.* lix. 7.

LXII. "And the black seventh waters which thou hast seen, this is the perversion (brought about) by the counsel of Jeroboam, who took counsel to make two calves of gold. 2. And all the iniquities which the kings who were after him iniquitously wrought. 3. And the curse of Jezebel and the worship of idols which Israel practised at that time. 4. And the withholding of rain, and the famines which occurred until women eat the fruit of their wombs. 5. And the time of their captivity which came upon the nine tribes and a half, because they were in many sins. 6. And Salmanasar king of Assyria came and led them away captive. 7. But regarding the Gentiles it were tedious to tell how they always wrought impiety and wickedness, and never wrought righteousness. 8. These are the black seventh waters which thou hast seen.

LXIII. "And the bright eighth waters which thou hast seen, this is the rectitude and uprightness of Hezekiah king of Judah and his benignity which came upon him. 2. For when Sennacherib was stirred up in order that he might perish, and his wrath troubled him in order that he might thereby

LXII. 4. Cf. 2 Kings vi. 28, 29.

5. The captivity of the nine and a half tribes 721 B.C. See lxxviii., note.

6. *I.e.* Shalmaneser, 2 Kings xvii. 3, 6. Cf. 4 Ezra xiii. 40.

7. *Wrought righteousness.* The text is ܐܙܕܕܩܘ = "have been justified." For the grounds for the above restoration, see xxi. 9, note.

LXIII. 1. *His benignity.* So ܘܛܒܘܬܗ. But the MS. originally read ܘܛܝܒܘܬܗ = "bounty, kindness." Both readings seem wrong.

2. This verse is translated as it stands in the Syriac. By omitting "for" the word "multitude" could be made the subject of the word "perish."

perish, for the multitude also of the nations which were with him. 3. When, moreover, Hezekiah the king heard those things which the king of Assyria was devising, (*i.e.*) to come and seize him and destroy his people, the two and a half tribes which remained: nay, more he wished to overthrow Zion also: then Hezekiah trusted in his works, and had hope in his righteousness, and spake with the Mighty One and said: 4. 'Behold, for lo! Sennacherib is prepared to destroy us, and he will be boastful and uplifted when he has destroyed Zion.' 5. And the Mighty One heard him, for Hezekiah was wise, and He had respect unto his prayer, because he was righteous. 6. And thereupon the Mighty One commanded Ramiel His angel who speaks with thee. 7. And I went forth and destroyed their multitude, the number of whose chiefs only was a hundred and eighty-five

3. *Hezekiah trusted in his works.* See xiv. 7, note. Observe the play on Hezekiah's name in these words when retranslated into Hebrew, חזקיה התחזק על. There appears to have been one also in Ecclus. xlviii. 22, *ἐποίησεν γὰρ Ἐζεκίας . . . καὶ ἐνίσχυσεν.* This conjecture as to the probable text in Ecclus. was made in March. It is now (June 20) confirmed by Dr. Neubauer's discovery last week in the Bodley of the Hebrew text of Ecclus. xl.-l. To his kindness and that of Mr. Cowley I owe the following passages where this play on the name occurs twice:—Ecclus. xlviii. 17, יחזקיהו חזק עירו=Ἐζεκίας *ὠχύρωσεν τὴν πόλιν αὐτοῦ*, and xlviii. 22, (כי עשה יחז)קיהו את הטוב (וי)תחזק בדרכי דוד=*ἐποίησεν γὰρ Ἐζεκίας τὸ ἀρεστὸν κυρίῳ, καὶ ἐνίσχυσεν ἐν ὁδοῖς Δαυείδ.*

4. *Lo, Sennacherib is prepared to destroy us.* There was a play here on the name Sennacherib in the Hebrew, והנה סנחריב עתיד להחריב אותנו.

5. In *Sifre*, 12*b*, and *Jalkut Shim.*, *Beresh.* 27, it is taught that men are heard by God on the ground either of their own merit or on that of others (Weber, 284, 285).

7. In 2 Kings xix. 35; Isa. xxxvii. 36, 185,000 is the complete number of the slain. In 2 Chron. xxxii. 21, only the slaughter of the chiefs is mentioned. From these two accounts the writer has worked up the present.

thousand, and each one of them had an equal number (at his command). 8. And at that time I burned their bodies within, but their raiment and arms I preserved outwardly, in order that the still more wonderful deeds of the Mighty One might appear, and that thereby His name might be spoken of throughout the whole earth. 9. Moreover, Zion was saved and Jerusalem delivered: Israel also was freed from tribulation. 10. And all those who were in the holy land rejoiced, and the name of the Mighty One was glorified so that it was spoken of. 11. These are the bright waters which thou hast seen.

LXIV. "And the black ninth waters which thou hast seen, this is all the wickedness which was in the days of Manasseh the son of Hezekiah. 2. For he wrought much impiety, and he slew the righteous, and he wrested judgment, and he shed the blood of the innocent, and wedded women he violently polluted, and he overturned the altars, and destroyed their offerings, and drave forth the priests lest they should minister in the sanctuary. 3. And he made an image with five faces: four of them looked to the

LXIV. 3. *He made an image with five faces: four of*, etc. This is a very peculiar version of 2 Chron. xxxiii. 7. וישם את-פסל הסמל—"he set the graven image of the idol." The LXX. implies the Hebrew just given. The Syriac, however, exhibits an early gloss which prepares the way for our text. Thus it gives ܘܣܡܗ ܠܨܠܡܐ ܕܐܪܒܥ ܐܦܝܢ = "and he set the four-fronted image." The Arabic goes still further; it = "and he set a statue having four heads with four faces." But the form of the tradition nearest to the text is found in the Talmud, *Sanh.* 103*b*: "At first he made for it (the idol) one face and in the end he made for it four faces, that the Shechinah might see and be provoked."

four winds, and the fifth on the summit of the image as an adversary of the zeal of the Mighty One. 4. And then wrath went forth from the presence of the Mighty One to the intent that Zion should be rooted out, as also it befell in your days. 5. But also against the two tribes and a half went forth a decree that they should also be led away captive, as thou hast now seen. 6. And to such a degree did the impiety of Manasseh increase, that it removed the praise of the Most High from the sanctuary. 7. On this account Manasseh was at that time named 'the impious,' and finally his abode was in the fire. 8. For though his prayer was heard with the Most High, finally, when he was cast into the brazen horse and the brazen horse was melted, it served as a sign unto him

6. *Removed the praise of the Most High from the sanctuary.* This may be explained by the statement in *Sanh.* 103*b*, that Manasseh erased the divine name and overturned the altar.

7. This verse runs counter to 2 Chron. xxxiii. 11-19, where it is clearly implied that Manasseh was really forgiven on his repentance. This writer declares, on the other hand, that Manasseh's experience in the brazen horse was only a foretaste of his future sufferings in hell.

In the fire. See xliv. 15, note.

8. *His prayer.* 2 Chron. xxxiii. 19; *The Prayer of Manasseh* in the Apocrypha.

Cast into the brazen horse and the brazen horse was melted. This tradition appears in the Targum of Chronicles after 2 Chron. xxxiii. 11: "And the Chaldeans made a copper mule and pierced it all over with little holes, and shut him up therein and kindled fire all around him. . . . And he turned and prayed before the Lord his God. . . . And He shook the world with His word, and the mule burst asunder and he went forth therefrom." Traces of this tradition are also found in the Apostolic Constitutions ii. 22: *καὶ ἐπήκουσε τῆς φωνῆς αὐτοῦ κύριος . . . καὶ ἐγένετο περὶ αὐτὸν φλὸξ πυρὸς καὶ ἐτάκησαν πάντα τὰ περὶ αὐτὸν σίδηρα.* Also in Anastasius on Ps. vi. (Canisius, *Thesaur. Monum.* iii. 112) *φασὶ οἱ ἀρχαῖοι τῶν ἱστοριογράφων, ὅτι ἀπενεχθεὶς Μανασσῆς κατεκλείσθη εἰς ζώδιον χαλκοῦν ἀπὸ βασιλέως Περσῶν καὶ ἔσω ὢν ἐν τοιούτῳ ζωδίῳ προσηύξατο μετὰ δακρύων.* In Suidas (see *Μανασσῆς*): *αἰχμάλωτος ἀπήχθη καὶ ἐς τὸ χαλκοῦν ἄγαλμα καθείρχθη . . . ἐδεήθη τοῦ κυρίου . . . καὶ τὸ μὲν ἄγαλμα θείᾳ δυνάμει διερράγη.*

Served as a sign. See note on ver. 7.

at the time. 9. For he did not live perfectly, for he was not worthy—but that thenceforward he might know by whom finally he should be tormented. 10. For he who is able to benefit is also able to torment.

LXV. "Thus, moreover, did Manasseh act impiously, and thought that in his time the Mighty One would not inquire into these things. 2. These are the black ninth waters which thou hast seen.

LXVI. "And the bright tenth waters which thou hast seen: this is the purity of the generations of Josiah king of Judah, who was the only one at that time who submitted himself to the Mighty One with all his heart and with all his soul. 2. And he cleansed the land from idols, and hallowed all the vessels which had been polluted, and restored the offerings to the altar, and raised the horn of the holy, and exalted the righteous, and glorified all that were wise in understanding, and brought back the priests to their ministry, and destroyed and removed the magicians and enchanters and fortune-tellers from the land. 3. And not only did he slay the impious that were living, but they also took from the sepulchres

9. Text is corrupt.

LXVI. 1. The writer thus appears to have believed that though Manasseh prayed, yet he did not really repent. This view is found in *Sanh.* 101: "Our Rabbis have taught: there are three who came *with cunning* (before God): they are Cain, Esau, and Manasseh. . . . Manasseh at first called upon many gods, and at last upon the God of his fathers" [Rashi: "He said: 'If Thou save me not, what doth it profit me that I have called on Thee, more than the other gods?'"] (quoted by Ball in his Comm. on *The Prayer of Manasses*). In *Sanh.* x. three kings are said to have no part in the future life, *i.e.* Jeroboam, Ahab, and Manasseh. Yet in the *Debarim rabba*, ii., salvation is ultimately said to be in store for Manasseh (Weber, 328).

the bones of the dead and burned them with fire. 4. [And the festivals and the sabbaths he established in their sanctity], and their polluted ones he burnt in the fire, and the lying prophets which deceived the people, these also he burnt in the fire, and the people who listened to them when they were living, he cast them into the brook Cedron, and heaped stones upon them. 5. And he was zealous with the zeal of the Mighty One with all his soul, and he alone was firm in the law at that time, so that he left none that was uncircumcised, or that wrought impiety in all the land, all the days of his life. 6. This, moreover, is he that shall receive an eternal reward, and he shall be glorified with the Mighty One beyond many at a later time. 7. For on his account and on account of those who are like him were the inestimable glories, of which thou wast told before, created and prepared. 8. These are the bright waters which thou hast seen.

LXVII. "And the black eleventh waters which thou hast seen: this is the calamity which is now befalling Zion. 2. Dost thou think that there is no anguish to the angels in the presence of the Mighty One, that Zion was so delivered up, and that lo! the Gentiles boast in their hearts, and assemble before their idols and say: 'She is trodden

4. The words which I have bracketed are either interpolated or misplaced. It would perhaps be best to read them after "to their ministry" in verse 2. In that case for "festival" we should read "festivals."

7. See note on xiv. 18.

LXVII. 2. *Boast.* Cf. v. 1; vii. 1; lxxx. 3. *Assemble.* The text ܟܢܫ̈ܐ = "crowds" is corrupt. I have emended it into ܟܢܫܘ = "assemble."

down who ofttimes trod down, and she has been reduced to servitude who reduced (others)?' 3. Dost thou think that in these things the Most High rejoices, or that His name is glorified? 4. But how will it serve towards His righteous judgment? 5. Yet after these things shall those that are dispersed among the Gentiles be taken hold of by tribulation, and in shame shall they dwell in every place. 6. Because so far as Zion is delivered up and Jerusalem laid waste, and idols prosper in the cities of the Gentiles, and the vapour of the smoke of the incense of righteousness which is by the law is extinguished in Zion and in the region of Zion, lo! in every place there is the smoke of impiety. 7. But the king of Babylon will arise who has now destroyed Zion, and he will boast over the people, and he will speak great things in his heart in the presence of the Most High. 8. But

5. "The dispersed" here seem to be the nine and a half tribes.

6-7. With the destruction of Jerusalem, godlessness is triumphant everywhere. In all the references in A^3 to this destruction of Jerusalem, *i.e.* in lxiv. 4; lxvii. 2, 6, 7, there is no trace of consciousness in the mind of the writer that there was any divine interposition to save the sacred vessels of the temple and to destroy Zion by the agency of angels after the manner described in B^1, *i.e.* in vi. 4-10; lxxx. 1-3. If, further, we remark that the declared object of this interposition was to prevent the enemies of Zion boasting before their idols that they had laid it waste and burnt the temple (vii. 1; cf. v. 1; lxxx. 3), and if at the same time we observe that the writer of A^3 represents the angel Ramiel as admitting that the Gentiles are boasting before their idols of their destruction of Zion (lxvii. 2), and that the king of Babylon makes the same vaunt (lxvii. 7), we can with tolerable certainty conclude that the ideas in B^1, *i.e.* in v. 1; vi. 4-vii. 1; lxxx. 1-3, were either unknown to him or else unacknowledged. These ideas seem foreign to B^2 also. This writer would have sympathised with the remonstrance in 4 Ezra v. 30: "Et si odiens odisti populum tuum, tuis manibus debet castigari." In the Assumpt. Mosis (iii. 2) the capture of the sacred vessels by Nebuchadnezzar is acknowledged.

Righteousness which is by the law. See xv. 5, note.

he also shall fall at last. 9. These are the black waters.

LXVIII. "And the bright twelfth waters which thou hast seen: this is the word. 2. For after these things a time will come when thy people shall fall into distress, so that they shall all run the risk of perishing together. 3. Nevertheless, they will be saved, and their enemies will fall in their presence. 4. And they will have in (due) time much joy. 5. And at that time after a little interval Zion will again be builded, and its offerings will again be restored, and the priests will return to their ministry, and again the Gentiles will come to glorify it. 6. Nevertheless, not fully as in the beginning. 7. But it will come to pass after these things that there will be the fall of many nations. 8. These are the bright waters which thou hast seen.

LXIX. "For the last waters which thou hast seen which were darker than all that were before them, those which were after the twelfth number, which were collected together, belong to the whole world. 2. For the Most High made division from the beginning, because He alone knows what will befall. 3.

LXVIII. 2, 3. The danger the Jews encountered according to the book of Esther, and their subsequent triumph over their enemies. We have here the second earliest allusion to this O. T. book. The earliest is in 2 Macc. xv. 36.

5. The rebuilding of the temple (535-515).

6. On the lower estimation in which the second temple was held see Mal. i.-ii.; Eth. En. lxxxix. 73, 74; Assumpt. Mos. iv. 8. This temple, therefore, was standing when chapters liii.-lxxiv. were written.

LXIX. 1. *Last.* I have here adopted Ceriani's suggestion and read ܐܚܪܝܐ instead of ܐܚܪܢܐ = "other."

The last waters, etc. See liii. 7.

For as to the enormities of the impieties which should be wrought before Him, He foresaw six kinds of them. 4. And of the good works of the righteous which should be accomplished before Him, He foresaw six kinds of them, beyond those which He should work at the consummation of the age. 5. On this account there were not black waters with black, nor bright with bright; for it is the consummation.

LXX. "Hear therefore the interpretation of the last black waters which are to come [after the black]: this is the word. 2. Behold! the days come, and it will be when the time of the age has ripened, and the harvest of its evil and good seeds has come, that the Mighty One will bring upon the earth and its inhabitants and upon its rulers perturbation of spirit and stupor of heart. 3. And they will hate one another, and provoke one another to fight, and the mean will rule over the honourable, and those of low degree will be extolled above the famous. 4. And the many will be delivered into the hands of the few, and those who are nothing will rule over the strong, and the poor will have abundance beyond the rich, and the impious

3, 4. This division of the periods of the world into six good and six evil recalls Ecclus. xlii. 24 πάντα δισσὰ ἐν κατέναντι τοῦ ἑνός (cf. also xxxiii. 15).

4. *Foresaw.* So Ceriani rightly emends from "foresees"—merely a change of pointing.

Beyond those which, etc. These woes—the travail pains of the Messiah—are developed at length in lxx.-lxxii. (see liii. 7; lxix. 1).

LXX. 1. I have bracketed the words "after the black" as interpolated. They misrepresent the scheme of the writer; for the "last black waters" come after the bright twelfth waters in lxviii.

2. *Its inhabitants.* See xxv. 2, note. *Stupor of heart.* Cf. xxv. 2.

3-10. With this notable description of the last woes, cf. xxv. 2-4; xxvii.; xlviii. 31-39; 4 Ezra v. 1-12; vi. 20-24; ix. 1-9; xiii. 29-31 (see xxvii. 1, note.

3. Cf. xlviii. 37; Jubilees xxiii. 19: 4 Ezra vi. 24.

will exalt themselves above the heroic. 5. And the wise will be silent, and the foolish will speak, neither will the thought of men be then confirmed, nor the counsel of the mighty, nor will the hope of those who hope be confirmed. 6. Moreover, it will be when those things which were predicted have come to pass, that confusion will fall upon all men, and some of them will fall in battle, and some of them will perish in anguish, and some of them will be destroyed by their own. 7. Then the Most High will reveal to those peoples whom He has prepared before, and they will come and make war with the leaders that shall then be left. 8. And it will come to pass that whosoever gets safe out of the war will die in the earthquake, and whosoever gets safe out of the earthquake will be burned by the fire, and whosoever gets safe out of the fire will be destroyed by famine. [9. And it will come to pass that whosoever of the victors and

5. Cf. xlviii. 33, 36 ; 4 Ezra v. 9-11.

The mighty. The text which here reads ܚܝܠܬܢܐ = "the Mighty One," is wrong. We must read the plural ܚܝ̈ܠܬܢܐ = "the mighty." In lxxiv. 1 we must change the plural into the singular.

The hope of those who hope, etc. Cf. 4 Ezra v. 12.

6. *Destroyed,* etc. Cf. Mic. vii. 6 ; Matt. x. 35, 36 ; Luke xii. 53. The Syriac text = "will be hindered" is corrupt; for the context requires a strong expression. The corruption is traceable to the Hebrew. Thus "will be hindered" = κωλυθήσονται, which would be the usual LXX. rendering of יִכָּלְאוּ. That יכלאו is a corruption of יכלו = "will be destroyed" is clear from the fact that these two verbs are often confused in Hebrew, combined with the further fact that יִכְלוּ = "will be destroyed" gives the exact sense we require.

7. *Whom He has prepared before.* Are these the hosts of Gog and Magog? if text in verse 9 is genuine.

8. *In the earthquake.* Cf. xxvii. 7 ; 4 Ezra ix. 3.

The fire. Cf. xxvii. 10 ; 4 Ezra, v. 8.

Will be destroyed. I have here followed Ceriani's emendation of ܢܘܣܦ = "he will add," into ܢܣܘܦ.

Famine. Cf. xxvii. 6.

9. I have with some doubt bracketed this verse as an inter-

the vanquished gets safe out of and escapes all these things aforesaid will be delivered into the hands of My servant Messiah.] 10. For all the earth will devour its inhabitants.

LXXI. "And the holy land will have mercy on its own, and it will protect its inhabiters at that time. 2. This is the vision which thou hast seen, and this is the interpretation. 3. For I have come to tell thee these things, because thy prayer has been heard with the Most High.

LXXII. "Hear now also regarding the bright lightning which is to come at the consummation after these black (waters): this is the word. 2. After the signs have come, of which thou wast told before, when the

polation. The appearance of the Messiah is premature. His advent does not really take place till lxxii. 2. Again verse 10 is the natural sequel to verse 8. Further, the extermination of the Gentiles is here implied, but only their partial destruction in lxxii. 4-6. Finally, since the Messiah is the defender of the righteous, lxxi. 1 is rather inappropriate. But lxxi. 1 is fitting if the Messiah has not yet come.

LXXI. See notes on xxix. 2. Observe that whereas God protects the inhabitants of Palestine in xxix. 2, and the Messiah protects them in xl. 2, it is the land that protects them here.

2. These words which should not occur till the end of the interpretation show that the text is dislocated. This will be obvious on other grounds as we proceed.

3. Cf. liv. 1.

LXXII. 1. *The bright lightning* = ܒܪܩܐ ܢܗܝܪܐ. So I have emended by means of liii. 8 the impossible text ܡ̈ܝܐ ܢܗܝܪ̈ܐ = "the bright waters." It will be remembered that in the vision in liii. the last blackest waters (liii. 7) were not succeeded by bright waters, but by the lightning which illuminated and healed the earth and ruled over it (liii. 8-11). The lightning thus symbolised the Messiah. But in the interpretation of the close of the vision, the lightning is not even mentioned according to the present text, but in its place bright waters are spoken of, though in the vision in liii. none such are seen and none such contemplated throughout the entire interpretation up to the present chapter. The scheme of the writer of A^3 was as we have seen above: twelve periods evil and good alternately, symbolised by black and bright waters respectively, followed by a period of woes—the blackest waters; and finally, the Messiah's kingdom which was prefigured by the lightning. The same emendation must be made in lxxiv. 4.

nations become turbulent, and the time of My Messiah is come, He will both summon all the nations, and some of them He will spare, and some of them He will slay. 3. These things therefore will come upon the nations which are to be spared by Him. 4. Every nation which knows not Israel, and has not trodden down the seed of Jacob, shall indeed be spared. 5. And this because some out of every nation will be subjected to thy people. 6. But all those who have ruled over you, or have known you, shall be given up to the sword.

LXXIII. "And it will come to pass, when He has brought low everything that is in the world, and has sat down in peace for the age on the throne of His kingdom, that joy will then be revealed, and rest appear. 2. And then healing will descend in dew, and disease will withdraw, and anxiety and anguish

Throughout lxxii. 1 the plurals are changed into the singular to agree with the singular subject.

4-6. The Messiah was to extend His dominion over the Gentiles (Ps. lxxii. 11, 17; Isa. xiv. 2; lxvi. 12, 19-21; Zech. xiv.; Eth. En. xc. 30; Pss. Sol. xvii. 32 καὶ ἕξει λαοὺς ἐθνῶν δουλεύειν αὐτῷ). But in the first century B.C. to which the Pss. Sol. belong, a harsher view of the destiny of the Gentiles began to prevail. In Eth. En. xxxvii.-lxx. and Assumpt. Mos. x. it seems to be that of annihilation; it is undoubtedly so in 4 Ezra xiii. 37, 38, 49, and all but universally in later Judaism; cf. Weber, 364-369, 376. A middle line is pursued in the text.

The Messiah here, as in xxxix. 7-xl.; 4 Ezra xii. 32, is a warrior who slays the enemies of Israel with His own hand. This view appears in the Targum of Jon. on Isa. x. 27, and of the pseudo-Jon. on Gen. xlix. 11. In Eth. En. lxii. 2; Pss. Sol. xvii. 27; 4 Ezra xiii. 38; as in Isa. xi. 4, He destroys them by the word of His mouth. But in the Eth. En. xc. 37; Ap. Bar. xxix. 2; 4 Ezra vii. 28, the conception of the Messiah is weak; he does not appear till evil has run its course; he has no active *rôle;* he reigns but does not rule.

LXXIII. 1. Cf. 1 Cor. xv. 24, 25.

Joy will be revealed. The text reads "will be revealed in joy," but this destroys the parallelism with "rest will appear." I have omitted the preposition before "joy."

2. *Healing will descend in dew.* Cf. xxix. 7.

and lamentation will pass from amongst men, and gladness will proceed through the whole earth. 3. And no one shall again die untimely, nor shall any adversity suddenly befall. 4. And judgments, and revilings, and contentions, and revenges, and blood, and passions, and envy, and hatred, and whatsoever things are like these shall go into condemnation when they are removed. 5. For it is these very things which have filled this world with evils, and on account of these the life of man has been greatly troubled. 6. And wild beasts will come from the forest and minister unto men, and asps and dragons will come forth from their holes to submit themselves to a little child. 7. And women will no longer then have pain when they bear, nor will they suffer torment when they yield the fruit of the womb.

LXXIV. "And it will come to pass in those days that the reapers will not grow weary, nor those that build be toilworn; for the works will of themselves speedily advance with those who do them in much tranquillity. 2. For that time is the consummation of that which is corruptible, and the beginning of that which is not corruptible. 3. Therefore those things which were predicted will belong to it: therefore it is far away from evils, and near to those things which die not. 4. This is the bright lightning which came after the last dark waters."

3. *Untimely.* See liv. 15.

4. Cf. *Or. Sibyl.* iii. 376-380, 751-755.

6. Cf. Isa. xi. 6-9; lxv. 25; *Or. Sibyl.* iii. 620-623, 743-750.

LXXIV. 2. Cf. xl. 2.

4. *This is the bright lightning.* Emended from "these are the last bright waters." See lxxii. 1, note.

LXXV. And I answered and said: "Who can understand, O Lord, Thy goodness? for it is incomprehensible. 2. Or who can search into Thy compassions, which are infinite? 3. Or who can comprehend Thy intelligence? 4. Or who is able to recount the thoughts of Thy mind? 5. Or who of those that are born can hope to come to those things, unless he is one to whom Thou art merciful and gracious? 6. Because, if assuredly Thou didst not have compassion on man, those who are under Thy right hand, they could not come to those things, but those who are in the numbers named can be called. 7. But if, indeed, we who exist know wherefore we have come, and submit ourselves to Him who brought us out of Egypt, we shall come again and remember those things which have passed, and shall rejoice regarding that which has

LXXV.-LXXVI. = B^2.

LXXV.-LXXVI. With these chapters we return again to B^2. We should observe that according to lxxv. 1 Baruch replies to the last speaker who has interpreted the vision in liii. for him. This speaker Baruch addresses as God. But the last speaker was not God but the angel Ramiel from whom is derived lv. 4-lxxiv. Thus we see that lxxv. does not belong to liii.-lxxiv.

LXXV. 1. *Can understand.* I have emended ܢܬܕܡܐ = "can be likened to" into ܢܬܒܝܢ = "can understand," and omitted the ܒ in ܒܛܝܒܘܬܟ.

2. The mercies of God are not dwelt upon much in this book. The righteous are fully conscious of their worth (cf. xiv. 7, note). We have, however, a prayer for God's mercy in xlviii. 18, and an acknowledgment of God's long-suffering in xxiv. 2, but this is shown alike to the righteous and the wicked. God is merciful (lxxvii. 7) and His compassions are infinite (lxxv. 2); He has dealt with Baruch according to the multitude of the tender mercies (lxxxi. 4); if God had not compassion on man, he could not attain to the world to come (lxxv. 5, 6). For references to mercy in 4 Ezra, see vii. 132-134; viii. 31, 32, 36, 45; xii. 48.

5, 6. *Those things.* Probably the blessed immortality described in li.

6. *Who are under Thy right hand.* Cf. Ps. lxxx. 17.

7. *We shall come again, i.e.* in the resurrection described in l. This verse deals with the destiny of the obedient and the righteous; the next with that of the disobedient.

been. 8. But if now we know not wherefore we have come, and recognise not the principate of Him who brought us up out of Egypt, we shall come again and seek after those things which were now, and be grieved with pain because of those things which have befallen."

LXXVI. And He answered and said unto me: [" Inasmuch as the revelation of this vision has been interpreted to thee as thou besoughtest], hear the word of the Most High that thou mayest know what is to befall thee after these things. 2. For thou shalt surely depart from this earth, nevertheless not unto death but thou shalt be preserved unto the consummation of the times. 3. Go up therefore to the top of that mountain, and there will pass before thee all the regions of that land, and the figure of the inhabited world, and the top of the mountains, and the depth of the valleys, and the depths of the seas, and the number of the rivers, that thou mayest see what thou art leaving, and whither thou art going. 4. Now this will befall after forty days. 5. Go now therefore during

LXXVI. 1. The earlier half of this verse is probably due to the final editor.

Hear the word of the Most High. This same mode of speech in which God speaks of Himself in the third person is found in xiii. 2: "Hear the word of the Mighty God," and also in xxv. 1, where the same statements are made in each case.

2. See note on xiii. 3.

Thou shalt be preserved until the consummation of the times. The Syr. here ܠܢܛܘܪܐ ܕܙܒܢܐ = "unto the observance of the times." If we compare the parallel passage, xxv. 1, we see that the above must be emended into ܬܬܢܛܪ ܠܙܒܢܐ, "thou shalt be preserved unto the times," or else into the fuller form we find in xvii. 3. I have done the latter in the text.

3. Cf. Deut. xxxiv. 1-3; Matt. iv. 8. Is the mountain here Nebo as in Deuteronomy?

4. *Forty days.* Cf. Exod. xxiv. 18; xxxiv. 28; Deut. ix. 9, 18. Analogous to this forty days to be

these days and instruct the people so far as thou art able, that they may learn so as not to die at the last time, but may learn in order that they may live at the last times."

LXXVII. And I, Baruch, went thence and came to the people, and assembled them together from the greatest to the least, and said unto them: 2. "Hear, ye children of Israel, behold how many ye are who remain of the twelve tribes of Israel. 3. For to you and to your fathers the Lord gave a law beyond all peoples. 4. And because your brethren transgressed the commandments of the Most High, He brought vengeance upon you and upon them, and He spared not

LXXVII.-LXXXII. = B^1.

spent by Baruch in teaching the people are the forty days assigned to Ezra, in which he was to restore the O.T. Scriptures (cf. 4 Ezra xiv. 23, 42, 44, 45).

5. *Live.* See xli. 1, note.

In LXXVIII. - LXXXVII. we have the conclusion of B^1. But of these chapters two are from other sources; LXXXIII. is from B^2, and LXXXV. from B^3. For the grounds for these conclusions, see the notes *in loc.* For a comprehensive treatment of the two sources, B^1 and B^2, the reader must consult the Introduction. The chief differences between B^1 and B^2 are: In the former an earthly felicity is looked for, in the latter not; in the former the dispersion is to return, in the latter not; in the former the earthly Jerusalem is to be rebuilt, in the latter not; in the former Baruch is to die, in the latter to be translated; in the former Jeremiah is not sent to Babylon, in the latter he is. Thus the portions derived respectively from B^1 and B^2 are as follows:— From B^1 i.-iv. 1; v.-ix. 1; xliii.-xliv. 7; xlv.-xlvi. 6; lxxvii.-lxxxii.; lxxxiv., lxxxvi., lxxxvii. From B^2 ix. 2-xii. (?); xiii. 1-3*a*; xx.; xxiv. 2-4; xiii. 3*b*-12; xxv., xiv.-xix.; xxi.-xxiv. 1; xxx. 2-5; xli., xlii.; xlviii. 1-47; xlix.-lii. 3; lxxv.; xxxi.-xxxii. 6; liv. 17, 18; xlviii. 48-50; lii. 5-7; liv. 16; xliv. 8-15; lxxxiii.; xxxii. 7-xxxv.; lxxvi. The portions derived from B^2 are restored to what seems to have been their original order in that source.

LXXVII. 1. *From the greatest to the least.* A favourite expression in Jeremiah (cf. vi. 13; viii. 10; xxxi. 34; xlii. 1, 8; xliv. 12; 4 Ezra xii. 40). Only in these it runs: "From the least to the greatest."

2. The twelve tribes which are here mentioned are treated of in their two main divisions in verse 4. Cf. lxxviii. 4; lxxxiv. 3.

3. *A law.* See xv. 5, note.

4. *Upon you. I.e.* the 2½ tribes = "the former" in the next line.

Upon them. The 9½ tribes = "the latter" in the next line.

the former, and the latter also He gave into captivity, and left not a residue of them. 5. And behold! ye are here with me. 6. If therefore ye direct your ways aright, ye also will not depart as your brethren departed, but they will come to you. 7. For He is merciful whom ye worship, and He is gracious in whom ye hope, and He is true, so that He shall do (you) good and not evil. 8. Lo! have ye not seen what has befallen Zion? 9. Or do ye perchance think that the place had sinned, and that on this account it was overthrown, or that the land had wrought foolishness, and that therefore it was delivered up? 10. And know ye not that on account of you who did sin, that which sinned not was overthrown, and, on account of those who wrought wickedly, that which wrought not foolishness was delivered up to (its) enemies." 11. And the whole people answered and said unto me: "So

Hath not left a residue of them. *I.e.* of the 9½ tribes. This denies the Samaritan claim.

5. Cf. lxxx. 5; 4 Ezra xiv. 33. 4 Ezra xiv. 30-33 seems to be dependent on lxxvii. 3-6. Those who are left with Baruch are a remnant of the 2½ tribes.

6. *As your brethren departed.* "The brethren" here embrace the 2½ tribes, and so we interpret the subsequent words, "and they will come to you." On the return of the 9½ tribes see note on lxxviii. 7.

7. *Do (you) good and not evil.* Cf. Jer. xxi. 10; Amos ix. 4.

8. =xliv. 5. Cf. x. 7; xiii. 3; lxxix. 1.

9. It was not the place that sinned. Hence it was destroyed by the hands of angels before it was delivered over to the king of Babylon, lest he should glory over it. Cf. v.-viii., lxxx.; see note on lxvii. 6.

10. Observe that the fall of Jerusalem is here attributed not only to the sins of the 2½ tribes but also of the 9½. This view appears first in Jer. xi. 17: "For the Lord of hosts that planted thee hath pronounced evil against thee, because of the evil of the house of Israel and of the house of Judah." Cf. Bar. ii. 26 *καὶ ἔθηκας τὸν οἶκον οὗ ἐπεκλήθη τὸ ὄνομά σου ἐπ' αὐτῷ, ὡς ἡ ἡμέρα αὕτη, διὰ πονηρίαν οἴκου Ἰσραὴλ καὶ οἴκου Ἰούδα.* Assumpt. Moyseos, iii. 5, where the two tribes say to the ten: "justus et sanctus Dominus, quia enim vos peccastis, et nos pariter abducti sumus vobiscum. Cf. also Targ. Jon. on Isa. liii. 5.

far as we can recall the good things which the Mighty One has done unto us, we do recall them; and those things which we do not remember He in His mercy knows. 12. Nevertheless, do this for us thy people: write also to our brethren in Babylon an epistle of doctrine and a scroll of good tidings, that thou mayest confirm them also before thou dost depart from us. 13. For the shepherds of Israel have perished, and the lamps which gave light are extinguished, and the fountains have withheld their stream whence we used to drink. 14. And we are left in the darkness, and amid the briers of the forest, and the thirst of the wilderness." 15. And I answered and said unto them: "Shepherds and lamps and fountains came (to us) from the law: and though we depart, yet the law abideth. 16. If therefore ye have respect to the law, and are intent upon wisdom, a lamp will not be wanting, and a shepherd will not fail, and a fountain will not dry up. 17. Nevertheless, as ye said unto me, I will write also unto your brethren in Babylon,

12. *To our brethren in Babylon, i.e.* the 2½ tribes. Cf. verse 19; lxxxv. 6. Observe that the writer does not conceive here of Jeremiah being at Babylon. If he had, he would have directed the letter to him. In the Rest of the Words of Baruch, on the other hand, the writer, conceiving Jeremiah to be in Babylon, directs to him the letter intended for the exiles there. This letter (cf. lxxvii. 17, 19; lxxxv. 6) to the 2½ tribes is lost.

Good tidings. Cf. xlvi. 6.

Depart. This refers to an ordinary death (cf. xliii. 2, note; see also xiii. 3, note; lxxviii. 5; lxxxiv. 1).

14. *We are left in darkness.* xlvi. 2; cf. 4 Ezra xiv. 20.

Briers. The text is ܗܘܠܐ = ὕλη, which is the LXX. rendering of שמיר in Isa. x. 17. I have supposed a similar rendering here. Or ὕλη may be a rendering of עֲצֵי = "trees," and this a corruption of צִנֵּי = "thorns." Something is wrong.

15. *The law.* See xv. 5, note.

16. *Shepherd.* The text reads ܪܥܝܢܐ = "mind," which Ceriani has rightly emended into ܪܥܝܐ = "shepherd."

and I will send by means of men, and I will write in like manner to the nine tribes and a half, and send by means of a bird." 18. And it came to pass on the one and twentieth day in the eighth month that I, Baruch, came and sat down under the oak under the shadow of the branches, and no man was with me, but I was alone. 19. And I wrote these two epistles: one I sent by an eagle to the nine and a half tribes; and the other I sent to those that were at Babylon by means of three men. 20. And I called the eagle, and spake these words unto it: 21. "The Most High hath made thee that thou shouldst be higher than all birds. 22. And now go and tarry not in (any) place, nor enter a nest, nor settle upon any tree, till thou hast passed over the breadth of the many waters of the river Euphrates, and hast gone to the people that dwell there, and cast down to them this epistle. 23. Remember, moreover, that, at the time of the deluge, Noah received from a dove the fruit of the olive, when he sent it forth from the ark. 24. Yea, also the ravens ministered to Elijah, bearing him food, as they had been commanded. 25. Solomon also, in the time

17. *A bird.* This is an eagle (cf. ver. 20). It is worth observing that whereas an eagle carries this letter to the 9½ tribes here, in the Rest of the Words of Baruch vii. it is an eagle that carries Baruch's letter to Jeremiah in Babylon.

18. *The oak.* See vi. 1, note; cf. 4 Ezra xiv. 1.

21. Cf. Rest of Words of Baruch vii. 3: "Elect above all the birds of heaven."

22. The 9½ tribes were carried away to Assyria and placed in Halah, and in Habor, on the river of Gozan (2 Kings xvii. 6). Their abode, according to 4 Ezra xiii. 40, 45, was Arzareth, *i.e.* ארץ אחרת of Deut. xxix. 28; Joseph. *Ant.* xi. 5, 2.

23. Cf. Gen. viii. 11; Rest of Words of Baruch vii. 10: "Be like the dove which three times brought back word to Noah."

24. Cf. 1 Kings xvii. 6.

of his kingdom, whithersoever he wished to send or seek for anything, commanded a bird (to go thither), and it obeyed him as he commanded it. 26. And now let it not weary thee, and turn not to the right hand nor to the left, but fly and go by a direct way, that thou mayest preserve the command of the Mighty One, according as I said unto thee."

26. Cf. Rest of Words vii. 12.

THE EPISTLE OF BARUCH WHICH HE WROTE TO THE NINE AND A HALF TRIBES

LXXVIII. These are the words of that epistle which Baruch the son of Neriah sent to the nine and a half tribes, which were across the river Euphrates, in which these things were written. 2. Thus saith Baruch the son of Neriah to the brethren carried into captivity: "Mercy and peace." 3. I bear in mind, my brethren, the love of Him who created us, who loved

LXXVIII. 1. *The nine and a half tribes.* In this book the tribes of Israel carried away by the king of Assyria are, except in i. 2, always so designated (cf. lxii. 5; lxxvii. 19). In 4 Ezra xiii. 40 they are called "the ten tribes" only in the Latin Version, but "the nine and a half tribes" in the Syriac and Arabic Versions; in Asc. Isa. iii. 2 and in the Ethiopic Version of 4 Ezra xiii. 40 they are called the "nine tribes."

2. *Mercy and peace.* 1 Tim. i. 2.

3. It is noteworthy that in the genuine parts of B[1] in chaps. lxxvii.-lxxxvii. Baruch speaks frequently in the first person sing. (see lxxvii. 1, 5, 11, 15, 17-20, 26; lxxviii. 3,

---

of Baruch the scribe'; *k*P, 'the Epistle of Baruch'; *mn*, 'the first Epistle of Baruch.'

LXXVIII. 1. ܗܠܝܢ ܐܢܘܢ 'these are,' *c*; ܘܗܠܝܢ 'and these,' *abdeghi*WP; *f*, ܗܠܝܢ. ܕܐܓܪܬܐ ܗܝ 'of that Epistle,' *c*; wrongly om. by *abdefghi*WP. ܥܒܪܗ *abcgh*; *def*WP, ܥܒܪܐ. ܦܪܬ 'Euphrates,' *abdefghi*WP. *c* om.

2. ܕܒܫܒܝܐ ܗܘܘ *c*; *abdefhi*WP, ܕܫ̈ܒܝܐ ܗ̈ܘܝܢ; *g*, ܕܒܫܒܝܐ ܗ̈ܘܝܢ. ܘܫܠܡܐ 'and peace,' *abdefghi*WP; *c*. reads ܐܦ ܫܠܡܐ ܢܗܘܐ ܠܟܘܢ 'and peace be unto you.'

3. ܕܒܪܢ 'who created us,' *abdefghil*WP; *c* wrongly ܕܒܪܝܢ

LXXVIII. ܐܓܪܬܐ ܕܒܪܘܟ ܒܪ
ܢܪܝܐ. ܕܫܕܪ ܠܬܫܥܐ ܫ̈ܒܛܝܢ

1 ܘܦܠܓܗ. ܗܠܝܢ ܐܢܘܢ
ܦܬܓ̈ܡܐ ܕܐܓܪܬܐ
ܗܘ ܕܫܕܪ ܒܪܘܟ ܒܪ ܢܪܝܐ
ܠܬܫܥܐ ܫ̈ܒܛܝܢ ܘܦܠܓܗ.
ܗܠܝܢ ܕܐܝܬܝܗܘܢ ܗܘܘ
ܒܥܒܪܗ ܕܢܗܪܐ. ܦܪܬ ܕܒܫܒܝܬܐ

2 ܗܘܘ ܒܗ ܗܠܝܢ. ܗܟܢܐ
ܐܡܪ ܒܪܘܟ ܒܪ ܢܪܝܐ.
ܠܐܚ̈ܐ ܕܐܫܬܒܝܘ. ܪ̈ܚܡܐ
ܘܫܠܡܐ.

3 ܕܟܝܪ ܐܢܐ ܐܚ̈ܝ ܠܚܘܒܗ
ܕܗܘ ܕܒܪܝ ܕܐܚܒܢ ܡܢ

For some account of the MSS. *abcdefghiklmn* see the General Introduction.

TITLE.—I have here given *c*, though what the title was is uncertain. *a* reads ܠܘܬ ܐܚ̈ܐ ܡܫܒܚܬܐ ܕܒܪܘܟ ܣܦܪܐ ܕܫܕܪ ܥܠ ܝܕ ܢܫܪܐ ܠܐܘܪܫܠܡ ܠܟܠܗܘܢ; so *g*, but that it om. ܢܫܪܐ, and *b*, but that it om. ܠܘܬ, ܡܫܒܚܬܐ and ܢܫܪܐ. *di* give ܠܘܬ ܐܚ̈ܐ ܡܫܒܚܬܐ ܕܒܪܘܟ ܣܦܪܐ ܡܫܠܡܢܐ ܕܝ; so w, but that it om. ܠܘܬ and ܕ before ܝ, and *ef*, but that they om. ܠܘܬ and ܕܝ ܡܫܠܡܢܐ. *l*, ܐܚ̈ܐ ܡܫܒܚܬܐ ܕܒܪܘܟ ܒܪ ܢܪܝܐ 'the first Epistle of Baruch, the son of Neriah'; *h*, 'the Epistle

us from of old, and never hated us, but above all educated us. 4. And truly I know that behold all we the twelve tribes are bound by one chain, inasmuch as we are born from one father. 5. Wherefore I have been the more careful to leave you the words of this epistle before I die, that ye may be comforted regarding the evils which have come upon you, and that ye may be grieved also regarding the evil that has befallen your brethren: and again, also, that ye may justify His judgment which He has decreed against you that ye should be carried away captive—for what ye have suffered is disproportioned to what ye have done—in order that, at the last times, ye may be found

4, 5; lxxx. 7; lxxxi. 2, 4; lxxxii. 1; lxxxiv. 1, 6, 7; lxxxvi. 3; lxxxvii.) In the interpolated portions this is not so.

4. *Twelve tribes.* lxxvii. 2; lxxxiv. 3.

5. *Before I die.* See xiii. 3, note.

Justify. See xxi. 9, note. Cf. Ps. li. 4; Dan. ix. 14; Baruch ii. 9.

For what ye . . . done is parenthetical. Cf. lxxix. 2.

That in the last times, etc. These words refer to the return of the 9½ tribes (see note on ver. 7).

---

4. ܕܗܐ 'that behold,' *abdefghiw*P; *c* wrongly ܕܠܐ 'that not.' ܡܬܚܒܫܝܢ ܚܢܢ *bcg*; *adefhiw*P, ܡܬܚܒܫܝܢܢ.

5. ܗܕܐ ܐܓܪܬܐ *abdefghiw*P; *c* trs. ܡܢ ܩܕܡ *defiw*P om. ܡܬܒܝܐܝܢ *abdefghilw*P; *c*, ܡܬܒܝܐܢ. ܒܝܫܬܐ ܕܓܕܫܬ 'evil that has befallen,' *abdefghiw*P; *c*, ܒܝܫ̈ܬܐ ܕܓܕܫ 'evils that have befallen.' ܐܦ ܕܝܢ ܬܙܕܩܘܢ *abdefghilw*P; *c*, ܕܝܢ ܘܬܙܕܩܘܢ. ܕܬܫܬܟܚܘܢ, *a* by a clerical error gives ܕܬܫܬܟܘܢ. ܕܢܫܬܟܚܘܢ *acdh*; *befgi*, ܕܬܫܬܟܚܘܢ. ܡܠܐ *c*; *abdefghiw*P, ܡܛܠ. ܚܘܒ *ch*; *b*, ܚܘܒܝ.

ܩܕܡܝܟ . ܘܪܒܐ ܡܫܡܫܢܘܬܟ
ܫܡܟ . ܐܢܐ ܡܠܥܠܐܝܬ ܪܒܐ
4 ܗܘܐ ܠܟ . ܘܡܪܝܡܐܝܬ ܡܪܘܡ
ܐܝܟ ܕܗܘܐ ܐܬܐܡܪ ܥܠܝܟ
ܬܪܥܝܢ ܡܫܒܚܝܢ ܒܥܝܢ
ܐܫܘܪܐ . ܕܐܡܪ ܕܡܢ
ܡܢ ܐܟܐ ܡܟܣܝܢ ܗܢܝܢ .
5 ܡܛܠ ܗܢܐ ܡܠܥܠܐܝܬ
ܐܬܒܛܠ ܠܟ ܕܐܫܬܡܥܘܢ
ܠܒܢܝ . ܩܕܝܫܘ ܕܐܝܪܬܐ
ܗܕܐ . ܡܢ ܩܕܡ
ܕܐܫܬܩܠ . ܕܬܗܘܘܢ ܡܫܬܒܚܝܢ
ܠܗ ܒܝܫܬܐ ܕܡܛܠܬܗܘܢ .
ܘܕܬܬܒܥܘܢ ܬܘܒ ܒܗ
ܒܝܫܬܐ ܕܚܪܝܦܐ ܠܐܢܫܘܬܗܘܢ .
ܬܘܒ ܕܝܢ ܐܦ ܕܬܐܕܫܘܢ
ܕܡܢܗ ܕܗܘ ܕܝܪܐ ܠܠܒܘܬܗܘܢ
ܕܬܬܒܥܘܢ . ܒܝܬ ܗܘ ܢܝܪ
ܡܢܝܟ ܕܫܒܘܩܝܢ ܡܢ ܡܢܐ
ܕܒܒܝܬܗܘܢ . ܡܛܠ ܕܟܒܪܝܐ
ܐܢܫܐ ܬܬܒܥܘܢ ܩܕܡ

who created me.' ܡܠܥܠܐܝܬ 'above all,' *abcgh*; *defi*WP om. ܪܒܐ *acdefi*; *bh*, ܪܘܪܒܐ.

worthy of your fathers. 6. Therefore if ye consider those things which ye have now suffered for your good, that ye may not finally be condemned and tormented, then ye will receive eternal hope; if above all ye destroy from your heart vain error, on account of which ye departed hence. 7. For if ye so do these things, He will continually remember you, He who alway promised on our behalf to those who were more excellent than we, that He will never forget or forsake us, but with much mercy will gather together again those who were dispersed.

6. *Departed hence. I.e.* from Palestine.

7. *Those who were more excellent.* The patriarchs.

With much mercy. In 4 Ezra xiv. 34, 35 the righteous are to obtain mercy after death. Here God's mercy will be shown to Israel by causing them to return from their captivity.

Gather together . . . those who were dispersed. Cf. lxxvii. 6; lxxxiv. 2, 8, 10. The promise that God would turn again the captivity of Israel is frequently made in the O. T. (cf. Deut. xxx. 3; Amos ix. 11-15; Isa. xi. 12; Jer. xxiii. 3; xxix. 14; xxxi. 10; xxxii. 37; Ezek. xxxvii. 21-28; Zeph. iii. 19, 20; also in Bar. iv. 36, 37; v. 5-7; Pss. Sol. xi.; 2 Macc. ii. 18). The prediction of the return of the exiles is found also in Tob. xiii. 13; Eth. En. lvii. 1, 2; xc. 33; *Or. Sibyl.* ii. 170-173; 4 Ezra xiii. 12, 39-47. Either as in the preceding passages God was to procure their return directly; or else indirectly (*a*) through the agency of the nations who should carry back to Jerusalem the dispersed as offerings (cf. Isa. xlix. 22; lx. 4, 9; lxvi. 20; Pss. Sol. xvii. 34); (*b*) by means of the Messiah (cf. Pss. Sol. xvii. 28, 30, 50; Targ. Jon. on Jer. xxxiii. 13); (*c*) by means of Elijah (cf. Ecclus. xlviii. 10). These different methods are not mutually exclusive. In the presence of this strongly attested hope of the restoration of the dispersed it is strange to find it positively denied by R. Akiba (*Sanh.* x. 3): "The ten tribes will nevermore return; for it is said of them (Deut. xxix. 28): 'He will cast them into another land, as this day.' Hence as this day passes away and does not return, so shall they pass away and not return. So R. Akiba."

The return of the exiles in B^1 accords well with the rebuilding of Jerusalem which is elsewhere expected in B^1. See i. 4; vi. 9, notes.

6 ܠܐ ܬܒܥܘܢ . ܡܛܠ̈ ܗܘܐ
ܐܢ ܬܬܚܫܒܘܢ ܗܠܝܢ
ܕܠܛܒ̈ܬܟܘܢ ܚܫܬܘܢ ܗܫܐ .
ܕܠܐ ܠܚܪܬܐ ܬܬܚܝܒܘܢ
ܘܬܫܬܢܩܘܢ . ܘܩܒܠܘܢ
ܬܡܟܠܘܢ ܣܒܪܐ ܕܠܥܠܡ .
ܐܢܗܘ ܕܡܬܪܐܡܬ ܬܪܥܝܬܟܘܢ
ܡܢ ܠܒܒܟܘܢ ܠܒܛܝܠܘܬܐ
ܫܪܝܬܐ . ܗܘ ܕܡܛܠܬܗ
7 ܐܬܐܠܨܬܘܢ ܡܢ ܗܪܟܐ . ܐܢ
ܓܝܪ ܬܥܒܕܘܢ ܗܠܝܢ ܗܟܢܐ .
ܐܡܝܢܐܝܬ ܡܬܕܟܪ ܗܘ
ܠܟܘܢ . ܗܘ ܕܒܩܕܡ ܙܒܢ
ܐܫܬܘܕܝ ܚܠܦܝܢ ܠܐܝܠܝܢ
ܕܡܝܬܪܝܢ ܡܢܢ . ܕܠܐ ܠܥܠܡ
ܢܛܥܢ ܐܘ ܢܫܒܩܢ .
ܐܠܐ ܒܪ̈ܚܡܐ ܣܓܝ̈ܐܐ
ܢܟܢܫ ܬܘܒ

6. ܕܠܛܒ̈ܬܟܘܢ *c*; *bdefgilWP*, ܕܠܛܒܬܟܘܢ ܗܘ; *ah* give conflate reading, ܕܠܛܒ̈ܬܟܘܢ ܗܘ.

7. ܡܬܕܟܪ, *c* adds ܗܘ. ܢܛܥܢ ܐܘ ܢܫܒܩܢ 'will not forget or forsake us,' *abdefghimWP*; *c*, ܢܛܥܐ ܐܘ ܢܫܒܘܩ ܠܙܪܥܢ 'will not forget or forsake our seed.' ܠܐܝܠܝܢ 'those,' *abdefghWP*; *c*, ܠܟܠܗܘܢ ܐܝܠܝܢ 'all those.'

LXXIX. Now, my brethren, learn first what befell Zion: how that Nebuchadnezzar king of Babylon came up against us. 2. For we have sinned against Him who made us, and we have not kept the commandments which He commanded us, yet He hath not chastened us as we deserved. 3. For what befell you we also suffered in a pre-eminent degree, for it befell us also.

LXXX. And now, my brethren, I make known unto you that when the enemy had surrounded the city, the angels of the Most High were sent, and they overthrew the fortifications of the strong wall, and they

LXXIX. 1. *What befell Zion.* See lxxvii. 8, note.

2. *We have sinned,* etc. Cf. Baruch i. 17, 18.

Chastened. Cf. i. 5; xiii. 10.

As we deserved. Cf. lxxviii. 5.

LXXX. This chapter closely resembles and implies vi.-viii., but lxvii. proceeds upon different presuppositions. See lxvii. 6, note.

1. *Fortifications of the strong wall.* Cf. vii. 1.

---

*bdefghi*WP. *bdefghi*WP read ܠܐ ܐܪܥܟܘܢ ܥܪܥܢ ܝܬܝܪܚܫܢ ܡܠܦܪܐܠ 'but likewise that which has befallen you has overtaken us: in a pre-eminent degree have we suffered also'; so also *a*, but that it inserts ܕ before ܡܠܦܪܐܠ, a conflate reading as in lxxviii. 6: all readings seem corrupt. ܚܫܢ *ce*; *bh*, ܢܚܫܢ; *fi*, ܢܚܫܢ. ܫܢܝܩܢ *abg*; *cdh*, ܫܢܝܩܢ; *fi*, ܫܢܝܩܢ; WP, ܫܢܝܩܢ 'our calamity.'

LXXX. 1. ܡܘܕܥ ܐܢܐ ܠܟܘܢ ܕ 'I make known unto you that,' *abdefghi*WP; *c* wrongly om. ܘܫܡܫܘ *abcdfghilm*; *e*WP om. ܘ 'and.' ܫܘܪܝܗܘܢ 'fortifications,' *abdefghilm*WP; *c*,

ܠܐܡܠܟܝܢ ܕܐܬܒܪܘ . — . ܡܕܡܐ 1 LXXIX.
ܐܢܫ ܕܩܡܬܘܢ ܩܕܡܝܗ
ܠܡܦܩ ܕܡܠܟܐ ܢܣܝܢܘ
ܠܩܘܡܘܝ . ܕܫܒܩ ܒܟܠܗ
ܢܬܒܥܬ ܦܠܓܐ ܕܒܟܠ .
ܒܠܐܬܐ ܡܢ ܠܗܘ ܕܒܢܝ . 2
ܘܠܐ ܢܛܪܝ ܦܘܩܕܢܐ
ܕܦܩܕ ܐܠܐ ܐܦ ܠܐ
ܪܕܝ ܐܝܟ ܕܚܛܝܢ ܗܘܝܢ .
ܡܛܠ ܡܢ ܕܡܛܝܢ ܗܘ 3
ܡܝܬܪܐܝܬ ܠܗܘ ܢܚܡ . ܀
. . ܐܦ ܠܢ ܡܢ ܕܡܛܐ ܀
ܘܗܫܐ ܐܚܝ ܡܘܕܥ ܐܢܐ ܠܟܘܢ ܕܟܕ ܐܚܕܘܗ 1 LXXX.
ܒܥܠܕܒܒܐ ܠܡܕܝܢܬܐ .
ܐܫܬܕܪܘ ܡܠܐܟܐ
ܕܡܪܝܡܐ ܘܣܚܦܘ ܫܘܪܝܗ

LXXIX. 1. ܠܡܦܩ *abdefghi*WP; *c*, ܡܦܩ. ܕܡܠܟܐ *abcgh*; *defi*WP, ܡܠܟܐ. ܢܬܒܥܬ *cfhi*; *bg*, ܢܬܒܥܬ.

2. ܒܠܐܬܐ *bdfghi*WP; *ac*, ܒܠܐܬܐ. ܕܒܢܝ *b(ad ?)efghi*WP; *c*, ܕܒܢܝ. ܦܘܩܕܢܐ 'commandments,' *ch*WP; *abdefgil*, ܦܘܩܕܢܐ 'commandment.'

2—3. ܡܝܬܪܐܝܬ . . . . ܠܐ 'yet He hath not chastened . . . . degree'; so *c*, save that I have om. ܕ before ܡܝܬܪܐܝܬ, with

destroyed the firm iron corners, which could not be rooted out. 2. Nevertheless, they hid all the vessels of the sanctuary, lest the enemy should get possession of them. 3. And when they had done these things, they delivered thereupon to the enemy the overthrown wall, and the plundered house, and the burnt temple, and the people who were overcome because they were delivered up, lest the enemy should boast and say: "Thus by force have we been able to lay waste even the house of the Most High in war." 4. Your brethren

Its . . . corners. Cf. vi. 4; viii. 1.

2. *Hid all the vessels.* Cf. vi. 7, 8. The ultimate motive for hiding the holy vessels can only be that given in vi. 9.

All the vessels of the sanctuary. The Syriac gives the impossible text, "the vessels of the vessels." The corruption becomes obvious when we retranslate into Hebrew. Thus the words = כלים מכלי הקדש corrupted from כל־כלי הקדש. I have emended accordingly.

Lest the enemy should get possession of them. The Syriac = "lest they should be polluted by the enemies." But the parallel passage in vi. 8, "So that strangers may not get possession of them," expresses the idea we should find here; for the object with which the vessels are hidden is their preservation for use in the restored temple (vi. 7-10). Further, we find that the corrupt text which = פן יחלו מאויבים becomes by the addition of a single letter פן ינחלום אויבים = "lest the enemy should get possession of them."

3. *Plundered house, and the burnt temple.* Cf. v. 3; vi. 6, 7.

Should boast. Cf. vii. 1. Contrast lxvii. 2, 7.

4. Cf. viii. 5. Observe that there is no mention here of Jeremiah

---

'who were overcome,' *abdefgi*WP; so *h*, but that it gives the plural; *c*, ܕܐܓܪܐ. ܡܛܠ ܕ 'because,' *abcgh*; *defi*WP, ܡܐ ܕ 'when.' ܕܐܫܬܠܡܬܘܢ, *b* reads ܕܐܫܬܠܡܬܘ. ܐܬܥܫܢܢ ܣܓܝ *b*; *adefghi*WP, ܐܬܥܫܢܝܢ; c, ܐܬܥܫܢܢ. ܒܚܝܠܐ 'by force,' *abdefghi*WP; *c* wrongly om. ܒܩܪܒܐ *bdefghi*WP; *a*, ܒܩܪ̈ܒܐ.

ܕܫܘܪܐ ܚܣܝܢܐ . ܘܗܦܟܘܗ
ܘܐܬܪ̈ܬܐ ܡܫܡܗܬܐ ܕܩܕ̈ܝܫܐ .
ܘܚܒܠܘ ܕܠܐ ܡܚܝܣܝܢ ܗܘܘ
2 ܕܢܬܒܣܪܘܢ . ܒܪܡ ܕܝܢ ܡܐܢܐ ܡܢ ܡ̈ܐܢܐ
ܕܩܘܕܫܐ ܠܩܛܘ . ܐܝܟ ܕܠܐ
ܢܬܛܡܘܢ ܡܢ ܒܥܠܕܒܒ̈ܐ .
3 ܘܟܕ ܓܡܪܘ ܗܠܝܢ . ܫܪܝܘ
ܐܫܠܡܘܗ ܠܗܘܢ ܠܒܥܠܕܒܒ̈ܐ ܫܘܪܐ .
ܟܕ ܫܚܩܘ ܘܒܝܬܐ ܟܕ
ܚܪܝܒ . ܘܗܝܟܠܐ ܟܕ ܡܟܝܟ .
ܘܐܪܥܐ ܕܐܬܕܒܪ ܡܟܝܠ
ܕܐܫܬܠܡܬ . ܕܠܐ ܢܗܘܘܢ
ܡܫܬܒܗܪܝܢ ܒܥܠܕܒܒ̈ܐ
ܘܐܡܪܝܢ ܕܗܟܢܐ ܐܙܟܝܢ ܚܣܝܢ ܒܩܪܒܐ
ܒܝܬܐ ܕܐܦ ܠܒܝܬܗ
ܕܥܫܝܢܐ ܢܨܚܢ ܒܩܪܒܐ .

ܚܣܝܢܘܬܗ ‘fortification.’ ܘܗܦܟܘܗ *abdefghiwP*; *c*, ܘܗܦܟܘ. ܐܬܪ̈ܘܬܐ *abdefgiwP*; *c*, ܐܬܪ̈ܘܬܗ. ܡܫܡܗܬܐ *abcgh*; *defgiwP*, ܡܫܡ̈ܗܬܐ.

2. ܡ̈ܐܢܐ ܡܢ ܡ̈ܐܢܐ ܕ ‘some vessels of the vessels,’ *abdefghiwP*; *c*, ܡ̈ܐܢܝܗ. ܢܬܛܡܘܢ ‘should be polluted,’ *abcdfghi*; *d*, ܢܬܛܡܣܘܢ; *ewP*, ܢܬܛܡܘܢ.

3. *f* om. ܘܟܕ . . . . ܠܒܥܠܕܒܒ̈ܐ through hmt. ܓܡܪܘ *abc'deghiwP*; *c*, ܓܡܪ. ܠܗܘܢ *abdeghiwP*; c om. ܕܐܬܕܒܪ

also have they bound and led away to Babylon, and have caused them to dwell there. 5. But we have been left here, being very few. 6. This is the tribulation about which I wrote to you. 7. For assuredly I know that the habitation of Zion gave you consolation: so far as ye knew that it was prospered (your consolation) was greater than the tribulation which ye endured in having departed from it.

LXXXI. But regarding consolation, hear ye the word. 2. For I was mourning regarding Zion, and I prayed for mercy from the Most High, and I said:

though, according to x. 5, he went with the captivity to Babylon. See x. 2, note.

5. From Jer. xlii. 2, where the words are spoken of the remnant in Jerusalem (cf. Deut. iv. 27; Baruch ii. 13). The two latter passages deal with the remnant among the Gentiles.

LXXXI. As in lxxx. 7 the 9½ tribes had consolation in the fact that Jerusalem prospered and were proportionately grieved on its overthrow, Baruch has now a word of consolation for them touching Zion (lxxxi. 1); for, when in his grief over it (lxxxi. 2), he asked God how long should this desolation last (lxxxi. 3), God, to give him consolation, vouchsafed a revelation as to the mysteries of the times and removed his anguish (lxxxi. 4).

1. *Regarding consolation.* This word refers to the restoration of Zion. Cf. xliv. 7; lxxxi. 4; lxxxii. 1.

---

*bdefghil*WP; *ac*, ܕܥܡ̈ܘܪܝܗ̇ 'habitations.' ܝܬܝܪ ܡܢ '(your consolation) was greater than,' *abcdeghi*; *f*WP, ܝܬܝܪܐ ܡܢ, which requires the following rendering: 'the more assured ye were that it prospered, the greater was the tribulation.'

LXXXI. 1. ܒܘܝܐܐ *abcefghi*; *d*WP, ܒܘܝܝܐ.

2. ܘܒܟܝܬ *c*; *abdefghi*WP, ܘܒܟܐ.

4 ܐܦ ܠܢ̈ܫܝܗܘܢ ܦܓܪܘ
ܘܐܘܒܠܘ ܠܒܢ̈ܝܗܘܢ . ܘܐܒܕܪܘ

5 ܐܢܘܢ ܠܡܢ . ܘܐܬܚܣܢܘ
ܣܓܝ ܗܪܟܐ . ܡܛܠ ܕܚܘ̈ܒܐ .

6 ܗܕܐ ܗܝ ܒܨܬܐ
ܕܥܠܬܗ ܠܒܗܝ ܒܠܚܘܕ .

7 ܡܫܪܪܐܬ ܓܝܪ ܡܪܢ ܐܠܐ .
ܕܡܒܒܝܐ ܗܘܐ ܠܒܗܝ
ܒܡܥܡܪܗ ܕܐܝܟܢ . ܒܨܒܐ
ܕܢܘܒܠܢ ܠܡܫܬܗܘܢ ܕܡܬܓܒܝܢܐ
ܗܘܐ ܡܬܒܪ ܡܢ ܒܨܒܐ
ܕܡܒܒܝܢ ܠܡܫܬܗܘܢ
ܕܐܢܫܬܗܘܢ ܡܕܢܚ . ܘ—ܘ . ܀ .

1 LXXXI. ܐܠܐ ܐܦ ܒܠ ܒܘܝܐܐ

2 ܡܫܒܚܘ ܡܠܬܐ . ܐܠܐ ܓܝܪ
ܡܠܐܟܠ ܢܘܡܬ ܒܠ
ܕܗܘܢ . ܘܒܫܡܬ ܕܝܡܟܐ ܡܢ

4. ܐܦ *acdefhiwp*; *bg*, ܘܐܦ. ܠܢ̈ܫܝܗܘܢ *bcdefghilwp*; *a*, ܠܢ̈ܫܝܗܘܢ. For ܘܐܘܒܠܘ *l* reads ܘܠܘܒܠ. ܠܒܢ̈ܝܗܘܢ *abc*; *defgiwp*, ܐܢܘܢ ܠܒܢܝܗܘܢ; *h*, ܠܒܒܢܝܗܘܢ.

5. ܘܐܬܚܣܢܘ *abcg*; *defhwp*, ܘܐܬܚܣܢܝܢ. ܣܓܝ *bc*; *adfhwp* om.

6. ܕܥܠܬܗ *cefghi*; *b*, ܕܒܥܠܬܗ.

7. ܕܡܒܒܝܐ *abcdfghi*; *lwp*, ܕܡܒܒܝܐܐ. ܒܡܥܡܪܗ 'habitation,'

3. "How long will these things endure for us? and will these evils come upon us always?" 4. And the Mighty One did according to the multitude of His mercies, and the Most High according to the greatness of His compassion, and He revealed unto me the word, that I might receive consolation, and He showed me visions that I should not again endure anguish, and He made known to me the mystery of the times, and the advent of the hours He showed me.

LXXXII. Therefore, my brethren, I have written to you, that ye may comfort yourselves regarding the multitude of your tribulations. 2. For know ye that our Maker will assuredly avenge us on all our enemies, according to all that they have done to us, also that

4. *The multitude . . . compassion.* Cf. Dan. ix. 18; Bar. ii. 27; cf. lxxvi. 6.
Consolation. See verse 1.
Mystery of the times. Cf. lxxxv. 8.

LXXXII. I am doubtful as to whether lxxxii. 2-9 belongs to B[1] or B[2]. I am inclined to believe the latter. But the evidence is not decisive either way.

---

4. ܘܥܒܕ 'and . . . did,' *c*; *abdefghi*WP, ܕܥܒܕ 'who did.' ܕܪ̈ܚܡܘܗܝ 'of His mercies,' *abcgh*; *defi*WP, ܕܪ̈ܚܡܐ 'of mercies.' ܕܐܬܒܝܐ *abgh*; *cdefil*WP, ܕܐܬܒܝܐܐ. ܕܐܙܐ 'mystery,' *abdefgi*WP; *ch*, ܕ̈ܐܙܐ 'mysteries.'

LXXXII. 1. ܕܐܘ̈ܠܨܢܝܟܘܢ 'of your tribulations,' *abgh*; *defi*WP, ܕܐܘܠܨܢܟܘܢ 'of your tribulation'; *c*, ܕܐܘ̈ܠܨܢܐ 'of tribulations.'

2. ܗܘܝܬܘܢ *abdfgh*WP; *c*, ܬܗܘܘܢ. ܬܒܥ *c*; *abefghlm*WP, ܬܒܥ; *di* om. point. ܠܢ 'us,' *abdefghilm*WP; *c* om. ܕܒܟܠ *c*; *abdefghi*WP, ܒܟܠ. ܠܢ 'to us'; *c* adds ܘܒܢ 'and in us,' against *abdefghi*WP. ܐܦ *abdefghi*WP; *c*, ܘ. ܗܘ

3 ܡܪܝܡܐ ܘܐܡܪܬ . ܕܥܕܡܐ
ܠܐܡܬܝܢ ܗܠܝܢ ܡܛܝܢ
ܥܠܝܢ . ܘܒܒܘܠܒܠܐ ܐܬܝܢ ܒܟܠܝܢ
4 ܕܒܥܬܐ ܗܠܝܢ . ܘܟܕ
ܡܣܬܟܠܢܐ ܐܝܟ ܗܘܝܬ
ܕܛܝܒܘܬܗ . ܘܡܪܝܡܘܬܗ
ܐܝܟ ܪܒܘܬܐ ܕܚܢܢܗ .
ܘܓܠܐ ܠܝ ܡܠܬܐ ܐܝܟ
ܕܐܬܒܝܐ . ܘܚܘܝܢܝ
ܚܙܘܢܐ ܐܝܟ ܕܬܘܒ ܠܐ
ܐܬܬܥܝܩ . ܘܐܘܕܥܢܝ
ܐܪܙܐ ܕܙܒܢܐ . ܘܡܐܬܝܬܗܘܢ
LXXXII. 1 .. ܕܥܕܢܐ ܚܘܝܢܝ . ܡܛܠ
ܗܢܐ ܐܚܝ ܟܬܒܬ ܠܟܘܢ
ܕܐܡܬܝ ܬܬܒܝܐܘܢ ܣܓܝ ÷
2 ܗܘܝܬ ܕܒܩܠܝܬܟܘܢ . ܗܘܦܬܘܢ
ܕܡܢ ܡܪܝܢ ܕܥܒܕܢ ܬܒܥ ܠܢ
ܒܟܘܠܗܘܢ ܥܡ ܒܥܠܝܗܘܢ
ܒܥܠܕܒܒܝܢ . ܐܝܟ ܕܟܠ ܡܐ
ܕܥܒܕܘ ܠܢ . ܐܦ ܕܫܘܬܦܘܬܐ

3. ܕܥܕܡܐ ܠܐܡܬܝܢ ܗܠܝܢ 'how long . . . these things?' *abdefghilm*WP ; *c*, ܕܗܠܝܢ ܥܕܡܐ ܠܫܘܠܡܐ '(will) these things . . . to the end?' ܥܠܝܢ 'upon us,' *acdefhi*WP ; *bg*, ܥܠܝ 'upon me.'

the consummation which the Most High will make is very nigh, and His mercy that is coming, and the consummation of His judgment, is by no means far off. 3. For lo! we see now the multitude of the prosperity of the Gentiles, though they act impiously, but they will be like a vapour. 4. And we behold the multitude of their power, though they do wickedly, but they will be made like unto a drop. 5. And we see the firmness of their might, though they resist the Mighty One every hour, but they will be accounted as spittle. 6. And we consider the glory of their greatness, though they do not keep the statutes of the Most High, but as smoke will they pass away. 7. And we meditate

3. *Like a vapour.* 4 Ezra vii. 61.

4. *Like unto a drop.* Isa. xl. 15; 4 Ezra vi. 56.

5. *Accounted as spittle.* Here כְּרֹק. certainly, and in 4 Ezra vi. 56, the text agrees with the LXX.; for in Isa. xl. 15 it has ὡς σίελος λογισθήσονται against the Hebrew יִטּוֹל.

---

bg, ܚܐܪܝܢ ܚܢܢ. ܗܫܐ 'now,' *abdfghi*WP; *c* om. here as it has already inserted ܗܫܐ in place of ܗܘ; *e* om. ܗܫܐ ܚܐܪܝܢܢ ܣܘܓܐܐ. ܕܡܨܠܚܢܘܬܐ *c*; *abdgh*WP, ܕܡܨܠܚܢܘܬܗܘܢ; *efi*, ܕܡܨ̈ܠܚܢܘܬܗܘܢ.

4. ܘܚܙܝܢܢ *cdefgim*WP; *abh*, ܘܚܙܝܢ ܚܢܢ. ܠܢܛܘܦܬܐ 'unto a drop,' *abdefghil*WP; *c* wrongly ܠܛܢܦܘܬܐ 'unto pollution.'

5. ܘܚܐܪܝܢܢ *cdefgh*WP; *ab*, ܘܚܐܪܝܢ ܚܢܢ. ܫܘܪܪܗ 'firmness,' *abdefghi*WP; *c* wrongly ܫܪܪܗ 'truth.' ܫܥܐ 'hour,' *abdefghi*WP; *c* wrongly ܫܢܐ 'year.'

6. ܘܡܬܒܩܝܢܢ *cdefghi*WP; *ab*, ܘܡܬܒܩܝܢ ܚܢܢ. ܦܘܩܕܢܝܗܘܢ 'commands,' *abdefgh*WP; *c*, ܦܘܩ̈ܕܝܗܘܢ 'statutes.'

ܡܪܝܡ ܗܘ ܣܘܟܠܐ ܕܟܠܗܝܢ

ܡܕܪܫܬܐ ܘܪ̈ܘܫܡܬܗܘܢ

ܕܐܬܬܘܢ . ܘܠܐ ܗܘܐ

ܪܫܡ ܣܘܟܠܗ ܕܕܝܢܗ .

3 ܗܐ ܓܝܪ ܡܬܪܡܝܢ ܗܢܐ ܫܘܓܢܐ

ܕܡܬܟܫܦܘܬܐ ܕܚܟ̈ܝܡܐ

ܟܕ ܗܕܝܢ ܡܬܪܡܝܢ . ܐܠܐ

4 ܠܗܘܟܠܐ ܗܘ ܕܦܠܚ . ܘܡܫܬܪܪܝܢ

ܒܫܘܓܢܐ ܕܐܘܚܝܬܗܘܢ

ܟܕ ܗܕܝܢ ܡܟܬܘܠܝܢ . ܐܠܐ

5 ܠܟܘܢܫܬܐ ܢܦܩܘܢ . ܘܡܬܪܡܝܢ

ܣܘܪܪܗ ܕܫܠܛܢܗܘܢ . ܟܕ ܗܕܝܢ

ܠܗܘܟܠܐ ܫܟܠܬܐ ܡܫܡܫܝܢ

ܟܕ ܟܠܐ ܗܟܐ . ܐܠܐ ܐܝܟ

6 ܪܘܡܐ ܢܦܩܘܢ . ܘܡܫܬܒܗܪܝܢ

ܟܠܐ ܠܡܫܘܫܬܐ ܕܪܡܘܬܗܘܢ .

ܟܕ ܗܕܝܢ ܠܐ ܢܛܪܝܢ

ܦܘܩܕܢܗܘܢ ܕܡܪܝܐ . ܐܠܐ

ܐܝܟ ܠܒܢܝ ܢܟܪ̈ܝܐ .

ܕܟܠܗܝܢ *acgh*WP; *bdefi*, ܗܘܐ. ܕܟܠܗܝܢ *abcdefhi*WP; *bg*, ܕܟܠܗܝܢ. ܣܘܟܠܗ *c*; *abdefhil*WP, ܣܘܟܠܐ.

3. ܗܐ 'lo!' *abdefghi*WP; *c*, ܗܫܐ 'now.' ܡܬܪܡܝܢ *acdfh*WP;

on the beauty of their gracefulness, though they have to do with pollutions, but as grass that withers will they fade away. 8. And we consider the strength of their cruelty, though they remember not the end (thereof), but as a wave that passes will they be broken. 9. And we remark the boastfulness of their might, though they deny the beneficence of God, who gave (it) to them, but they will pass away as a passing cloud.

LXXXIII. = B².

[LXXXIII. For the Most High will assuredly hasten His times, and He will assuredly bring on His hours. 2. And He will assuredly judge those who are in His

7. *As grass*, etc. Isa. xl. 6, 7.

LXXXIII. This chapter seems to belong to B². Thus the times will be cut short (lxxxiii. 1, 6), and everything brought into judgment (lxxxiii. 2, 3, 7); let not, therefore, earthly interests engage them (lxxxiii. 4), but let them fix their thoughts on the promised consummation (lxxxiii. 4, 5), and devote themselves to their faith of aforetime, lest to their captivity in this world there should be added torment in the next (lxxxiii. 8); for the world passeth away with its strength and its weakness, its virtues, and its lusts (lxxxiii. 9-23).

The connection between lxxxiii. and xx. is close. Cf. lxxxiii. 1, 6; xx. 1; lxxxiii. 2; xx. 2; lxxxiii. 7; xx. 4. This chapter seems to have formed originally part of Baruch's address to the people (xxxi. 3 - xxxii. 6; xliv. 8 - 15), and to have followed immediately on xliv. 8-15.

1. This and verse 6 are related to xx. 1. Cf. liv. 1; Ep. Barn. iv. 3.

---

8. ܘܡܬܒܩܝܢ ܚܢܢ *c*; *abdefghi*WP, ܘܡܬܒܩܝܢ. ܠܚܝܠܐ ܕܟܒܪ *cdefhi*; *abg*, ܕܟܒܪ ܠܚܝܠܐ; WP give plural.

9. ܘܡܬܟܠܡܝܢ *cdfghi*; *ab*, ܘܡܬܟܠܡܝܢ ܚܢܢ; *e*WP, ܘܡܬܟܠܡܝܢ. ܫܘܒܗܪܐ 'the boastfulness,' *c*; *abdefghi*WP, ܫܘܦܪܐ 'the beauty.' ܕܐܠܗܐ ܗܘ 'of God—Him,' *c*; *abdefghi*WP, ܕܝܠܗ 'of Him.'

LXXXIII. 2. ܘܕܐܢ ܕܐܢ 'will assuredly judge,' *acdefhi*WP;

7 ܘܢܚܙܝܢ ܠܟܠ ܫܘܦܪܐ
ܕܓܐܝܘܬܗܘܢ . ܐܝܟ ܗ̇ܢܘܢ
ܒܛܢܘ̈ܦܘܬܐ ܡܕܡ ܕܥܒܪܝܢ . ܐܠܐ
ܐܝܟ ܥܣܒܐ ܕܝܒܫܐ

8 ܢܐܒܕܘܢ . ܘܢܬܚܫܒܘܢ ܚܝܠ
ܠܟܠ ܥܘܫܢܐ ܕܫܘܠܛܢܗܘܢ .
ܐܝܟ ܗ̇ܢܘܢ ܣܪܝܬܐ ܠܐ
ܡܕܡ ܕܥܒܪܝܢ . ܐܠܐ ܐܝܟ
ܓܠܠܐ ܕܥܒܪ ܢܬܚܫܒܘܢ .

9 ܘܢܬܒܛܠܝܢ ܠܟܠ ܫܘܒܗܪܐ
ܕܚܝܠܗܘܢ . ܐܝܟ ܗ̇ܢܘܢ ܥܒܪܝܢ
ܒܛܝܒܘܬܗ ܕܠܒܐ ܗܘ
ܕܡܘܕܥ ܠܗܘܢ . ܐܠܐ ܐܝܟ
.. ܚܢܢܐ ܕܥܒܪܐ ܢܥܒܪܘܢ . ܡܢܗ .

LXXXIII. 1 ܡܪܗܛܐ ܓܝܪ ܡܪܗܛܗܘ
ܡܪܗܛ ܙܒ̈ܢܘܗܝ . ܘܡܝܬܝܘ

2 ܡܝܬܐ ܠܥܕ̈ܢܘܗܝ . ܘܕܝܢ
ܕܐܢ ܠܐܝܠܝܢ ܕܒܥܠܡܗ .

7. ܘܢܚܙܝܢ *abdefgi*WP; *bhl*, ܘܢܚܙܐ ܚܢܢ. ܕܓܐܝܘܬܗܘܢ 'of their gracefulness,' *c*; *abdefghil*WP, ܕܚܝܘܬܗܘܢ 'of their life.' ܒܛܢܘ̈ܦܘܬܐ 'with pollutions,' *c*; *abdefghil*WP, ܒܛܢܘܦܘܬܐ 'with pollution.'

world, and will visit in truth all things by means of all their hidden works. 3. And He will assuredly examine the secret thoughts, and that which is laid up in the secret chambers of all the members of man, and will make (them) manifest in the presence of all with reproof. 4. Let none therefore of these present things ascend into your hearts, but above all let us be expectant, because that which is promised to us will come. 5. And let us not now look unto the delights of the Gentiles in the present, but let us remember what has been promised to us in the end. 6. For the ends of the times and of the seasons and whatsoever is together with them will assuredly pass

2. *Visit.* See xx. 2, note.

3. See 4 Ezra xvi. 65. Cf. 1 Cor. iv. 5; also Heb. iv. 12; 1 Cor. xiv. 25.

4. *Let none therefore*, etc. Cf. Col. iii. 3: τὰ ἄνω φρονεῖτε.

That which is promised, etc. See xiv. 13, note; xxi. 25; xliv. 13.

6. See xx. 1, note.

---

which in all'; *dei*WP, ܕܒܟܠܗܘܢ. ܕܒܟܠܗ̈ܘܢܐ. ܕܒܪܢܫܐ 'of man,' *abdefghil*WP; *c*, ܕܒܪܘܫܥܐ 'which in wickedness.' ܐܢܫ ܟܘܠ *cdh*; *abgil*, ܟܠܢܫ.

4. ܡܟܝܠ, *bdefghi*WP add ܢܣܩ against *ac*. ܕܩܢܘܡܢ *cl*; *bgh*, ܕܡܬܢܟܝܢ. ܗܘ̇ *ach*WP; *bdegi*, ܗܘ; *f*, ܗܘ̣. ܠܢ 'to us,' *abdefghi*WP; *c* om.

5. ܗܫܐ 'now,' *abdfghi*WP; *c*. om. *e* om. ver. 5 through hmt. ܒܒܘ̈ܣܡܝܗܘܢ 'the delights,' *c*; *abdfghi*WP, ܒܒܘܣܡܗܘܢ 'the delight.' ܕܥܠܡܐ, *c* adds ܕܗܫܐ against *abdefghi*WP.

6. ܘܙܒܢ̈ܐ *bcdefghi*WP; *a*, ܘܙܒܢܐ. ܐܝܟ ܗܝ *c*; *abdefghi*WP, ܐܟܚܕܐ.

ܘܢܒܩܐ ܒܫܪܪܐ ܠܟܠܡܕܡ .
ܒܐܝܕܐ ܕܟܠ ܥܒܕܝܗܘܢ
3 ܕܡܛܫܝܢ ܘܢܒܩܐ
ܢܒܩܐ ܡܚܫܒܬܐ ܟܣܝܬܐ
ܘܟܠ ܕܒܬܘܢܐ . ܕܗܕܡܝܗܘܢ
ܗܕܡܐ ܕܒܪܢܫܐ ܢܦܩ .
ܘܒܓܠܝܐ ܡܢܗ ܟܠ ܐܢܫ
4 ܟܕ ܐܟܐ ܒܚܣܡ . ܡܛܠ ܠܐ
ܢܣܩ ܥܠ ܠܒܟܘܢ ܡܕܡ
⁘ ܡܢ ܗܠܝܢ ܕܩܝܡܝܢ . ܐܠܐ
ܢܬܡܪܐܡܬ ܢܦܫܐ . ܡܛܠ
ܕܐܬܐ ܗܘ ܡܕܡ
5 ܕܡܠܟܝܢ ܠܢ . ܘܠܐ ܢܚܘܪ ܗܫܐ
ܒܦܘܢܩܝܗܘܢ ܕܥܡܡܐ
. ܐܠܐ ܢܬܕܟܪ ܡܕܡ
6 ܕܠܚܪܬܐ ܡܠܟܝܢ ܠܢ . ܡܛܠ
ܕܡܥܒܪܢ ܥܒܪܝܢ ܠܙܒܢܝܗܘܢ
. ܕܙܒܢܐ ܘܡܫܢܝܐ . ܘܟܠ
ܕܐܝܬ ܒܗܘܢ ܐܝܟ ܚܙܝܐ .

bg, ܘܢܕܘܢ ܡܪܢ 'our Lord will judge.' ܕܡܛܫܝܢ 'hidden,' *abdefghi*WP; *c*, ܕܚܛܗܐ ܗܘܘ 'which were sins.'

3. ܕܒܬܘܢܐ ܕܗܕܡܝܗܘܢ 'which in the secret chambers of all,' c; *abfghl*, ܕܒܬܘܢܐ ܕܒܗܕܡܝܗܘܢ 'which in the secret chamber

by. 7. The consummation, moreover, of the age will then show the great might of its ruler, when all things come to judgment. 8. Do ye therefore prepare your hearts for that which before ye believed, lest ye come to be in bondage in both worlds, so that ye be led away captive here and be tormented there. 9. For that which exists now or which has passed away, or which is to come in all these things, neither is the evil fully evil, nor again the good fully good. 10. For all healthinesses of this time are turning into diseases. 11. And all might of this time is turning into weakness,

7. Cf. xx. 4.

8. *Prepare your hearts.* See xxxii. 1, note.

That which ye before believed. This seems to refer to apostates, *i.e.* Christians who had left Judaism. Cf. xli. 3; xlii. 4.

Come to be in bondage, etc. Cf. lxxxv. 9.

10. Contrast xxix. 7.

11. *All might of this time*, etc. Cf. xxi. 14.

ܕܬܫܬܒܘܢ ܗܪܟܐ ܘܬܬܢܓܕܘܢ 'that ye be led away captive and . . . there,' *c*; *abdefghik*WP, ܕܗܪܟܐ ܐܫܬܒܘܢ ܘܬܬܢܓܕܘܢ. *e* om. ܘܬܬܢܓܕܘܢ.

9. At the beginning of this verse *ef* insert ܒ in red, w inserts ܒ ܘܡܛܠܘܢ, as also *di*, but that they add ܕ before ܒ. ܕܩܝܡ *ch*; *bg*, ܕܩܝܡ; *efi*, ܕܩܝܡ; *k*, ܕܩܐܡ. ܕܒܪܝ *cefh*; *b*, ܕܒܪܝ; *adgik*WP, ܕܒܪܝ. ܠܘܬ ܚܕܬܐ ܡܫܬܚܠܦܬ *c*; *abdefgik*WP, ܡܫܬܚܠܦܝܢ ܠܘܬ ܚܕܬܐ; *h*, ܡܫܬܚܠܦܝܢ ܠܘܬ ܚܕܬܐ. ܚܕܬܐ.

10. ܠܟܘܪܗܢܐ 'diseases,' *abcdeghk*; *d'fi*WP, ܠܟܘܪܗܢܐ 'disease.'

11. ܠܡܐܘܢܐ 'to misery,' *bg*: so also *a*, ܠܡܐܘܘܢܐ and *defhi*,

7 ܫܘܠܡܗ ܕܝܢ ܕܥܠܡܐ
ܘܢܚܘܐ ܗܘܐ ܚܝܠܗ ܪܒܐ
ܕܡܕܒܪܢܗ . ܟܕ ܟܠܡܕܡ
8 ܠܕܝܢܐ ܐܬܐ . ܐܢܬܘܢ
ܗܟܝܠ ܐܬܛܝܒܘ ܒܠܒܘܬܟܘܢ
ܠܡܕܡ ܕܡܢ ܩܕܡ
ܘܡܬܒܥܬܘܢ ܕܠܐ ܡܢ
ܬܬܒܗܬܘܢ ܒܥܠ̈ܡܐ ܬܬܚܝܒܘܢ
ܕܐܬܛܥܝܬܘܢ ܗܪܟܐ . ܘܬܬܢܚ
9 ܬܐܬܢܝܚܘܢ . ܡܕܡ ܓܝܪ
ܕܡܢܗ ܗܫܐ ܐܘ ܕܥܒܪ
ܐܘ ܕܐܬܐ ܒܟܘܠܗܝܢ
ܗܠܝܢ . ܐܦ ܠܐ ܒܝܫܬܐ
ܒܝܫܐ ܓܡܝܪܐܝܬ . ܐܦ ܠܐ
ܬܘܒ ܛܒܬܐ ܡܓܡܪܐܝܬ
10 ܛܒܬܐ ܐܝܬܝܗ̇ . ܟܠ ܓܝܪ
ܚܘܠܡܢ̈ܐ ܕܗܫܐ ܗ̇ܘܝܢ
11 ܠܟܘܪܗܢܐ . ܘܟܠ
ܚܠܝܡܘܬܐ ܕܗܫܐ ܗ̇ܘܝܐ

7. ܫܘܠܡܗ 'the consummation,' *c*; *e*, ܘܫܘܠܡܗ; *abdfghik*WP, ܒܫܘܠܡܗ 'in the consummation.'

8. ܥܠ̈ܡܐ 'worlds,' *abdefghik*WP; *c*, ܥܠܡܐ 'world.'

and all force of this time is turning into misery. 12. And every energy of youth is turning into old age and consummation, and every beauty of gracefulness of this time is turning faded and hateful. 13. And every proud dominion of the present is turning into humiliation and shame. 14. And every praise of the glory of this time is turning into the shame of silence, and every splendour and insolence of this time is turning into voiceless ruin. 15. And every delight and joy of this time is turning to worms and corruption. 16. And every clamour of the pride of this time is turning into dust and stillness. 17. And every possession of riches of this time is being turned into Sheol alone.

12. *Every beauty*, etc. Cf. xxi. 13. Cf. xlviii. 35. 14; xlviii. 35.

---

so also *i*, but defectively; *c* reads corruptly ܥܘܬܪܐ ܕܡܫܬܒܪܢܘܬܐ 'swelling of pride': we must emend ܕܡܫܬܒܪܢܘܬܐ into ܕܡܫܬܒܗܪܢܘܬܐ.

14. *e*WP om. ܘܟܠ . . . ܠܒܗܬܬܐ through hmt.

15. ܦܘܢܩܐ ܘܒܘܣܡܐ 'delight and joy,' *bdefghi*WP; *ack*, ܦܘ̈ܢܩܐ ܘܒܘ̈ܣܡܐ 'delights and joys.' ܠܪ̈ܡܬܐ 'to worms,' *abdefghik*WP; *c*, ܠܪܚܩܘܬܐ 'to rejection.' For ܘܠܚܒܠܐ *f* reads ܘܠܚܒ̈ܠܐ.

16. ܕܫܘܒܗܪܐ ܕܗܢܐ 'of the pride of this time,' *abdefghik*WP; *c*, ܕܫܒܗܪ̈ܢܐ 'of the proud.' ܠܥܦܪܐ ܘܠܫܠܝܘܬܐ 'to dust and stillness,' *abdefghikm*WP; *c*, ܠܥܦܪܐ ܫܠܝܐ 'to the still dust.'

17. ܕܥܘܬܪܐ 'of riches,' *cdefi*WP; *abghk*, ܘܥܘܬܪܐ 'and riches.'

ܠܡܣܟܢܘܬܐ . ܘܟܠ ܒܘܣܡܐ

ܕܗܫܐ . ܗܦܟ ܠܐܘܢܐ .

12 ܘܟܠ ܒܘܙܐ ܕܒܠܡܣܟܘܬܐ

ܗܦܟ ܠܫܒܘܬܐ ܘܫܘܠܡܐ .

ܘܟܠ ܫܘܦܪܐ ܕܓܐܘܬܐ

ܕܗܫܐ ܗܦܟ ܚܣܕܐ

13 ܘܡܫܬܒܚܢܐ . ܘܟܠ ܐܘܚܕܢܐ

ܕܡܪܘܪܒܢܘܬܐ ܕܗܫܐ ܗܦܟ

14 ܠܫܦܠܐ ܘܠܟܘܢܬܬܐ . ܘܟܠ

ܫܘܒܚܐ ܕܪܡܘܬܐ ܕܗܫܐ

ܗܦܟ ܠܒܗܬܬܐ ܕܫܬܩܐ .

ܘܟܠ ܦܐܝܘܬܐ ܘܫܬܡܪܘܬܐ

ܕܗܫܐ ܗܦܟܐ ܠܡܚܒܠܘܬܐ

15 ܕܫܠܝܐ . ܘܟܠ ܫܘܢܝܐ

ܘܒܘܫܡܐ ܕܗܫܐ . ܗܦܟ

16 ܠܪܡܬܐ ܘܠܫܪܟܐ . ܘܟܠ

ܡܬܠܐ ܕܫܘܒܗܪܐ ܕܗܫܐ ܗܦܟܐ

17 ܠܟܦܪܐ ܘܠܫܬܩܐ . ܘܟܠ ܡܫܚܐ

ܕܟܘܬܪܐ ܕܗܫܐ ܗܦܟ

ܠܕܘܘܢܐ; *c*, ܠܐܘܘܢܐ 'to miseries.' *k* om. . . . ܠܐܘܢܐ
ܗܦܟ through hmt.

12. ܘܫܘܠܡܐ *c*; *abfghik*WP, ܘܠܫܘܠܡܐ.

13. ܐܘܚܕܢܐ ܕܡܪܘܪܒܢܘܬܐ 'proud dominion,' *abdefghk*WP;

18. And all the rapine of passion of this time is turning into involuntary death, and every passion of the lusts of this time is turning into a judgment of torment. 19. And every artifice and craftiness of this time is turning into a proof of the truth. 20. And every sweetness of unguents of this time is turning into judgment and condemnation. 21. And every love of lying is turning to shame through truth. 22. Since therefore all these things are done now, does any one think that they will not be avenged? 23. But the consummation of all things will come to the truth.]

LXXXIV = B[1]. LXXXIV. Behold! I have therefore made known unto you (these things) whilst I live: for I said that

---

19. ܕܢܟܠܐ *c*; *abdefghiklw*P, ܕܢܟܠܬܐ. ܘܡܣܪܟܘܬܐ 'and craftiness,' *abdefghiklnw*P; *c*, ܕܡܣܪܟܘܬܐ 'of craftiness.' *f* om. ܗܘܐ ܗܘ ܕܡܬܩܢܐ . . . ܠܡܬܡܣܟܢܘܬܐ through hmt.

20. ܘܠܡܣܟܢܘܬܐ *c*; *h*, ܘܠܡܣܟܢܐ.

21. ܕܫܘܩܪܐ 'of lying,' *abdefghikw*P; *c* wrongly om. ܠܒܢܝ̈ܢܫܐ *c*; *abdefghikw*P, ܠܒܢܝܢܫܐ. ܒܩܘܫܬܐ 'through truth,' *abdefgikw*P; *c*, ܒܫܬܩܐ 'in silence.'

22. ܗܟܝܠ ܗܠܝܢ ܗܘܝܢ *c*; *abhk* trs.; *di*, ܗܟܝܠ ܗܟܝܠ; *efglw*P, ܗܟܝܠ. For ܗܘܝܢ *efilw* read ܗ̈ܘܝܢ. ܣܒܪ ܐܢܫ 'does anyone think?' *abdefghiklw*P; *c*, ܣܒܪ ܐܢܬ 'dost thou think?'

23. ܕܟܠ 'of all,' *abcdefghik*; *w*P, ܟܠ 'all.'

LXXXIV. 1. ܗܘ *abdefghikw*P; *c* om. ܕܐܘܕܥܬ ܠܟܠܟܘܢ

18 ܠܡܫܘܠ ܒܠܫܢܘܗܝ . ܘܟܠ
ܡܬܗ̈ܦܟܐ ܕܪ̈ܓܬܐ ܕܗܢܐ
ܗܦܟܝܢ ܠܡܥܒܘܬܐ ܕܠܐ
ܒܪܚܡܬܗܘܢ . ܘܟܠ ܪ̈ܓܬܐ
ܕܚܫ̈ܐ ܕܗܢܐ ܗܦܟܐ ܠܓܒܐ .
19 ❖ ܕܬܫܡܫܐ . ܘܟܠ ܓܕܠܬܐ
ܘܣܪܘܚܘܬܐ ܕܗܢܐ
ܗܦܟܐ ܠܡܥܒܫܘܬܐ
20 ܕܫܪܪܐ . ܘܟܠ ܣܟܠܘܬܐ
ܕܡܫܬܢܝܐ ܕܗܢܐ ܗܦܟܐ
21 ܠܓܒܐ ܘܠܣܡܟܘܬܐ . ܘܟܠ
ܙܢܝܘܬܐ ܕܫܘܦܪܐ ܗܦܟܐ
ܠܢܟܦܘ ܒܟܘܣܝܬܐ . ܒܝ
22 ܗܒܝܠ ܗܠܝܢ ܟܠܗܝܢ ܗ̈ܘܝ
ܗܘܐ . ܫܒܩ ܐܢܫ ܕܠܐ
23 ܡܬܬ̈ܥܒܪܢ . ܡܘܠܦܢܐ ܕܝܢ
. . ܕܟܘܠ ܠܡܙܪܐ ܠܐܬܐ . ____ . .
LXXXIV. 1 ܐܢܐ ܗܘܝܬ ܗܘ ܐܘܪܚܬܟܘܢ
ܒܝ ܡܢ ܐܢܐ . ܐܦܪܬ

18. ܡܬܗ̈ܦܟܐ *abc*WP; *defghi*, ܡܬܗܦܟܐ. ܕܚܫ̈ܐ 'of the lusts,' *abcegh*; *dfi*WP, ܕܚܫܐ 'of the lust.' ܕܗܢܐ 'of this time,' *abdefghik*WP; *c* wrongly om. *k* om. ܘܟܠ . . . ܒܪܚܡܬܗܘܢ through hmt., and for ܕܚܫ̈ܐ ܪ̈ܓܬܐ reads ܕܪ̈ܓܬܐ ܚܫܫܬܐ.

ye should above all things learn the commandments of the Mighty One, wherein I shall instruct you: and I will set before you some of the commandments of His judgment before I die. 2. Remember that formerly Moses assuredly called heaven and earth to witness against you, and said: "if ye transgress the law ye shall be dispersed, but if ye keep it ye shall be kept." 3. And other things also he used to say unto you when ye the twelve tribes were together in the desert. 4. And after his death ye cast them away from you: on this account there came

LXXXIV. 1. *Before I die.* See lxxviii. 5.

The commandments of the Mighty One (cf. ver. 7; xliv. 3).

2. See xix. 2, 3, note. In this verse there are several traces of the Hebrew original. First the Syr. for "assuredly called . . . to witness" = *διαμαρτυρόμενος διεμαρτύρατο* = העד העיד. Next we have the play on the two senses of שמר: "if ye keep it, ye shall be kept" = אם תשמרוה תשמרו. Finally, there seems to be a paronomasia intended in "if ye transgress the law, ye shall be dispersed" = אם תסורו מתורה תזורו.

3. *Twelve tribes.* Cf. lxxviii. 4; James i. 1.

ܦܘܩܕ̈ܢܝ, *e* save in reading ܦܘܩܕܝ, *f* save in reading ܦܩܕ̈ܢܝ, and *k* save in reading ܕܐܬܬܠܡܕܘܢ (for ܕܐܬܪܠܡܕܘܢ). ܦܘܩ̈ܕܢܐ *ce*; *dfgi*WP, ܦܘܩܕ̈ܢܐ; *k*, ܦܘܩ̈ܕܢܘܗܝ.

2. ܣܗ̇ܕ *abcefghil*WP; *b*, ܐܣܗ̇ܕ. ܒܟܘܢ *abdefghi*WP; *c* om. ܬܬܢܛܪܘܢ 'ye shall be kept,' *abdefghi*WP; *c*, ܬܬܢܨܒܘܢ 'ye shall be planted.'

3. ܐܠܐ ܐܦ *abdefghi*WP; *c*, ܘܐܦ. ܟܕ *ach*; *bdefgi*WP, ܕܟܕ. ܫܒ̈ܛܐ *c*; *abdefghi*WP, ܫܒ̈ܛܝܢ.

4. ܡܛܠܗܢܐ 'therefore,' *abdefgi*WP; *ch*, ܘܡܛܠܗܢܐ 'and

ܓܝܪ ܕܝܬܝܪܐܝܬ ܬܠܦܘܢ

ܦܘܩܕܢܝ ܚܝܠܬܢܐ

ܕܐܠܦܟܘܢ . ܘܐܣܝܡ

ܩܕܡܝܟܘܢ ܩܠܝܠ ܡܢ ܦܘܩܕܢܐ

ܕܕܝܢܗ ܡܢ ܩܕܡ ܕܐܡܘܬ .

2 ܐܬܕܟܪܘ ܕܒܙܒܢ ܡܣܗܕ

ܗܘ̣ ܒܟܘܢ ܡܘܫܐ

ܫܡܝܐ ܘܐܪܥܐ ܘܐܡܪ .

ܕܐܢ ܬܥܒܪܘܢ ܥܠ ܢܡܘܣܐ

ܬܬܒܕܪܘܢ . ܘܐܢ

ܬܛܪܘܢܗ ܬܬܢܨܒܘܢ .

3 ܐܠܐ ܐܦ ܐܚܪܢܝܬܐ ܐܡܪ

ܗܘܐ ܠܟܘܢ ܟܕ ܐܝܬܝܟܘܢ

ܗܘܝܬܘܢ ܐܚܝܕܐ ܬܪܬܥܣܪ

4 ܫܒ̈ܛܐ ܒܡܕܒܪܐ . ܘܡܢ

ܒܬܪ ܡܘܬܗ ܫܕܝܬܘܢ

ܐܢܘܢ ܡܢܟܘܢ . ܡܛܠܗܕܐ

ܦܘܩܕܢܝ ܚܝܠܬܢܐ ܕܐܠܦܟܘܢ 'that ye should above all things learn the commandments of the Mighty One wherein I shall instruct you'; so *c*, save that I have with Ceriani emended ܚܝ̈ܠܬܢܐ into ܚܝܠܬܢܐ ; *bdghil*WP read ܕܡܝܬܪܬܐ ܬܠܦܘܢ ܦܩܕܢܝ ܓܝܪ ܚܝܠܬܢܐ ܕܐܠܦܟܘܢ 'that ye should learn the things that are excellent; for the Mighty One hath commanded me to instruct you'; *a* agrees with *bdghi*WP save in reading

upon you what had been predicted. 5. And now Moses used to tell you before they befell you, and lo! they have befallen you: for you have forsaken the law. 6. Lo! I also say unto you after ye have suffered, that if ye obey those things which have been said unto you, ye will receive from the Mighty One whatever has been laid up and reserved for you. 7. Moreover, let this epistle be for a testimony between me and you, that ye may remember the commandments of the Mighty One, and that also there may be to me a defence in the presence of Him who sent me. 8. And remember ye the law and Zion, and the holy

4. Cf. xix. 3.

6. The 9½ tribes must endure chastisement before they could attain unto the promised happiness. This chastisement was for their well-being (lxxviii. 6); it was less than they deserved (lxxix. 2); and its aim was to make them worthy of their fathers in the last days (lxxviii. 5, see note).

8. They were to remember Zion and the Holy Land; for they were one day to return thither (cf. ver. 10 and lxxviii. 7, note).

---

5. ܐܦܪܢ *c*; *abdefghi*WP, ܐܡܪܢ.

6. ܬܬܡܟܣܘܢ *ac*; *bdefghi*WP, ܬܬܬܡܟܣܘܢ. ܕܐܬܐܡܪ *abcgh*; *d*, ܕܐܬܐܡܪܝܢ; *efi*WP, ܕܐܬܐܡܪܝܢ. ܡܫܡܠܝܐ, *def* add ܗܫܐ.

7. ܒܢܝܟܘܢ *c*; *abdefghi*WP, ܒܟܠ. ܠܣܗܕܘܬܐ *abcgh*; *defi*WP, ܣܗܕܘܬܐ. ܠܦܘܩܕܢܝܗ *abdefghi*WP; *c*, ܠܦܘܩܕܢܗ. ܘܦܘܩܕܢܘܗܝ *c*; *abdefghil*WP, ܠܦܘܩܕܢܘܗܝ. ܘܕܐܢܚܢܐ ܐܦ *c*; *abdfghi*WP, ܐܢܚܢܐ ܕܐܦ.

8. ܠܢܡܘܣܐ ܘܠܨܗܝܘܢ 'the law and Zion,' *abefghil*WP;

ܗܢܐ ܡܠܬܡܟܘܢ ܐܡܠܟܝܢ
ܕܦܩܝܕܝܢ ܗ̈ܘܘ ܐܒܗ̈ܬܢ .
5 ܘܗܫܐ ܡܟܘܫܐ ܐܡܪܢ
ܗܘܐ ܠܟܘܢ ܡܢ ܩܕܡ
ܕܠܐ ܬܥܒܪܘܢ . ܘܗܐ
ܥܒܪܬܘܢ . ܘܡܫܛܬܘܢ ܥܠ
6 ܢܡܘܣܐ . ܐܦ ܐܢܐ ܗܐ
ܐܡܪ ܐܢܐ ܠܟܘܢ ܡܢ
ܒܬܪ ܕܣܛܝܬܘܢ . ܕܐܦ
ܬܬܚܣܣܘܢ . ܠܐܡܠܟܝܢ ܕܐܬܐܡܪ
ܠܟܘܢ . ܬܫܡܥܘܢ ܡܢ
ܚܝܠܬܢܐ ܕܠܥܠܡ ܕܒܫܡܐ
7 ܘܢܛܪ ܠܟܘܢ . ܬܗܘܐ ܕܝܢ
ܗܕܐ ܐܓܪܬܐ ܒܝܢܝ ܠܟܘܢ
ܘܠܟܘܢ ܠܣܗܕܘܬܐ . ܕܬܗܘܘܢ
ܥܗܝܕܝܢ ܒܦܘܩ̈ܕܢܘܗܝ
ܕܚܝܠܬܢܐ . ܘܕܐܡܟܝܢܐ ܐܦ
ܠܝ ܢܗܘܐ ܠܝ ܡܦܩ
ܒܪܘܚܐ ܩܕܡ ܗܘ ܕܫܕܪܢܝ .
8 ܘܗܘܝܬܘܢ ܥܗܝܕܝܢ
ܠܢܡܘܣܐ ܘܠܨܗܝܘܢ

therefore.' ܗܢܐ *abcgh*; *defiwP*, ܗܕܐ. ܐܡܠܟܝܢ *c*; *abdefghiwP*, ܗܡܠܟܝܢ.

land and your brethren, and the covenant of your fathers, and forget not the festivals and the sabbaths. 9. And deliver ye this epistle and the traditions of the law to your sons after you, as also your fathers delivered (them) to you. 10. And at all times make request perseveringly and pray diligently with your whole heart that the Mighty One may be reconciled to you, and that He may not reckon the multitude of your sins, but remember the rectitude of your fathers. 11. For if He judge us not according to the multitude of His mercies, woe unto all us who are born.

LXXXV. = B[3]. [LXXXV. Know ye, moreover, that in former

9. *The traditions of the law*, *i.e.* the unwritten law.

10. *That the Mighty One may be reconciled to you.* Cf. 4 Ezra x. 24: "ut tibi repropitietur Fortis." Here this reconciliation is to lead up to their return to Palestine; for in lxxviii. 7 it is declared that He that promised their fathers that He would not fail their posterity, would gather them together from their dispersion, should they become faithful.

The rectitude of your fathers. On the merit of the fathers see xiv. 7, note.

11. *His mercies.* See lxxv. 2, note.

Woe unto all, etc. See x. 6, note.

LXXXV. This chapter is certainly an interpolation. I shall designate it B[3] It belongs neither to B[1] nor

---

traditions,' *c*; *abcdefghiw*P, ܡܫܠܡܢܘܬܗ 'the tradition.' ܠܒܢܝܟܘܢ *bcdefghiw*P; *a*, ܠܒܢܝܗܘܢ. ܐܝܟ *c*; *abdefghiw*P, ܐܝܟܢܐ.

10. ܐܡܝܢܐܝܬ 'perseveringly,' *abdeghiw*P; *c* om. ܕܚܛܗܝܟܘܢ 'of your sins,' *abdefghiw*P; *c*, ܕܚܛܝܝܟܘܢ 'of your sinners.' ܠܐ ܢܚܫܘܒ *abcgh*; *defiw*P, ܕܠܐ ܢܚܫܘܒ.

11. ܠܟܠܗܘܢ *abdefghilmw*P; *c*, ܠܟܠܢ. ܡܝܠܕܐ *cdefghilmw*P; *ab*, ܐܬܝܠܕܢ.

ܘܠܐܪܥܐ ܩܕܝܫܬܐ . ܘܠܐܚ̈ܝܟܘܢ
ܘܠܕܝܬܩܐ ܕܐܒ̈ܗܝܟܘܢ ❖
ܘܠܥܐܕ̈ܐ ܘܠܫܒ̈ܐ ܠܐ
9 ܬܛܥܘܢ . ܘܐܫܠܡܘ ܗܕܐ
ܐܓܪܬܐ ܘܡܫܠܡܢܘܬܗ
ܕܢܡܘܣܐ ܠܒ̈ܢܝܟܘܢ ܡܢ
ܒܬܪܟܘܢ . ܐܝܟ ܕܐܦ ܠܟܘܢ
ܐܫܠܡܘ ܠܟܘܢ ܐܒ̈ܗܝܟܘܢ .
10 ܘܒܟܠܙܒܢ ܐܡܝܢܐܝܬ ܒܥܘܬܟܘܢ ܒܥܘ
ܘܨܠܘ ܚܦܝܛܐܝܬ ܡܢ
ܟܠܗ ܠܒܟܘܢ . ܐܝܟ ܕܢܬܪܥܐ
ܠܟܘܢ ܚܝܠܬܢܐ . ܘܠܐ ܢܚܫܘܒ
ܣܘܓܐܐ ܕܚܛ̈ܗܝܟܘܢ . ܐܠܐ
ܢܬܕܟܪ ܠܬܪܝܨܘܬܐ ܕܐܒ̈ܗܝܟܘܢ .
11 ܐܢ ܓܝܪ ܐܝܟ ܣܘܓܐܐ
ܕܪ̈ܚܡܘܗܝ ܠܐ ܕܐܢ
1 LXXXV. . . ܘܝ ܠܢ ܠܟܠܢ ܝܠܝ̈ܕܐ . ܬܘܒ
ܕܝܢ ܕܥܘ ܕܒܙ̈ܒܢܐ . ܕܩ̈ܕܡܝܐ

d, ܘܠܐܚ̈ܝܟܘܢ ܠܕܝܬܩܐ ; c trs. wrongly. ܘܠܐܪܥܐ abdefghiwP; c, ܐܦ ܠܐܪܥܐ. ܕܐܒ̈ܗܝܟܘܢ 'of your fathers,' abdefghiwP; c, ܘܠܐܒ̈ܗܝܟܘܢ 'and your fathers.' ܘܠܥܐܕ̈ܐ bcg; adefhiwP, ܘܠܥܐܕ̈ܐ.

9. ܘܐܫܠܡܘ bcdefghiwP; a, ܘܫܠܡܘ. ܘܡܫܠܡܢܘܬܗ 'the

times and in the generations of old those our fathers had helpers, righteous men and holy prophets. 2. Nay more, we were in our own land, and they helped us when we sinned, and they prayed for us to Him who made us, because they trusted in their works, and the Mighty One heard their prayer and was gracious unto us. 3. But now the righteous have been gathered and the prophets have fallen asleep, and we also have gone forth from the land, and Zion has been taken

B^3. In B^1 there is a strong national hope which embraces a restored Jerusalem and the return of the dispersion. This hope is here implicitly denied. Although B^3 and B^2 differ in important respects, they agree in despairing of any national restoration. They regard this world as lost, and look only for spiritual blessedness in the world of incorruption (lxxxv. 4, 5). On the other hand, there is a deeper strain of individualism in B^3 than in B^2; the writer's interest centres mainly in the destiny of the individual; let each see that he is ready when the end comes (lxxxv. 11), and that end is at hand for all (lxxxv. 10). Again, whereas B^2 seems to have been written in Jerusalem, B^3 was written in Babylon or some other land of the Dispersion. Thus in lxxxv. 3 the writer says: "We also have gone forth from our own land, and Zion has been taken from us"; and in lxxxv. 2: "Nay more, we were in our own land, and they (the righteous) helped us when we sinned." Again, whereas according to B^2 Jeremiah was with the exiles in Babylon (see x. 2, note), it is here definitely stated that the righteous and the prophets are dead and the exiles have none to intercede for them (lxxxv. 2). B^3 and S (x. 6-xii. 4) are the most pessimistic parts of this book.

1. The generation of Jeremiah seems to be in the far past.

2. This verse conflicts with lxxvii. 5 and lxxx. 5. The writer implies that he is one of the exiles in Babylon or elsewhere. This is still more evident from the next verse.

They helped us when we sinned, and they prayed for us, etc. This thought reappears in the Rest of the Words of Baruch ii. 3: "For when the people transgressed, Jeremiah . . . prayed on behalf of the people until the transgressions of the people were forgiven them."

Trusted in their works. See xiv. 7, note; lxiii. 3. Observe that whereas in lxxxiv. 10 the merits of the patriarchs are regarded as a stay of Israel, no such belief appears here. According to this verse and the next it is implied that only the intercessions of the living righteous avail, and now there are none such. Yet it is shown that there were many such in ii. Hence this seems a later production.

3. *We also have gone forth*, etc. See verse 2.

ܡܩ̈ܕܡܝܐ ܘܒܕܪ̈ܐ ܕܥܠܡ
ܡܢܡܛ ܐܝܬ ܗܘܐ ܠܗܘܢ
ܐܒܗ̈ܝܢ ܡܥܕܪ̈ܢܐ ܙܕܝ̈ܩܐ .
2 ܘܢܒ̈ܝܐ ܩܕܝ̈ܫܐ . ܐܠܐ ܐܦ
ܚܢܢ ܗ̤ܘܝܢ ܒܐܪܥܢ . ܘܗܢܘܢ
ܡܥܕܪܝܢ ܗܘܘ ܠܢ ܡܐ
ܕܚܛܝܢ ܗ̤ܘܝܢ . ܘܒܥܝܢ ܗܘܘ
. ܚܠܦܝܢ ܡܢ ܗܘ ܕܒܪܢ . ܡܛܠ
ܕܬܟܝܠܝܢ ܗܘܘ ܥܠ
ܥܒ̈ܕܝܗܘܢ . ܘܫܡܥܗ ܠܗ ܚܝܠܬܢܐ
ܗܘܐ ܠܨܠܘܬܗܘܢ . ܘܡܚܣܢܐ
3 ܗܘܐ ܠܚܛܗܝܢ . ܗܫܐ ܕܝܢ
ܙܕܝ̈ܩܐ ܐܬܟܢܫܘ . ܘܢܒ̈ܝܐ
ܫܟܒܘ . ܘܐܦ ܚܢܢ ܡܢ ܐܪܥܢ

LXXXV. 1. ܐܒܗ̈ܝܢ *c*; *abdefghiw*P, ܠܗܢܘܢ ܐܒܗ̈ܝܢ. ܡܥܕܪ̈ܢܐ ܙܕܝ̈ܩܐ . *cg*; *adefhiw*P insert the punctuation between these words; *b* has no punctuation. ܢܒ̈ܝܐ ܩܕܝ̈ܫܐ 'holy prophets,' *abdefghiw*P; *c*, ܢܒ̈ܝܐ ܘܩܕܝ̈ܫܐ 'prophets and holy (men).'

2. ܐܠܐ ܐܦ 'nay, more,' *abdefghiw*P; *c*, ܐܠܐ ܕܝܢ 'moreover.' ܨܠܘܬܗܘܢ 'their prayer,' *abdefghiw*P; *c*, ܠܗܘܢ 'them.' ܗܘܐ *c*; *abdefghiw*P om. For ܚܠܦܝܢ *h* reads ܠܗܘܢ.

3. ܘܐܦ 'and also,' *abdefghiw*P; *c* om. 'and.' ܐܪܥܢ 'our land,' *c*; *abdefghiw*P, ܐܪܥܐ 'the land.' ܗܫܐ ܡܟܝܠ, *a* trs.

from us, and we have nothing now save the Mighty One and His law. 4. If therefore we direct and dispose our hearts, we shall receive everything that we lost, and much better things than we lost (yea, better) by many times. 5. For what we have lost was subject to corruption, and what we shall receive will not be corruptible. [6. Moreover, also, I have written thus to our brethren to Babylon, that to them also I may attest these very things.] 7. And let all those things aforesaid be always before your eyes, because we are still in the spirit and the power of

We have nothing now save the Mighty One and His law. The law was Israel's everlasting possession. This sentiment appears also in Josephus, *Apion*, ii. 38: κἂν πλούτου καὶ πόλεων καὶ τῶν ἄλλων ἀγαθῶν στερηθῶμεν, ὁ γοῦν νόμος ἡμῖν ἀθάνατος διαμένει. In the Talmud, further, we find (*Mechilta*, 68*b*) that whereas the land, the sanctuary, and the kingdom of David, were given conditionally to Israel, the law was given unconditionally. Hence Israel could exist without the former, but not without the latter. This thought combined with that in xlviii. 22 that, so far as Israel observed the law, it could not fall, became the inspiration of Rabbinic Judaism and the safeguard of the race through the storms of later times. On the law see xiv. 7, note.

5. See xxi. 19, note.

6. This verse is due to the final editor.

7. *The power of our liberty*, *i.e.* enjoy freewill. Cf. 4 Ezra ix. 11: "Qui fastidierunt legem meam, cum adhuc erant habentes libertatem" (also viii. 56). For the diction compare 1 Cor. vii. 37 ἐξουσίαν δὲ ἔχει περὶ τοῦ ἰδίου θελήματος: Acts i. 7; v. 4; Pss. Sol. ix. 7: τὰ ἔργα ἡμῶν ἐν . . ἐξουσίᾳ τῆς ψυχῆς ἡμῶν. On the doctrine see liv. 15, note.

---

6. ܠܒܒܠ ܕܐܦ 'to Babylon that also,' *abcg*; *h*, ܠܒܒܝܠ ܕܐܦ; *defi*WP, ܠܒܒܝܠ ܘܐܦ 'to Babylon and also.'

7. ܡܫܡܫܝܢ ܗܠܝܢ. ܟܠܗܘܢ *c*; *abdfghi*WP, ܡܫܡܫܝܢ. ܗܠܝܢ ܟܠܗܘܢ. ܘܫܘܠܛܢܐ 'and the power,' *abdefghi*WP; *c*, ܕܫܘܠܛܢܐ 'of the power.'

ܢܦܩܢ . ܘܨܗܝܘܢ ܐܫܬܩܠܬ
ܡܢܢ . ܘܠܝܬ ܠܢ ܡܕܡ
ܗܫܐ ܐܠܐ ܐܢ ܚܝܠܬܢܐ
4 ܘܢܡܘܣܗ . ܐܢ ܗܟܝܠ
ܢܬܪܨ ܘܢܬܩܢ ܠܒܘܬܢ
ܢܣܒܝܢ ܟܠܡܕܡ ܕܐܘܒܕܢ
ܘܕܡܝܬܪܢ ܣܓܝ ܡܢ ܐܝܠܝܢ ܕܐܘܒܕܢ
5 ܒܟܦܠܐ ܣܓܝܐܐ . ܡܕܡ
ܓܝܪ ܕܐܘܒܕܢ ܕܚܒܠܐ
ܗܘܐ . ܘܡܕܡ ܕܢܣܒܝܢ ܠܐ
6 ܡܬܚܒܠܢ . ܐܦ ܠܐܚܝܢ
ܕܝܢ ܗܟܢܐ ܟܬܒܬ ܠܒܒܠ .
ܕܐܦ ܠܗܘܢ ܬܢܝܬ ܗܠܝܢ
7 ܐܣܗܕ . ܢܗܘܘܢ ܕܝܢ ܒܟܠ
ܙܒܢ ܩܕܡ ܥܝܢܝܟܘܢ ܗܠܝܢ .
ܒܟܠܗܘܢ ܕܡܫܩܒܠܝܢ ܐܠܗܝܢ .
ܡܛܠ ܕܥܕܟܝܠ ܒܪܘܚܐ ܚܝܠ

4. ܢܣܒܝܢ *acdefghi*WP; *b*, ܢܣܒܝܢ ܣܓܝ. ܡܕܡ *c*; *abdefghi*WP om. ܘܕܡܝܬܪܢ ܣܓܝ ܡܢ ܐܝܠܝܢ ܕܐܘܒܕܢ 'and much better things than we lost,' *abdefghi*WP; *c* ܣܓܝ omitting by hmt.

5. ܕܐܘܒܕܢ *abfdgh*WP; *c*, ܕܐܘܒܕܝܢ; *e* om. ܕܚܒܠܐ *acdef*; *bgh*, ܕܚܒܠܐ; WP, ܒܚܒܠܐ. ܗܘܐ *c*; *abdefghi*WP, ܗܘ. ܡܬܚܒܠܢ *c*; *abdefghi*WP, ܡܬܚܒܠܐ.

our liberty. 8. Again, moreover, the Most High also is long-suffering towards us here, and He hath shown to us that which is to be, and hath not concealed from us what will befall in the end. 9. Before therefore judgment exact its own, and truth that which is its due, let us prepare our soul that we may enter into possession of, and not be taken possession of, and that we may hope and not be put to shame, and that we may rest with our fathers and not be tormented with our enemies. 10. For the youth of the world is past, and the strength of the creation is already exhausted, and the advent of the times is very short, yea, they have

8. *Hath shown to us . . . and hath not concealed from us.* In B[1] Baruch does not use the plural in this connection (cf. lxxxi. 4; see lxxviii. 8, note).

9. *Judgment . . . its due.* Cf. v. 2; xlviii. 27.

Let us prepare our soul. xxxii. 1, note.

That we may enter into possession of, and not be taken possession of = ܕܢܚܣܢ ܘܠܐ ܕܢܬܚܣܢ. These words are obscure, probably corrupt.

That we may rest with our fathers. Cf. xi. 4; also lxxxv. 11.

Tormented. Cf. lxxxiii. 8.

10. *The youth of the world is past.* Cf. 4 Ezra xiv. 10: "saeculum perdidit juventutem suam et tempora appropinquant senescere;" also xiv. 16; v. 50-56.

---

parallel expressions in v. 2 and xlviii. 27; *bdefghil*WP are wrong here, as they give ܕܝܢܐ 'the Judge.' Next, for ܕܡܕܡ 'of anything,' of *ac*, I follow *bdefghi*WP in reading ܡܕܡ, for ܫܪܪܐ is clearly the subject and not the object of the verb. The text of *bdefgi*WP = 'before therefore the Judge exact His own and truth that which is its due.' ܕܠܗ ܙܕܩ *c*; *abdefghi*WP, ܕܙܕܩ ܠܗ. ܕܢܚܣܢ ܘܠܐ ܢܬܚܣܢ *c*; *bfh*, ܢܚܣܢ ܘܠܐ ܕܢܬܚܣܢ. ܘܕܢܬܢܝܚ *abcdefh*; WP, ܕܢܬܢܝܚ; *h*, ܘܕܢܬܢܝܚ.

10. ܘܡܐܬܝܬܗܘܢ 'and the advent,' *abcdefghil*; WP,

8 ܘܡܫܬܠܛܢܐ ܕܐܒܗܬܢ . ܬܘܒ

ܕܝܢ ܡܪܝܡܐ ܢܓܝܪ

ܪܘܚܗ ܠܘܬܢ ܗܪܟܐ .

ܘܐܘܕܥܢ ܡܕܡ ܕܥܬܝܕ

ܘܠܐ ܟܣܐ ܡܢܢ ܡܕܡ

9 ܕܒܚܪܬܐ ܢܗܘܐ . ܡܢ ܩܕܡ

ܗܟܝܠ ܕܬܦܪܘܥ ܕܝܢܐ ܀

ܕܝܠܗ . ܘܫܪܪܐ ܡܕܡ

ܕܠܗ ܙܕܩ . ܢܛܝܒ ܢܦܫܢ

ܕܢܣܒ ܘܠܐ ܕܢܬܢܣܒ

ܘܕܢܣܒܪ ܘܠܐ ܕܢܒܗܬ .

ܘܕܢܬܢܝܚ ܥܡ ܐܒܗܬܢ .

ܘܠܐ ܕܢܫܬܢܩ ܥܡ

10 ܣܢܐܝܢ . ܕܥܠܝܡܘܬܗ ܓܝܪ

ܕܥܠܡܐ ܥܒܪܬ . ܘܚܝܠܗ

ܕܒܪܝܬܐ ܡܢ ܟܕܘ ܫܠܡ

ܠܗ . ܘܐܬܝܬܗܘܢ

ܕܙܒܢܐ ܩܪܝܒ ܛܒ ܘܥܒܪܘ .

8. ܬܘܒ 'again,' *abdefghi*WP; *c*, ܘܬܘܒ 'and again.' ܡܪܝܡܐ 'the Most High,' *abdefghi*WP; *c*, ܐܦ ܡܪܝܡܐ 'also the Most High.'

9. ܡܢ ܩܕܡ . . . . ܙܕܩ. The text follows *c* save in two cases: instead of ܕܝܢܗ 'His judgment,' of *c*, I read ܕܝܢܐ 'the judgment,' with *a*; this is manifestly required by the

passed by; and the pitcher is near to the cistern, and the ship to the port, and the course of the journey to the city, and life to consummation. 11. And again prepare your souls, so that when ye sail and ascend from the ship ye may have rest and not be condemned when ye depart. 12. For lo! when the Most High will bring to pass all these things, there will not there be again an opportunity for returning, nor a limit to the times, nor adjournment to the hours, nor change of ways, nor place for prayer, nor sending of petitions, nor receiving of knowledge, nor giving of love, nor place

12. *An opportunity for returning.* The Syr. here = "place" or "opportunity for repentance." But as this idea is found again in this verse, and obviously in its right context, it cannot be right here. The difficulty can be resolved as follows:—In early post-classical Hebrew תשובה meant both "return" and "repentance." The Greek translator followed the latter meaning when he ought to have followed the former.

Place of repentance. Cf. 4 Ezra ix. 12: "cum adhuc esset eis apertus poenitentiae locus, non intellexerunt." This is the universal teaching in the Books of Enoch and 4 Ezra.

---

11. ܬܣܩܘܢ *abceghiw*P; *d*, ܬܣܩܢ. ܕܐܠܦܐ *c*; *abdeghiw*P, ܐܠܦܐ. ܬܬܚܝܒܘܢ 'be condemned,' *abcgh*; *ef*wP, ܬܬܢܝܚܘܢ 'may have rest'; *di*, ܬܬܢܚܘܢ.

12. ܟܕ 'when,' *abdefghiw*P; *c* om. ܠܝܬ ܬܘܒ *c*; *abdefghiw*P, ܬܘܒ ܠܝܬ. ܠܬܝܒܘܬܐ *abcefghiw*P; *d*, ܠܬܝܒܘܬܐ. ܕܐܘܪ̈ܚܬܐ 'of ways,' *bgw*P; *dei*, ܕܐܘܪܚܬܐ 'of way'; *acfl*, ܕܐܘܪܚܬܐ; *h*, ܠܘܪ̈ܚܬܐ. ܡܨܠܬܐ *bcdefghiw*P; *a*, ܐܡܨܠܬܐ. ܡܘܗܒܐ ܕܚܘܒܐ 'giving of love,' *cd*; *abcefghiw*P, ܡܗܘܒܐ ܕܚܘܒܐ 'giving of love,' or 'pardoner of guilt,' accord-

ܠܗܘܢ . ܘܩܪܝܒܐ ܗܘ ܫܘܠܡܐ
ܠܓܘܒܐ . ܘܐܠܦܐ
ܠܠܡܐܢܐ . ܘܡܪ̈ܕܝܬܗ
ܕܐܘܪܚܐ ܠܡܕܝܢܬܐ . ܘܚ̈ܝܐ
11 ܠܫܘܠܡܐ . ܬܘܒ ܕܝܢ ܛܝܒܘ
ܢܦ̈ܫܬܟܘܢ ܕܡܐ ܕܪ̈ܕܝܬܘܢ
ܘܣܠܩܬܘܢ ܡܢ ܐܠܦܐ
ܬܬܢܝܚܘܢ . ܘܠܐ ܕܡܐ
12 ܕܐܙܠܬܘܢ ܬܬܚܝܒܘܢ . ܗܐ
ܓܝܪ ܟܕ ܢܝܬܐ ܡܪܝܡܐ
ܗܠܝܢ ܟܠܗܝܢ . ܬܡܢ ܠܝܬ
ܬܘܒ ܐܬܪܐ ܠܬܝܒܘܬܐ .
ܘܠܐ ܬܚܘܡܐ ܠܙ̈ܒܢܐ .
ܘܠܐ ܢܘܓܪܐ ܠܫܥ̈ܝܐ . ܘܠܐ
ܫܘܚܠܦܐ ܕܘܒ̈ܪܐ . ܘܠܐ
ܐܬܪܐ ܠܨܠܘܬܐ . ܘܠܐ
ܡܫܕܪܢܘܬܐ ܕܒܥ̈ܘܬܐ .
ܘܠܐ ܠܡܣܒ ܝܕܥܬܐ . ܘܠܐ
ܝܗܒܐ ܕܚܘܒܐ . ܘܠܐ
ܐܬܪܐ ܠܬܝܒܘܬ ܢܦܫܐ .

ܡܬܚܡܗܘܢ 'the space.' ܗܘ *c*; *abdefhiw*P om. ܘܡܪ̈ܕܝܬܗ *c*; *abdefghiw*P. ܘܡܪ̈ܕܝܬܐ.

of repentance, nor supplication for offences, nor intercession of the fathers, nor prayer of the prophets, nor help of the righteous. 13. There there is the sentence of corruption, the way of fire, and the path which bringeth to Gehenna. 14. On this account there is one law by one, one age and an end for all who are in it. 15. Then He will preserve those to whom He finds He may be gracious, and at the same time destroy those who are polluted with sins.]

LXXXVI. When therefore ye receive this my epistle, read it in your congregations with care. 2.

Intercession of the fathers. Cf. 4 Ezra vii. 102-115; Slav. En. liii. 1.

13. *Way of fire.* Cf. xliv. 15, note.

In the Ass. Moyseos, iii. 12, Moses is called the mediator of the law.

14. *One law by one.* Moses seems to be here referred to. The remark seems directed against the Christians (cf. xlviii. 24). This verse seems either to be interpolated or in its wrong place.

ܕܚܒܠܐ 'of corruption,' *abdefghi*WP; *c*, ܠܚܒܠܐ 'to corruption.' ܐܘܪܚܐ 'the way,' *abdefghi*WP; *c*, ܕܐܘܪܚܐ 'of the way.' ܠܓܗܢܐ 'to gehenna,' *abefghi*; so *d*WP, ܠܓܝܗܢܐ; *c*, ܠܓܘܡܪ̈ܐ 'to coals.'

14. ܚܕ ܢܡܘܣܐ *cg*; *defh*WP, ܚܕ . ܚܕ ܢܡܘܣܐ

15. ܗܝܕܝܢ 'then,' *bcgh*; *adefil*WP, ܘܗܝܕܝܢ 'and then.' ܢܚܣ *acdefi*WP; *bgh*, ܚܝ̈ܐ. ܐܠܝܢ 'those,' *c*; *adefghi*WP, ܘܐܠܝܢ 'and those.' ܕܛܢܦܐ *abdefgh*WP; *c*, ܘܛܢܦܐ. ܡܛܘܫܠܫܠܝܢ ܒܚܛܗ̈ܐ *c*; *abdefghi*WP trs.

LXXXVI. 1. ܗܟܝܠ ܬܣܒܘܢ *c*; *abdefghi*WP trs. ܗܕܐ 'this,' *abdefghi*WP; *c* om. ܐܓܪܬܝ *abdefghi*WP; *c*, ܐܓܪܬܐ.

ܘܠܐ ܦܝܣܐ ܕܥܠ ܣܟܠ̈ܘܬܐ .

ܘܠܐ ܒܥܘܬܐ ܕܐܒ̈ܗܐ .

ܘܠܐ ܨܠܘܬܐ ܕܢܒ̈ܝܐ . ܘܠܐ

13 ܥܘܕܪܢܐ ܕܙܕ̈ܝܩܐ . ܐܝܬ

ܬܡܢ ܓܙܪ ܕܝܢܐ ܕܚܒܠܐ

ܐܘܪܚܐ ܕܢܘܪܐ ܘܫܒܝܠܐ

14 ܕܡܩܪܒ ܠܓܗܢܐ . ܡܛܠ

ܗܢܐ ܚܕ ܒܚܕ ܚܕ

ܢܙܕܗܪ ܚܕ ܒܟܠܡܕܡ .

ܘܠܐܝܠܝܢ ܕܐܝܬ ܒܗ ܚܛܗܐ

15 ܠܟܠܗܘܢ . ܗ̇ܘܝܢ ܚܝܐ

ܠܐܝܠܝܢ ܕܡܫܟܚ ܕܢܟܦܐ

ܒܟܠܗܘܢ ܘܐܒܕܐ ܢܘܒܕ

ܠܐܝܠܝܢ ܕܡܛܠܫܝܢ ܒܚܛܗ̈ܐ .

LXXXVI. 1 ܟܕ ܗܟܝܠ ܬܩܒܠܘܢ

ܗܕܐ ܐܓܪܬܐ ܩܪܘܗ̇

ܒܟܢܘܫܬܟܘܢ ܒܚܦܝܛܘܬܐ .

ing as we vocalise the phrase. ܦܝܣܐ 'supplication,' *abdeghil*WP; *c*, ܦܝ̈ܣܐ 'supplications'; *f* om. ܦܝܣܐ . . . ܐܬܪܐ. ܣܟ̈ܠܘܬܐ, *d* repeats; *e* reads singular. ܒܥܘܬܐ 'intercession,' *bdefghi*WP; *ac*, ܒܥ̈ܘܬܐ 'intercessions.'

13. ܬܡܢ, *c* adds above the line in first hand ܕܝܢ against *abdefgi*WP; *h* adds ܓܙܝܪ. ܓܙܪ ܕܝܢܐ *abdefghi*WP; *c*, ܓܙܪܐ ܕܕܝܢܐ.

And meditate thereon, above all on the days of your fasts. 3. And bear me in mind by means of this epistle, as I also bear you in mind in it, and always fare ye well.

LXXXVII. And it came to pass when I had ended all the words of this epistle, and had written it sedulously to its close, that I folded it, and sealed it carefully, and bound it to the neck of the eagle, and dismissed and sent it.

HERE ENDS THE BOOK OF BARUCH THE SON OF NERIAH.

LXXXVII. *Bound it to the neck of the eagle.* These words reappear in the Rest of the Words of Baruch vii. 8, *τὴν ἐπιστολὴν . . . ἔδησεν εἰς τὸν τράχηλον τοῦ αἰετοῦ* (cf. vii. 30).

---

the first epistle'; in WP, ܫܠܡܬ ܐܓܪܬܐ ܕܒܪܘܟ '(here) ends the epistle of Baruch'; *f* om. subscription.

LXXXVII. Found only in *c*, but undoubtedly a part of the original work, as is clear from a comparison of lxxvii. 17, 20—26. As all the other MSS. began with lxxviii., and gave only a fragment of the book for ecclesiastical reading, they naturally omitted this chapter, since it would have been unintelligible without lxxvii., and simply closed the section with the words ܗܘܠܝܢ ܡܫܠܡܝܢ.

2 ܘܗܘܝܬܘܢ ܡܬܗܓܝܢ ܒܗ̇ .
ܝܬܝܪܐܝܬ ܒܨܘ̈ܡܝܟܘܢ
3 ܀ ܘܕܘܩ̈ܕܡܝܟܘܢ . ܘܗܘܝܬܘܢ ܘܗܘܝܬܘܢ
ܡܬܕܟܪܝܢ ܠܝ ܒܗܝ ܐܓܪܬܐ
ܗܕܐ . ܐܝܟ ܕܐܦ ܐܢܐ
ܡܬܕܟܪ ܐܢܐ ܠܟܘܢ ܒܗ̇ .
LXXXVII. 1 .. ܘܒܟܠܥܕܢ ÷ ܘܗܘܐ ܕܟܕ
ܫܠܡܬ ܟܠܗܘܢ ܡ̈ܠܝܗ̇
ܕܐܓܪܬܐ ܗܕܐ ܘܟܬܒܬܗ̇
ܒܫܠܡܘܬܐ ܥܕܡܐ ܠܫܘܠܡܗ̇
ܘܟܪܟܬܗ̇ ܘܚܬܡܬܗ̇
ܒܙܗܝܪܘܬ . ܘܩܛܪܬܗ̇ ܒܨܘܪܗ
ܕܢܫܪܐ . ܘܫܪܝܬ ܘܫܕܪܬܗ̇ .

ܫܠܡ ܟܬܒܐ ܕܒܪܘܟ ܒܪ

܀ ܀ ܀ ܢܪܝܐ . ܀ ܀ ܀

2. ܝܬܝܪܐܝܬ, c adds ܕܝܢ against *abdefghi*wP.

3. ܐܝܟ *c*; *abdfgh*wP, ܐܝܟܢܐ. ܐܢܐ *bcdfgh*wP; *a* om. ܒܗ̇ ܘܒܟܠܥܕܢ 'in it and always,' *c*; *abdefghi*wP, ܒܗ̇ . ܘܒܟܠܥܕܢ ܗܘܝܬܘܢ ܫܠܝܡܝܢ 'in it, and always fare ye well': with these words all MSS. but c close. The subscription in *bgh* is ܫܠܡܬ ܐܓܪܬܐ ܩܕܡܝܬܐ ܕܒܪܘܟ ܣܦܪܐ '(here) ends the first epistle of Baruch the scribe'; so *a*, but that it writes ܐܝܓܪܬܐ for ܐܓܪܬܐ; in *dei*, ܫܠܡܬ ܐܓܪܬܐ ܩܕܡܝܬܐ '(here) ends

APPENDIX ON VI. 7-10

In 2 Macc. ii. 4-8 there is a tradition closely related to the account in vi. 7-10. Here Jeremiah is warned of God to hide, in a cave-like dwelling in the mountain where Moses climbed up, "the tabernacle and the ark and the altar of incense" (*τὴν σκηνὴν καὶ τὴν κιβωτὸν καὶ τὸ θυσιαστήριον τοῦ θυμιάματος*). This place was to remain unknown till God should gather His people again together (*ἄγνωστος ὁ τόπος ἔσται ἕως ἂν συναγάγῃ ὁ Θεὸς ἐπισυναγωγὴν τοῦ λαοῦ*).

The mention here of the "altar of incense" supports the rendering I have given of ܦܪܝܣܐ in vi. 7. This word implies *θυμιατήριον* in the Greek. In the LXX. this word means "censer," but in Philo, Josephus, Clem. Alex., and Origen it is the ordinary appellation of the "altar of incense." Now as regards the first meaning, there is no mention of any particular censer in the Old Testament, not even in Lev. xvi. 12. The only mention of the golden censer is found in the Mishna, *Joma*, v. 1, vii. 4 (quoted by Lünemann on Heb. ix. 4), which the High Priest took with him into the Holy of Holies on the Day of Atonement. Since, however, in the frequent earlier and contemporary enumerations of the holy vessels in 2 Macc. ii. 5; Philo, *Quis rerum divin. haer.* i. 504; *de Vita Mos.* ii. 149; Heb. ix. 1-5 (?); Joseph. *Ant.* iii. 6, 8; *Bell. Jud.* v. 5. 5, *this censer is nowhere given, but the altar of incense always*, it seems right to conclude that *θυμιατήριον* should be taken here in its meaning of "altar of incense," and not in that of "censer," as it was by the Syriac translator.

INDEX I

Passages from the Scriptures and other Ancient Books Directly Connected or Closely Parallel with the Text.

Only the more important are given except in the case of 4 Ezra, and the two books of Enoch.

See pp. lxxvi.-lxxix.

Apocalypse of Baruch.	Ethiopic Enoch.
lix. 10	xxii. 5-9
„ 10	xli. 3 ; xliii. 1, 2, etc.
lxviii. 6	lxxxix. 73, 74

Apocalypse of Baruch.	Slavonic Enoch.
x. 6	xli. 2
xviii. 2	xxx. 15, 16
xxi. 4	xxiv. 2
„ 6	xxix. 1
„ 7	xlvii. 5
xxiii. 4	xlix. 2 (lviii. 5)
xlviii. 10	xvii.
li. 11	„
liv. 15, 19	xxx. 15
lvi. 11-13	xviii. 4-6
lix. 5	xxviii. 3
„ 5	xli. 4
„ 8	lxi. 1-4 ; lxx. 3, 4
„ 10	x. ; xc. 12
„ 10	xx. 1, 3
„ 11	xi. 9

Apocalypse of Baruch.	Apocryphal Book of Baruch.

See pp. xiv.-xv. ; lxv.-lxvii.

Apocalypse of Baruch.	4 Ezra.
ii. 1	iv. 36 ; viii. 51, 62 ; xiv. 9, 49
iii. 1	„ 38 ; v. 23, 38 ; vi. 11, 38 ; vii. 17, 58, 75 ; xii. 7 ; xiii. 51
„ 1	x. 7
„ 2 (xxviii. 6)	v. 56 ; vii. 102 ; viii. 42 ; xii. 7
„ 7	vii. 30
iv. 3	„ 26 ; xiii. 36
v. 1	iv. 28
„ 1	„ 25
ix. 2	v. 20 ; vi. 35 ; ix. 26, 27 ; xii. 51
x. 6 (xi. 6, 7)	iv. 12 ; vii. 66, 116, 117
xi. 3	iii. 30
xiii. 8	iv. 34
xiv. 7	vii. 77 ; viii. 33
„ 11 (xlviii. 15)	viii. 5
„ 17	vi. 38
„ 18	„ 54
„ 18	„ 55, 59 ; vii. 11 ; viii. 44 ; ix. 1
xv. 6	vii. 72
xvii. 4	iii. 19
xix. 1, 2	vii. 121-130
xx. 1 (liv. 1)	iv. 26 ; vi. 18
xxi. 6	viii. 21
„ 19	vii. 113 (iv. 11 ; vii. 111)
„ 21	v. 27

Apocalypse of Baruch.	Psalms of Solomon.
ix. 1	xvii. 41
xx. 3	xiv. 5
xlii. 4	xvii. 17
xlviii. 9	xix. 2, 3
lx. 1	ii. 15
lxxviii. 7	viii. 34
lxxxv. 7	ix. 7

INDEX II

Names and Subjects

Printed by R. & R. Clark, Limited, *Edinburgh*

Printed in the United States
99492LV00002B/97/A